What Is Systematic Theology?

Bernard Lonergan left many questions unanswered in regard to his treatment of systematics in his classic work *Method in Theology*. In *What Is Systematic Theology?* Robert M. Doran attempts to articulate and respond to these questions.

Doran begins by accepting four emphases presented by Lonergan concerning systematics: first, that its principal function is the hypothetical and analogical understanding of the mysteries of faith; second, that it should begin with those mysteries of faith that have received dogmatic status; third, that it must proceed in the 'order of teaching' rather than the 'order of discovery'; and last, that it must be explanatory rather than merely descriptive. He then replies to the questions that are raised by each of these emphases.

What Is Systematic Theology? is the most thorough attempt thus undertaken to advance Lonergan's program for systematics, fully in the spirit of his work but addressing issues that he left to others. Doran's idea of a core set of meanings for systematics – or a 'unified field structure' – is highly original, as is the integration of the systematic ideal and contemporary historical consciousness.

(Lonergan Studies)

ROBERT M. DORAN is the director of the Lonergan Research Institute and professor emeritus of systematic theology at Regis College, University of Toronto.

ROBERT M. DORAN

What Is Systematic Theology?

UNIVERSITY OF TORONTO PRESS
Toronto Buffalo London

Reprinted 2012
Reprinted in paperback 2016

ISBN 978-0-8020-9041-6 (cloth)
ISBN 978-1-4875-9146-5 (paper)

Printed on acid-free paper

Lonergan Studies

Library and Archives Canada Cataloguing in Publication

Doran, Robert M., 1939–
What is systematic theology? / Robert M. Doran

(Lonergan studies)
Includes index.
ISBN 978-0-8020-9041-6 (bound). 978-1-4875-9146-5 (pbk.)

1. Theology, Doctrinal. I. Title. II. Series.

BT75.3D67 2005 230 C2005-902194-2

This volume was published with the aid of a grant from the Jesuit Community of Regis College, Toronto.

University of Toronto Press acknowledges the financial assistance to its publishing program of the Canada Council for the Arts and the Ontario Arts Council.

University of Toronto Press acknowledges the financial support for its publishing activities of the Government of Canada through the Book Publishing Industry Development Program (BPIDP).

Contents

Preface

Bernard Lonergan is reported to have said once, 'When is a book finished? When its author is sick and tired of revising it!' I have been working on various elements of this short manuscript since the publication in 1990 of the much longer preliminary work, *Theology and the Dialectics of History.*[1] Thus this small book has taken me at least as long to write as did the earlier much larger work. Many of the ideas recorded here have been published in article form over the years, but in the present work I am trying to bring together under one cover, not all of the thoughts I have had on expanding Lonergan's notion of systematic theology, but those that I have judged worth preserving because upon critical reflection I found that they merit affirmation.

Some might ask, Why systematics? Couldn't you turn your attention to something more interesting? Why not continue to develop the notion of psychic conversion, for example?

Well, in fact there is a development of the notion of psychic conversion to be found in these pages. But from the beginning, my thinking on psychic conversion, on the integration of the psychological with Lonergan's intentionality analysis, has had a theological objective. For nearly thirty years, I have been heading toward clarifying the method, objectives, and grounds of systematic theology in this new and precarious stage of meaning on which, sometimes kicking and screaming, we have entered. The opportunity is enormous for a complete reconstruction of the discipline or functional specialty of systematic theology, and I would be less than candid if I did not say that these present reflections ambition nothing short of such an achievement. The achievement, of course, will not be that of any individual, but of a community engaged in what Lonergan loved to call 'ongoing collaboration.' I only hope that the present pages manage to convey something of the vision of what this new systematics can be. It will, of course, be entirely continuous with the permanent achievements of the past, but those permanent achievements were reached in stages of meaning that are now part of history. They must be transposed into a stage in which the ultimate arbiters of meaning are found in what Lonergan calls interiorly and religiously differentiated consciousness, that is, in the personally appropriated structure of one's own cognitive and deliberative operations and in the gift of God's love as one has made that gift one's own and followed it where it leads one.

The sea change that Lonergan's work makes possible is here only envisioned from afar. But at least now, perhaps, I can begin to do what for thirty years I have been talking about doing. That will be the real proof, the genuine indication of whether and to what extent these reflections have been on the mark.

My work is cumulative, and so the present book builds on previous work. And that previous work in turn built on the achievements of Bernard Lonergan. This has been a difficulty for me from the beginning: not only does my work presume familiarity with Lonergan's, but my later work presumes familiarity with my earlier work. I have always attempted to ground my own insights in a careful reading of Lonergan's texts, and I will continue to do so here. But obviously I cannot repeat previous efforts over and over again, and so I will have to rely on the good will of my readers and beg their indulgence as I ask them when necessary to become familiar with the earlier work on which this later work depends.

I wish to thank a number of people who have read earlier versions of this manuscript and by their encouragement and criticism have helped me toward the final draft. I mention in particular Neil Ormerod, Gordon Rixon, Daniel Monsour, John Dadosky, and Frederick Lawrence. My students at Regis College, Toronto School of Theology, and my colleagues at Regis and in the Lonergan Research Institute have been constant sources of both challenge and consolation. I have a set of serious administrative responsibilities for the Institute, but the burden is rendered lighter because I work with such an amazing group of people: Deborah Agnew, Frederick E. Crowe, Robert C. Croken, Michael Shields, Daniel Monsour, and Greg Lauzon. The mission of the Institute is fourfold: to preserve, promote, develop, and implement the work of Bernard Lonergan. It is my hope that this book is a step towards contributing especially to the last two of these objectives.

Finally, let me thank Rev. Joseph Schner, s.j., and the Regis College Jesuit Community for a generous subsidy to support publication.

Robert M. Doran
28 December 2004

What Is Systematic Theology?

1

The Question

In this book I will confront basic methodological issues in systematic theology and take a position in their regard. While I do so relying on and continually referring to the enormous contributions of Bernard Lonergan to the clarification of those issues, still I begin with the assumption that there is a certain amount of unfinished business in what Lonergan wrote about systematic theology. That unfinished business sets my agenda. My purpose here is not to present an exhaustive interpretation and evaluation of Lonergan's writings on systematic theology. I have begun that sort of study, but have decided that it must be published separately.[1] As Lonergan found it impossible to include in the same volume both his interpretations of Aquinas on understanding and inner word and his own transposition and development of Aquinas's views in the light of contemporary issues, so I have found it necessary to assign to distinct texts work in indirect and direct discourse. Thus while the present effort rests on a long period of research in the principal texts and in Lonergan's private papers, I am speaking in my own voice and not principally as an interpreter of Lonergan. A recent book by Ivo Coelho presents some of the essential moments of Lonergan's development regarding theological method.[2] I can leave many of the relevant details about Lonergan's intellectual history in Coelho's able hands and concentrate on the issue of developing the notion of systematic theology. I found in studying Lonergan's writings on the issue that there is a series of problems that just will not go away, despite both my admiration for his relentless presentation of one particular notion of systematics and my general agreement with his views. The present book represents one theologian's answer to those problems. I will give a broad outline of Lonergan's notion of systematics, raise some questions about it, and propose an answer to these questions that I think will serve to develop the notion and, most importantly, the practice of systematics. The suggested development will be consistent, I believe, with the dynamic thrust of Lonergan's differentiated notion of theological specializations; in fact, it will be seen that some of the developments that the book suggests are already suggested in Lonergan's explicit statements about systematics.

While Lonergan's own intellectual development is marked by a series of genetic developments on many of the most important issues in his thinking, his notion of systematics remained remarkably unchanged throughout his career. But, I believe, his very development in other areas raises further questions about systematics. Facing these questions will promote a development in the notion of systematics itself that, while preserving Lonergan's emphases, also includes more among the tasks of systematics than he ever explicitly acknowledged. I believe, too, that the proposed development brings the account of systematics into greater harmony with the dynamism of Lonergan's method than does his own chapter on systematics in *Method in Theology*.[3] The general form of my questions emerges from the dynamic movement of that now classic work. Lonergan's conception of theology in terms of the functional specialization of the operations that theologians perform requires that more be said about systematic theology than is available in the book's chapter on systematics. The chapter, in my view, does not say enough. More precisely, there are operations that systematic theologians perform that Lonergan does not account for at any point in his presentation of the method of systematics, or for that matter anywhere else. The chapter does not represent even some of Lonergan's own documented reflections on what systematics would become under the direction of the overall method that is presented in *Method in Theology*. It reverts, on my reading, to a pre-*Method* mentality that interrupts the dynamic movement that the book would promote. If there is a particular development that I would like to effect here, it would be to move the presentation of systematics more completely into the full historical and methodological context that *Method in Theology* not only addresses but also modifies and transforms.

One result of this effort, if it is successful, would be to open the presentation of systematics to the issues of cultural and religious pluralism and interreligious dialogue that Lonergan addressed in a quite sensitive manner in papers written subsequently to *Method in Theology*.[4] Perhaps no area of theology in direct discourse is of greater importance at the present time and for the foreseeable future than this, and I am convinced that Lonergan's own suggestions concerning the direction that Christian theology must take on these issues are still the clearest I have seen and make more sense than any others, even as they are compatible with the best thinking on the part of people who have specialized in this set of questions.

Thus, even as I register broad agreement with Lonergan on the nature and function of systematics, in fact even as I insist on the necessity of preserving his distinct emphases, I will also be suggesting certain refinements and arguing that they are required by the very dynamic exigencies that gave rise in the first place to his developed account of theological method. At times I will be picking up on hints found in Lonergan's own writings or notes, while at other times I will introduce my own concerns and suggestions.

I must make clear from the outset, however, that I have no quarrel with what Lonergan *does* say about systematics. I am rather noting the absence of certain key elements from his work. I want him to say more. He *can* say more. The 'more' is waiting to be said. Clearly, I cannot make him say more, so I will try to say more myself.

Let me go into more detail on the principal question that drives this work. The first chapter of Lonergan's *De Deo trino, Pars systematica,* written for his course on the Trinity at the Gregorian University in the 1950s and 1960s,[5] provides by far the most detailed single exposition in Lonergan's work of an understanding of systematics. It deserves to be regarded as something of a classic exposition of one particular option regarding what systematics is and does. In fact, it is perhaps the most relentlessly consistent presentation of that option to be found anywhere in theological literature. Its position regarding systematics did not undergo radical revision when Lonergan wrote *Method in Theology*. There is, of course, in the latter work a vastly expanded notion of theology as a whole, and so a far more nuanced and differentiated presentation of the relation of systematics to other theological tasks. There are in Lonergan's unpublished notes from the period in which he arrived at the notion of functional specialization suggestions that would greatly expand and enrich his notion of systematics. But in fact there is little change between *De Deo trino* and *Method in Theology* with regard to the basic notion of what systematics is and how it is to be done. And that is precisely the problem. Most of what we find in the first chapter of *De Deo trino* appeared for the first time in 1957,[6] eight years before Lonergan was to arrive at the notion of functional specialization, and at least a few years before he was to grasp with articulate clarity that systematics is grounded in conversion[7] and that theology mediates between faith and culture. Yet the understanding of systematics presented in this earlier manuscript survives essentially unchanged in the new framework opened up in *Method in Theology*. And my main question, in general terms, will be whether that is what ought to have happened. Is it not rather the case that the framework for the whole of theology that is provided by functional specialization and the notion of mediation demands a more extensive notion not only of that whole – this Lonergan certainly does provide – but also of the functional specialty 'systematics'?

I have said that the exposition in *De Deo trino* is classic. But when Lonergan speaks of the classic text, he speaks also of the traditions that the classics ground and in which they are received. A genuine tradition displays 'a long accumulation of insights, adjustments, re-interpretations, that repeats the original message afresh for each age.'[8] It is my suggestion that functional specialization, mediation, and the new notion of foundations call for an accumulation of insights, adjustments, and reinterpretations around the notion of systematics that do not find their way into the chapter on that functional specialty in *Method in Theology*. I do not in the least dispute Lonergan's contention that the principal function of systematics is *intelligentia mysteriorum*, an understanding of the mysteries of faith affirmed in ecclesial and theological doctrines. But functional specialization and the notions of mediation and foundations have an impact on systematics that has not, to my mind, been adequately expressed in *Method in Theology*.

My intention, then, is not to question whether Lonergan's affirmation that the principal function of systematics is an understanding of the mysteries of faith is correct. It is. But he should have said more in *Method in Theology*, where, for all practical purposes, he intends to draw the entire map of theological operations. His conception of the whole of theology in terms of the functional specialization of operations is radical. It is concrete. It represents the fruit of years of profound reflection, teaching, and writing. It is utterly Catholic in the best and only genuine sense of that term. In principle it is meant to anticipate heuristically every operation performed by every person making any contribution to the theological enterprise. It establishes a 'framework for collaborative creativity.'[9] But its presentation is, throughout, just a beginning, a sketch, a program that still needs fine-tuning before it can bear fruit for the centuries, as I believe it is destined to do. Our own age is, by and large, more interested in hermeneutics and history than in doctrines and systematics, and so we are more apt to see the mutually self-mediating advantages of dialogues between Lonergan and, say, Gadamer, Heidegger, and Ricoeur than we are to turn to the development of the direct discourse found in doctrines and systematics. While I have no doubt at all of the developments that could occur as Lonergan is brought into ever more explicit dialogue with the great hermeneutical thinkers of the twentieth century, the specialties of direct discourse are also areas that require particular attention in our time. I hope here to make a contribution to a set of fundamental refinements.

2

The Principal Function of Systematics and the Issues This Raises

1 Lonergan's Emphases

There are four emphases in Lonergan's writings about systematics that I regard as crucial; they must continue to be affirmed even as we attempt to develop the notion of systematics found in his work.

1.1 The Principal Function

The first emphasis is the insistence that the principal function of systematics, around which the other functions are assembled, is precisely what Lonergan says it is, namely, the hypothetical, imperfect, analogical, obscure, and gradually developing understanding of the mysteries of faith.[1] The theologian has already affirmed these mysteries in the statements in which one expresses one's own positions or 'doctrines,' and has done so on grounds other than either systematic argumentation, which has a function quite distinct from doctrinal affirmation, or proof and demonstration, which are not the appropriate ways of arriving at affirmations made in faith. Lonergan's is perhaps the most relentlessly consistent presentation of this option regarding systematic theology. The option remained essentially unchanged throughout his career, from his doctoral dissertation on Aquinas to his writings even after *Method in Theology*. His vision of the whole of theology underwent dramatic change with the idea of functional specialization. His understanding of what constitutes scientific knowledge moved to ever more nuanced qualifications on the position that classical Catholic theology had inherited from Aristotle.[2] But through all of these developments, systematic theology (or systematics) remains the imperfect, analogical, obscure, but extremely fruitful understanding of the mysteries of faith, precisely that understanding recommended and praised by the First Vatican Council.

> Out of the Augustinian, Anselmian, Thomist tradition, despite an intervening heavy overlay of conceptualism, the first Vatican council retrieved the notion of understanding. It taught that reason illumined by faith, when it inquires diligently, piously, soberly, can with God's help attain a highly fruitful understanding of the mysteries of faith both from the analogy of what it naturally knows and from the interconnection of the mysteries with one another and with man's last end (DS 3016).
>
> The promotion of such an understanding of the mysteries we conceive to be the principal function of systematics.[3]

Perhaps a clarification by contrast will be helpful. Let us compare this emphasis of Lonergan's with the procedures followed by Wolfhart Pannenberg in his *Systematic Theology*. Pannenberg conceives truth as coherence.[4] This is an idealist conception of truth entailing a less than adequate distinction between insight and judgment. Within such a conception there is no ground for distinguishing doctrines from systematics, for there is no acknowledgment of judgment as a distinct constitutive element in human knowing. On Lonergan's account doctrines are correlated with judgment, systematics with understanding. Doctrines are affirmations. Systematics attempts to understand what has been affirmed. The affirmations are reached in other ways than by systematic argumentation. On Pannenberg's account doctrines and systematics are one, because on his account judgment and understanding are one; as in all idealisms, they are not adequately distinguished. Thus we have the title of the first chapter of Pannenberg's *Systematic Theology*: 'The Truth of Christian Doctrine as the Theme of Systematic Theology.' On Lonergan's account, again, affirming Christian doctrine as true is one thing, while understanding what one has affirmed to be true is something else. For Lonergan, it is the *meaning* of Christian doctrine, not its truth, that is 'the theme of systematic theology.' It is 'how it *can* be true' that is at stake in systematics. *That* it is true is already affirmed. Or, to be more precise, by the time the theologian begins to do systematics, he or she has already determined precisely what are the doctrines that are to be affirmed. These may or may not be completely coincident with the official doctrines of a particular communion, but the point is that systematics is an attempt on the part of the theologian to state as clearly as possible the meaning of what one has already affirmed to be the case. And at this point, we are concerned with the principal function of systematics, namely, the understanding of the mysteries of faith affirmed in church doctrines. The truth of doctrine pertains to the functional specialty 'doctrines,' while the meaning of what has already been affirmed as true is the concern of systematics. To affirm certain statements as true and to attempt to understand what these statements mean entail distinct sets of operations. The first set of operations Lonergan calls 'doctrines,' and the second 'systematics.' In Lonergan's words, people 'know what church doctrines are. But they want to know what church doctrines could possibly mean. Their question is the question to be met by systematic theology.'[5]

1.2 Dogma and Systematics

A second emphasis, one that Lonergan makes most explicitly in *De Deo trino*, is that the systematic theologian does best to take as his or her core or central problems those mysteries of faith that have been defined in the church's dogmatic pronouncements.[6] If we can generalize from Lonergan's own example, it would seem that he would single out especially the mysteries of the Trinity, the hypostatic union, and grace.[7] The aim of systematics is to present an 'assimilable whole,'[8] and so a unified understanding of Christian doctrine; but the core meanings that were explicitly affirmed by the Christian church in the kairos moments of its self-constitution are to form the core of that synthetic statement.

1.3 The Order of Teaching

The third emphasis is that systematic understanding should proceed as much as possible according to what Lonergan, following Aquinas, calls the *ordo disciplinae* or *ordo doctrinae*, the order of learning and teaching. Lonergan distinguishes the order of teaching from the order of discovery, the *via inventionis*. '[T]he course of discovery is roundabout. Subordinate issues are apt to be solved first. Key issues are likely to be overlooked until a great deal has been achieved. Quite distinct from the order of discovery is the order of teaching. For a teacher postpones solutions that presuppose other solutions. He begins with the issues whose solution does not presuppose the solution of other issues.'[9] The difference of the two ways can be grasped perhaps most clearly in the contrast between what happens in the history of a science and, on the other hand, the way in which the science is presented in a contemporary textbook. To use what is perhaps Lonergan's most frequent example, the history of chemistry shows that the science established its conclusions by moving step by step toward the understanding of sensible data; but a contemporary textbook begins, not by repeating these experiments and so going through the whole history of discovery, but with the periodic table of chemical elements from which over 300,000 compounds can be derived. The way of analysis, the way of discovery, led to the formulation of the periodic table. The way of teaching begins from the periodic table and proceeds to compose from it the various compounds that it allows us to understand. Scientific investigations begin from the sensibly manifest, but a teacher starts with those notions the understanding of which does not presuppose the understanding of anything else but rather makes possible the understanding, in the limit, of everything else in the science.[10] And on this basis, we may formulate one of our key questions in the following form: *What will stand to systematic theology as the periodic table stands to chemistry?* Answering that question will enable us to proceed in the *ordo doctrinae* that is appropriate to systematics.[11]

We may refer once again to the work of Pannenberg in order to make our point. For Lonergan, as long as one is moving in the way of discovery, one may be moving toward systematic reflection, but one is not doing systematics. One is working in one or more of the first six functional specialties: research, interpretation, history, dialectic, foundations, doctrines. Pannenberg's three-volume *Systematic Theology* proceeds almost entirely in this *via inventionis.* It is good *via inventionis* work, in some places quite outstanding. For the most part, it leads to, represents, or supports 'sound doctrine.' But it is not what Lonergan means by systematics. In fact, I think it is no exaggeration to say that Pannenberg is working at one time or other in every other functional specialty, and hardly, if at all, in systematics as Lonergan conceived the latter.

And yet even in Lonergan the distinction of the two ways as it affects systematics is not absolute. For there is a history to systematics. There is, if you want, systematics *in fieri,* systematics on the way, and, occasionally and rarely, there is the production of a systematics *in facto esse,* a finished product. The latter, in fact, will in our time be at best the work of a community of theologians, not of any one theologian working alone. There is also a series of movements from particular sets of systematic achievements to further, more complete sets, that is, from one systematics *in facto esse* (relatively) to another systematics *in facto esse* (again, relatively). Most systematic efforts, in fact, are part of systematics *in fieri,* and every systematics *in facto esse* is destined to be replaced by new syntheses, as questions arise that cannot be treated adequately within the framework provided by the old system. In Lonergan's words, the principal 'question to be met by systematic theology' is 'what church doctrines could possibly mean,' and 'the answer to that question is a gradual increase of understanding. A clue is spotted that throws some light on the matter in hand. But that partial light gives rise to further questions, the further questions to still further answers. The illuminated area keeps expanding for some time but eventually still further questions begin to yield diminishing returns. The vein of ore seems played out. But successive thinkers may tackle the whole matter over again. Each may make a notable contribution. Eventually perhaps there arrives on the scene a master capable of envisaging all the issues and of treating them in their proper order.'[12] Yet, as Lonergan makes clear especially in his 1959 course 'De intellectu et methodo,' even such a synthesis will be gone beyond as yet further questions emerge, questions that in many instances could not even have been asked had not the systematic synthesis been achieved. The questions are raised within the framework of a particular systematic achievement, and yet they cannot be answered within the confines of that same framework. In the work of one who presents such a synthesis, systematic theology would follow the *ordo doctrinae,* in a manner analogous to the way in which a chemistry textbook composes the compounds from the periodic table. But in the work that leads up to and makes possible such a synthesis *and* in the work that follows once the synthesis that once satisfied now proves inadequate to respond to later questions, both ways of ordering ideas are employed. The *ordo doctrinae* remains the systematic ideal, of course. But it is crucial that the theologian acknowledge which of these two 'ways' he or she is working in at any given point. And when it becomes clear that a particular systematic framework is too narrow to handle the further questions that arise within it, then holding fast to the *ordo doctrinae* of that systematic framework is, at best, a logical-deductivist mistake and, at worst, obscurantist rejection of those further questions. The move has to be made to the systematics *in fieri* that employs the *ordo inventionis,* until there is reached the new vantage point that will account for and respond to the new questions. The irreversible 'upper blade,' the source of all permanent achievements, lies in the dynamism of the minds that raise the further questions. Permanent achievements, both doctrinal and theological, have been reached along the way, but the only arbiter of such achievements lies in the authenticity that acknowledges them.

1.4 Explanation on the Level of One's Own Time

The fourth emphasis has to do with the crucial importance of making the move in systematics from description to explanation, and of doing so on the level of one's own time.

First, there is the move itself from description to explanation. 'Not only does the order of teaching or exposition differ from the order of discovery, but also the terms and relations of systematic thought express a development of understanding over and above the understanding had either from a simple inspection or from an erudite exegesis of the original doctrinal sources. So in Thomist Trinitarian theory such terms as procession, relation, person have a highly technical meaning. They stand to these terms as they occur in scriptural or patristic writings much as in modern physics the terms, mass and temperature, stand to the adjectives, heavy and cold.'[13]

Second, there is the contemporary context of what is essentially the same move: '[T]he basic terms and relations of systematic theology will be not metaphysical, as in medieval theology, but psychological ... General basic terms name conscious and intentional operations. General basic relations name elements in the dynamic structure linking operations and generating states. Special basic terms name God's gift of his love and Christian witness. Derived terms and relations name the objects known in operations and correlative to states ... For every term and relation there will exist a corresponding element in intentional consciousness.'[14] So one must ground or root one's categories in what Lonergan calls interiorly and religiously differentiated consciousness. Moreover, a systematic theology on the level of its own time must include the 'general categories' that theology shares with other contemporary disciplines, as well as the 'special categories' proper to theology itself.[15] The insistence on general categories remains one of the most contentious issues in theology, even as it was in the medieval context that formed the fateful conflict between Aristotelians and Augustinians. While the issue is not always formulated as an issue about categories, it is a central feature in many of the most serious disputes in theology, contemporary and past. While the debate over John Milbank's so-called 'radical orthodoxy' is perhaps the most notable instance on the contemporary scene,[16] a refusal to recognize the necessity and validity of the general categories affects other debates in a more or less subterranean way. Many of the tendencies of doctrinaire authorities to absolutize positions that would be threatened by the development of knowledge surrounding the realities named in the general categories are well known. Positions that themselves are not at the core of Christian belief have been elevated to such prominence for reasons other than doctrinal integrity. I refer to such categories as those that help us understand social and institutional organization, gender, sexual relations, power relationships, and so on.

The base of the general categories is the interiorly differentiated consciousness promoted by Lonergan's intentionality analysis; Lonergan indicates that his earlier work *Insight* shows how the general categories are derived. The base of the special categories is the religiously differentiated consciousness that would be promoted by an exploration of religious love and a differentiation of the spiritual life.

This fourth point could equally well be called an insistence on honouring the systematic, critical, and methodical exigences.[17] The turn to theory and explanation is in accord with the systematic exigence. The turn to the subject meets the critical exigence. And the return in communications to the natural and human sciences and the varieties of commonsense language and insight prevailing in one's own cultural matrix satisfies the methodical exigence.[18]

1.5 A Theological Qualification

A further point with regard to both the third and the fourth emphasis is that, unlike work in the other sciences, the movement from the descriptive to the explanatory is, at least when the talk is about God, not a movement from the causes of knowing to the causes of being. In God there are no causes of being. The move in theology is a reversal within the causes of knowing themselves.

> [I]n theology, whenever God is the object of inquiry, we have only the causes of knowing, since for God, who is utterly simple and necessary, there are no causes of being whether intrinsic or extrinsic. However, since our knowledge of God consists of numerous truths related to one another by various reasons, a truth that is the reason for another truth is also the cause of our knowing that other truth. And since there is a twofold ordering among all truths, namely, from what is more evident with respect to us to what is more evident with respect to itself, and from what is more evident with respect to itself to what is more evident with respect to us, there are in theology some causes of knowing that are more evident with respect to us, namely, those from which we begin when faith is enlightening reason by the way of theological discovery, and there are other causes of knowing that are more evident with respect to themselves, namely those from which we begin when reason enlightened by faith acquires some understanding of the mysteries of the faith by the way of theological teaching.[19]

2 Questions about Each Emphasis

Despite my firm agreement with Lonergan in these four regards, I am asking whether he says enough. Let me expand on this question by focusing on related questions that arise out of each of these areas of agreement.

First, then, if the principal function of systematic theology is clear – the hypothetical, imperfect, analogical, obscure, gradually developing understanding of the mysteries of faith – what are the other functions, how are they related to the principal function, and how are they related to the other functional specialties? To speak of a 'principal function' implies that there are other functions. What are they? Unless I am mistaken, we are not told, at any point in Lonergan's writings, beyond the references to the inclusion of the philosophy of God in systematics.[20]

Second, while the core problems are set by the dogmas that express some of the revealed mysteries, still there are also aspects of revealed mystery that have not received, perhaps never will receive, and even cannot receive dogmatic status in the church. How are these to be related in systematics to the dogmatic elements?

Third, if the *ordo doctrinae* is the appropriate ideal mode of exposition of systematic understanding, nonetheless it is clear even from Lonergan's own account, as we have seen, that much systematics is not done exclusively in this mode. Moreover, the other functions of systematics to which we are pointing might introduce still more of an element of the *via inventionis* into systematics itself. But the relation of the *via inventionis* components to the *ordo doctrinae* needs further elaboration than is provided in Lonergan's account of theological operations in *Method in Theology*. In particular, entering on the way of discovery will involve one in other functional specialties besides systematics. The *via inventionis* includes the tasks fulfilled in the first six functional specialties: research, interpretation, history, dialectic, foundations, and doctrines.[21] But when these operations are performed by a *systematic* theologian in service of systematic understanding, they have a finality other than the one that is proper to the given functional specialty itself. The ulterior aim of some work in biblical exegesis or historical investigation, for example, might be systematic understanding. The dynamics that are operative when one is engaging in one functional specialty in order to meet the demands of another functional specialty – surely a legitimate task – stand in need of further explanation. While the *ordo doctrinae* is the proper method of procedure in systematic exposition, a question arises as to the element of the *via inventionis* that is engaged in precisely for the sake of systematics, an element that is different from simple interpretation or history, for example. These operations in the *via inventionis* will be performed by a systematic theologian because of an ulterior motive, a further and not at all hidden agenda, namely, systematic understanding. What are the dynamics that are operative here, when one is doing, for example, interpretation or history or dialectic or even doctrines, not for their own sake but in order to prepare the way for systematics? And how does one guarantee that one's integrity in these other functional specialties is not compromised by one's ulterior objective?[22]

Finally, in many instances the meaning of some of the mysteries of faith is perhaps *permanently* best expressed in categories that are symbolic, aesthetic, dramatic, narrative. Even if a technical explanation is possible in, for example, metaphysical terms, nonetheless the value of aesthetic, dramatic, and narrative theologies of the same mysteries is unmistakable. But in that case the question arises, Are these aesthetic, dramatic, narrative theologies also to be explanatory? And if so, how does one move from description to explanation with regard to such expressions of meaning? Is an explanatory employment of symbolic categories possible, and if so what are its grounds? At this point we are moving in the area addressed by Hans Urs von Balthasar's theological aesthetics and dramatics.[23] But we are attempting to relate the positive gains of these works to Lonergan's systematics while complementing each of them by the other. If Balthasar speaks of 'theological dramatic theory,'[24] we must inquire into his meaning of the word 'theory.' If its explanatory potential remains under-emphasized in Balthasar's work, as I think it does, then we must ask how it can be developed. It is an important emphasis that should be promoted, not reversed, and yet it will not be promoted *for systematics* unless a move can be made from description to explanation. To give a concrete illustration, the second volume of Balthasar's *Theo-drama*[25] is concerned with precisely the same problem that Lonergan addresses in his study of Aquinas on *Grace and Freedom*,[26] namely, the interrelationship of divine and human freedom. The categories in which the problem is expressed are remarkably different: Balthasar's are dramatic, while Lonergan's are metaphysical. The problem yet to be answered is just how the two treatments are related to one another.

Needless to say, when the issue is the very mystery of God, which cannot be explained in the strict sense of the term, the word 'explanatory' has to be understood in the sense employed above, when I spoke of the *priora quoad se* among the causes of knowing, not among causes of being, of which there are none in God. But many of the mysteries to which I am here referring are mysteries of the economy, not of the immanent Trinity. And for those we may perhaps speak of explanation in a more strict sense.

For example, will there be, can there ever be, a word or phrase that has even the tincture of systematic meaning that informs the term *homoousios*, when one is seeking a systematic understanding, not of the kind of question forced on the church by the Arian heresy, but of the dramatic deed enacted on Calvary for our redemption? I do not think so. I believe that this particular mystery will be permanently best expressed in symbolic, dramatic, narrative categories. But in that case can we arrive at an understanding of the redemption that is more than descriptive of the *priora quoad nos*? Lonergan is very clear in *Insight* that explanatory understanding of non-explanatory meanings is possible.[27] At least once in his discussion of modern psychologies he stated that the depth psychologies of Freud and Jung were seeking precisely this kind of understanding; as contrasted with other psychologies, at least the depth psychologies were in pursuit of explanatory understanding.[28] But to my knowledge he never shifted these hermeneutical affirmations into a theological context so as to face the question, Is an explanatory employment of symbolic, dramatic categories possible *in systematic theology*, as a way of talking about the mysteries of faith? And if it is, what are its grounds? In fact, in the introductory chapter of the *pars systematica* of *De Deo trino*, the contribution even of depth psychology to the transcultural problem is still regarded as descriptive.[29] The most difficult point for some Lonergan students to grasp in what I have written about symbols and psychic conversion is my insistence that it is possible to attain an explanatory understanding of symbolic meaning, an understanding that relates the symbols to one another. This emphasis can be extended to narrative, so that it is possible to have an explanatory grasp of narrative. But that is still a hermeneutic affirmation, even if it bears principally upon the interpretation of the reality of the self. My present questions are such questions as the following: Can that possibility be carried over into systematic theology? If it can be, is it desirable to do so, or should systematics under all circumstances seek to move to technical language? If it is possible and desirable to pursue an explanatory use of symbolic categories or of narrative, how would one begin to ground this use?

Concretely, then, we might ask, Is Balthasar's aesthetic-dramatic approach genuinely systematic? If not (and I do not think it is), then what has to be done to make it so? Again, do Balthasar and some of Lonergan's students (if not Lonergan himself) set up a false dichotomy between such an approach and explanation? If so, what has to be done to overcome such a dichotomy?

These are but some of the questions that I want to raise in this exploration of methodological issues in systematic theology. The questions will not all be answered in this book. Many of them must be resolved *ambulando* in constructing a systematic theology on the basis that I am here suggesting. My basic concern in the present book is simply stated. The mysteries affirmed as true by the community, and so given the status of doctrines, are constitutive of the community that gathers in the world in the name of Christ Jesus. Systematics is a particular form of witness to the truth of the doctrines, the witness of understanding.[30] As such it is a witness to realities whose affirmation in doctrines establishes the core meanings constitutive of the Christian community. The understanding that it reaches is, primarily, an understanding of the revealed divine mystery. The synthesis that it expresses is centred in meanings that we would not attain at all were the realities (the mysteries) that they intend not revealed. As such, systematic understanding must remain permanently imperfect, hypothetical, analogical, and open to development. But if we find ourselves agreeing with Lonergan on this crucial methodological point, we must also indicate several points on which his notion of systematics calls for development. The development does not run counter to Lonergan's notion of systematics, but rather brings to the fore some elements in that notion that otherwise are all too easily overlooked and promotes others that have been left undeveloped.

3

Dogma and Mystery

We have indicated areas of fundamental agreement with Lonergan on the method and objectives of systematics, as well as the questions that arise even from these points of agreement. It is time to turn to developments on what is explicitly given us by Lonergan in his writings on systematics.

The first point I would make by way of expanding upon Lonergan's emphases has to do with the relationship between dogmas and the mysteries of faith. It is a complex point.

First, what is dogma? On Lonergan's interpretation, the doctrine about doctrine of the First Vatican Council correlates 'dogmas' with 'mysteries.' The use of the term 'dogma' in this context refers to doctrines that express a mystery that is otherwise so hidden in God that we could not know it at all had it not been revealed by God.[1]

Second, while doctrines are of various sorts,[2] my concern is with a twofold differentiation. First, among the church's doctrines some express mysteries of faith and some do not. Second, among the church doctrines that do express mysteries of faith, some have received dogmatic status and some have not. Dogma is thus a subset, twice removed, of the more basic category 'church doctrines.'

Third, systematic theology is organized around that subset, around those church doctrines that are also dogmas. However much systematic theology will attempt also to understand doctrines that are not dogmas, whether they be ecclesial or theological doctrines or both, and even to propose new theological doctrines, some of which may some day become church doctrines, at its core lies the attempt to present a synthetic understanding of the mysteries that have been expressed in the dogmatic judgments of the church. This is, again in Lonergan's words, its principal function.

One of the central elements in these proposals for systematic theology will serve as an example. There appears in Lonergan's work a four-point systematic hypothesis that I will take as a part of the organizing systematic conception, the unified field structure, of systematic theology. It is expressed in a statement that has been buried for nearly fifty years in a Latin manual of Trinitarian theology. I refer to it now simply in order to indicate what I mean when I say that systematics attempts a synthetic understanding of those mysteries that have received dogmatic status; eventually we will see how the hypothesis is part of the basic systematic conception of an overall systematic view, part of what stands to systematic theology as the periodic table stands to chemistry. The hypothesis reads as follows.

> [T]here are four real divine relations, really identical with the divine substance, and so four special ways of grounding an imitation or participation *ad extra* of God's own life. And there are four absolutely supernatural created realities [four created graces]. They are never found in an unformed or indeterminate state. They are: the secondary act of existence of the Incarnation, sanctifying grace, the habit of charity, and the light of glory.
>
> Thus it can appropriately be maintained that the secondary act of existence of the Incarnation is a created participation of paternity, and so that it has a special relation to the Son; that sanctifying grace is a created participation of active spiration, and so that it bears a special relation to the Holy Spirit; that the habit of charity is a created participation of passive spiration, and so that it has a special relation to the Father and the Son; and that the light of glory is a created participation of filiation that brings the children of adoption perfectly back to the Father.[3]

We will not linger on this statement at the moment. I present it here simply in order to show that a systematic theology can be organized around a synthetic statement of *dogmatic* materials. The hypothesis expresses a synthetic understanding of specifically dogmatic affirmations regarding Trinity, Incarnation, grace, and the last things.

But my concern now is still preliminary to systematic considerations as such. The community that gathers in the name of Christ Jesus is, like every other community, constituted by meaning. It is a community only to the extent that it is the achievement of common meaning. The common meaning that constitutes the community intends objects that the community affirms as real and good. Systematic theology attempts to understand the realities intended in that common meaning, and to do so in a synthetic fashion. At the heart of that common meaning are the realities intended in judgments that the community holds to be true. When the community is forming those judgments, it is establishing its doctrines. Among the doctrines some regard mysteries so hidden in God that they could not be known at all unless they were revealed. And among the doctrines that regard such mysteries some (only a few, in fact) have been given dogmatic status. Dogma is limited to such doctrines, at least for our present purposes and in accord with Lonergan's usage of the term 'dogma' in this context. Systematic theology is centred on an understanding precisely of those mysteries of faith that have received such dogmatic status in the church, in the manner embodied in the four-point hypothesis that we have cited. The hypothesis expresses a synthetic understanding of the mysteries affirmed in dogmas regarding the Trinity, the Incarnation, grace, and the life everlasting, and so it is duly equipped to serve as an initial systematic theorem and as part of the basic systematic conception or unified field structure of a contemporary synthetic construction.

Fourth, however, systematic theology is more than an understanding of dogmas. And this is the principal point of this chapter. Systematic theology is the ordered, coherent, hypothetical, gradually developing, structured, synthetic, and in places analogical and obscure understanding, in the limit, of all the realities intended in the meanings actually or ideally constitutive of the community that is the church. It is centred around those meanings that express the realities intended in the theorem of the supernatural, that is, the mysteries so hidden in God that we could not know them at all unless they were revealed. More precisely, it is centred around those mysteries of faith that have received dogmatic status in the church. Its other functions are subordinate to the task of understanding the mysteries of Christian faith, and centrally those mysteries to which the church has granted dogmatic status. But the correlation of dogma and mystery is a one-way correlation. That is, 'dogma' is limited here to certain affirmations, and at times (as in the conciliar definitions establishing Christological and Trinitarian dogmas) clarifications, of mysteries of faith. But the 'mysteries of faith,' even some of those included in the creed, include more than the realities affirmed and clarified in explicitly dogmatic pronouncements.[4] While dogma affirms mysteries, mysteries extend far beyond what has been clarified or perhaps ever will be expressed in dogmatic statements, and this in at least two ways. First, there are elements of Christian constitutive meaning, and indeed of the mysteries of faith in the strict sense of 'mysteries,' that have not received, and perhaps never will receive, dogmatic status. Second, and just as important, the element of mystery is a permanent feature even of those elements of Christian constitutive meaning that *have* received such status in the church, no matter how clear their conceptual formulation will be. The meaning of the Nicene *homoousion*, for example, is clear: the same things are to be said of the Son as are said of the Father, except that that Father is Father and the Son is Son.[5] But the mystery of the Incarnate Word is inexhaustible. And the principal function of systematics is the understanding of the mysteries of faith, whether these mysteries have been explicitly affirmed in dogmatic pronouncements or not.

Really, then, the issue is one of mystery, and of how mystery is preserved in systematic theology. What are the grounds that will enable systematic theology to remain in touch with the mystery that it is attempting to stutter about (however systematic the stuttering may be)? What are the grounds that will prevent systematic theologians from entering again the vast arid wasteland of theological controversy over inconsequential issues? What are the grounds that will prevent both systematic theologians and church teachers from neglecting the proclamation of the mysteries in favour of focusing on issues that are not central to the gospel? If we agree with Lonergan that systematics does best to draw its central problems from dogmatic statements, we also ask about the rest. And the rest consists in part of (1) the mysteries that have not received, and in some cases perhaps will not, even cannot, receive, such dogmatic formulation, and (2) the element of mystery that will remain permanent even after a particular dogmatic pronouncement has been made.

None of this, of course, is alien to Lonergan's concerns. He even draws on Pope Pius XII's encyclical *Humani generis* to affirm that the fonts of revealed doctrine contain so many and such great treasures of truth that they will never adequately be exhausted (DS 3886).[6] And in *Insight*, even prior to discussing explicitly theological themes, he affirms and emphasizes the permanence of an element of mystery no matter how clear and precise our concepts become, an element that will be expressed not in technical language but in dynamic images.[7] Surely such an affirmation applies as well to theology as to the pre-theological elements that he is discussing at that point in the book. Theologians too must pay heed to the following statement: 'The achievement ... of full understanding and the attainment even of the totality of correct judgments would not free man from the necessity of dynamic images that partly are symbols and partly are signs. This necessity ... remains despite complete and fully conscious rejection of counterpositions, of the attempt to confine explanation within a descriptive mold, of gnosticism and of magic. It is a necessity that has its ground in the very structure of man's being.'[8] Thus, while it is true, for example, that after Athanasius the meaning of the *homoousion* is clear, still there is an infinite sea of meaning surrounding the Trinitarian and Christological mysteries that never will be captured in expressions like this, in propositions about propositions, no matter how clear either set of propositions may be. To do theology in abstraction from that abyss of inexhaustible intelligibility is to betray the very mystery that theology attempts to understand. Hans Urs von Balthasar calls to our attention the aesthetic and dramatic character of the categories that express that element of permanent, abiding mystery. While a number of questions have to be put to his work, still we may draw on that work for appropriate leading threads that can be woven into a more or less seamless whole with the writings of Lonergan.[9]

There are, then, mysteries expressed in the scriptures and in the church's tradition, in the creeds and in other doctrines affirmed as constitutive of the community of faith, that never have been, and in some cases perhaps never will be, defined as dogma. There is no defined dogma regarding the resurrection of Jesus, though there may be need of such a definition in our time. There is no defined dogma that does for the *pro nobis* of the redemption what Nicea and Chalcedon do for the incarnation and the ontological constitution of Christ. There are scriptural doctrines on both resurrection and redemption, and there are theological doctrines found in many forms in the church's tradition with regard to the meaning, the immanent intelligibility, of both resurrection and redemption. But there is no explicit church dogma that does for either of these mysteries what Nicea and Chalcedon do for the mystery of the Incarnation, the divinity of the incarnate Word, and the ontological constitution of Christ. And yet the resurrection and the redemption are also at the core of the constitutive meaning of the Christian community, just as much as are the definitions of Nicea and Chalcedon; and they are there precisely as mysteries of faith. Positions can be taken in their regard that are just as heretical as denials of Nicea or Chalcedon. Thus, while dogma defines mysteries of faith, the mysteries of faith extend beyond what has been or, perhaps, will be formulated in explicit dogmatic pronouncements, and systematic understanding must include these mysteries as well as those that have been dogmatically affirmed. If systematics is an understanding of the mysteries of faith, it includes an understanding of these nondogmatic elements. A statement on method in systematics must account for such understanding. And so we ask, What grounds the synthetic inclusion in systematic theology of elements of the Christian mystery that have not been and perhaps never will be formulated in dogmatic pronouncements?

Let us consider in more detail the example of the *pro nobis* of the redemption. The exact nature of the *pro nobis*, the immanent intelligibility of 'for us and for our salvation,' remains for theologians a question that is open in a manner that simply is not true of the issue of Christ's ontological constitution.[10] Nicea and Chalcedon express, not a systematic meaning, but definitely at least a 'post-systematic meaning.'[11] It is quite possible that there may never be this kind of dogmatic definition of the redemption, in fact that there *cannot* be such a definition. Perhaps its meaning is forever the meaning of a dramatic deed, a deed that is true but that will never be defined. There are scriptural doctrines about the redemption. There are theological doctrines found in many and sometimes conflicting forms in the church's tradition; they have to do with its meaning, its immanent intelligibility. But when Lonergan, precisely as systematic theologian, expresses that immanent intelligibility in terms of the just and mysterious law of the cross,[12] the affirmed truth, the doctrine, that he is attempting to understand is not one that has ever been given the conceptual, post-systematic, defined doctrinal clarity that the *homoousion*, correctly understood, provided in answer to the questions that it resolved. The affirmed truth of the redemption, the doctrine of redemption, lies rather in the domain of *permanently elemental meaning*. That is to say, it is possible that its meaning will always be better expressed in the symbolic, aesthetic, and/or dramatic terms of scripture, literature, and drama, and be lived forward from the narrative, than it will be formulated in the quasi-technical type of formulation that most dogmas provide. The principal issue may always be something like, How best do we tell this story? rather than searching for some technical formulation in the realm of system and theory. But even then, as I will argue when I speak later about psychic conversion, there can be an explanatory grasp of the narrative itself, where its inner constituents are related not just to us but to one another.[13]

Lonergan discusses elemental meaning in the context of his discussion of *art* and *symbols* as carriers of meaning.[14] The *permanence* of mystery that he affirms in *Insight* and to which we have already drawn attention is equivalent to what we are here calling 'permanently elemental meaning.' That is, it is meaning that remains permanently just like that of an 'experiential pattern' that does not intend something else that is meant. Again, it is meaning just like that of a symbol whose meaning 'has its proper context in the process of internal communication in which it occurs' and not in some subsequent interpretation.[15] It is always possible to set elemental meaning within a conceptual field, but never by so doing to reproduce the elemental meaning itself. 'The proper expression of the elemental meaning is the work of art itself'[16] or the developing or declining conscious intentionality of the imagining or perceiving subject.[17] It may be that the most that dogma could, even in principle, do for the truth of the redemption is to protect it against error or aberration. Again, it may be that a dogma that would affirm the need of redemption would be salutary at the present time. But *homoousion* does considerably more regarding the ontological status of the incarnate Word, since it responds to an exigence for positive clarification that could not be satisfied without the move to at least a 'tincture of systematic meaning.'[18] It may be that the mystery of redemption is one whose articulation, precisely as a mystery, remains forever the *symbolic* expression of a 'position,' the *aesthetic* and *dramatic* presentation of a truth that, affirmed as truth, is constitutive of the community of believers. Perhaps its truth is primarily what Balthasar calls the truth of a divine *deed.*[19] The sense, Balthasar hastens to add, is quite different from Faust's and Fichte's 'In the beginning was the Deed,' since 'the drama between God and man is itself already *logos,* meaning, word ... in the sense of a word that happens, *a word that possesses one dimension more than the word that is witness.*'[20]

Perhaps we may note in this connection, and extend to the mystery of redemption, what Lonergan says about a theological understanding of the Marian dogmas.

> [T]he dogmas of the Immaculate Conception and of the Assumption of our Lady differ from those defined in ecumenical councils. The latter settle controverted issues. The former repeat what was already taught and celebrated in the whole Catholic church. Accordingly they are named ... 'cultic.' Their sole effect was that the solemn teaching office now proclaims what formerly was proclaimed by the ordinary teaching office. Perhaps I might suggest that human psychology and the refinement of human feelings is the area to be explored in coming to understand the development of Marian doctrines.[21]

This is in contrast to the refinement and appropriation of cognitional operations required to understand the development of the Christological and Trinitarian doctrines. And if this is the case with regard even to some elements of the church's constitutive meaning that *have* received dogmatic expression, then surely it might be true also of other elements that, while constitutive of the community, have never been given, and perhaps will never be given, such dogmatic articulation.

Thus, while dogma defines mysteries of faith, the element of mystery extends beyond what has been or perhaps even will be formulated in explicit dogmatic pronouncements. Systematic theological understanding must find a way to include these elements. If systematics is an understanding of the mysteries of faith, it includes an understanding of what may remain nondogmatic elements. Methodological reflection on systematic understanding must specify the grounds on which such inclusion is justified and adjudicated. What is it that makes possible the synthetic inclusion in systematic theology of elements of the Christian mystery that have not and perhaps never will be formulated in dogmatic pronouncements? Where do these elements belong within a systematic theology that would be a *Glaubenslehre,* an understanding of the mysteries of faith? How are they related intelligibly to those elements of the mysteries of faith that in fact have been given dogmatic formulation? How does one reach a *systematic* understanding of meanings that perhaps will remain expressed in elemental, symbolic, aesthetic, dramatic, narrative carriers of meaning? There is at least a possibility, as I indicated earlier, that an adaptation of René Girard's work on violence and the sacred can contribute in a major way to soteriology. But the adaptation will not consist in moving from symbolic discourse to metaphysical categories, unless the metaphysics is an ontology of meaning and value.[22] There must be some kind of explanatory employment of symbols themselves through a further immersion into the symbols that enables one *to grasp in their relations to one another first the symbolic meanings, and through those meanings the elements of the drama that are affirmed precisely by employing these symbols.*

Again, particular parameters around resurrection and redemption are just as central to the constitutive meanings of the Christian community as are the *homoousion* of Nicea and the 'one person in two natures' of Chalcedon. Other ways of understanding resurrection and redemption in fact amount to a denial of the community's constitutive meaning.[23] To affirm that Jesus rose only in the consciousness of the disciples, so that they are the ones who in fact came alive, is in fact to deny the resurrection that is affirmed in the New Testament and in the creed. To affirm a purely revelational soteriology, so that 'salvation in Jesus' means *only* that Jesus reveals the salvation that God is always working in the world, is in fact to deny the efficacy meant when we confess '*pro nobis*' regarding the redemption wrought in the concrete historical events of the death and resurrection of Jesus. That part of the meaning of the resurrection is the transformation of the disciples is clear. That part of the meaning of redemption lies in the revelation of God's constant activity is clear. But to reduce either mystery to such a partial component is to venture on the way of heresy. The conversion of the disciples is the easy part of resurrection doctrine. The revelational aspect of soteriology is the easy part of soteriology. The hard work of determining precisely in what lies the resurrection of Jesus and the salvation that God has wrought in Jesus remains to be done, even after one has affirmed the transforming power of the resurrection and the revelatory value of the redemptive act.

But what enables one to tell the difference between an understanding that witnesses to the truth constitutive in the formation of the community and an understanding that denies or waters down that truth? And once such nondogmatic elements of Christian constitutive meaning have been properly (*convenienter*) understood, what enables one to relate them systematically to those elements that are strictly dogmatic? Such questions push us back to the grounds of systematic understanding. If those grounds at times have to do with 'the refinement of human feelings,' with the emergence of a Christian religious *sensibility*, with the aesthetic and dramatic constitution of Christian living, then there is perhaps a dimension to theological foundations that Lonergan did not expressly articulate. It is the dimension that I have attempted to indicate in my various attempts to speak of a 'psychic conversion.'[24]

The issue can be approached in another way, namely, by asking whether all derived categories in systematic theology must be metaphysical. Clearly, on Lonergan's account, no basic terms and relations are metaphysical. '[F]or every term and relation there will be a corresponding element in intentional consciousness,'[25] and it is in that corresponding element that basic terms and relations are to be located. But must all systematic theological construction eventually take a metaphysical turn? Again, where are the analogies to be found through whose help the mysteries of faith are understood? Surely metaphysical analogies have proven most helpful in the search for theological understanding of the mysteries of faith. Even in a dimension that is as laden with dramatic significance as the theology of grace, Aquinas has demonstrated the power of metaphysical analogies. Sanctifying grace is understood by Aquinas by analogy with the Aristotelian metaphysical analysis of the habit. Actual grace, *auxilium divinum* as Aquinas calls it, is understood by analogy with the Aristotelian metaphysical analysis of operation.[26] But Lonergan himself says in the epilogue of *Insight*, '[T]he theologian is under no necessity of reducing to the metaphysical elements, which suffice for an account of this world, such supernatural realities as the Incarnation, the indwelling of the Holy Spirit, and the beatific vision.'[27] The basis of this statement is 'a very relevant distinction between the more detailed metaphysics of proportionate being and the generalities that alone are available a priori on ... supernatural elements.'[28] And so, if there is no absolute requirement that theological analogies be metaphysical, then presumably there is nothing to prevent the analogies that would enable a properly theological understanding of at least some of these mysteries of faith from being aesthetic and dramatic analogies.

The affirmed truth of the redemption, and so the doctrine of the redemption, remains perhaps in the domain of permanently elemental meaning, that is, the kind of meaning that is carried in symbols, art, narrative, dance, sculpture, poetry, and not in technical or post-technical language. 'Elemental meaning' is a category that Lonergan introduces when speaking of art and symbols as carriers of meaning. Permanently elemental meaning is meaning that remains permanently like that of the artistic objectification of a purely experiential pattern, where the meaning does not intend something else that is meant, as in conceptual formulations and explicit propositional judgments. Again, it is meaning that is like that of a dream symbol, where the proper context of the meaning is supplied by the process of internal communication in which it occurs, and not in some subsequent interpretation. Setting elemental meaning within a subsequent conceptual field is always possible, of course, but such a procedure can never reproduce the elemental meaning itself, and may easily distort it.[29]

I am not claiming, of course, that systematic theology must reproduce elemental meaning in the manner of a work of art. Systematic theology is technical discourse, and technical discourse can never reproduce elemental meaning. The issue is rather one of remaining faithful to the elemental meaning, not distorting it, and the question recurs in this context, *Whence the analogies that will render such technical discourse possible?*

It is at this point that systematic theology even in the tradition of someone like Lonergan can legitimately turn to one of the basic inspirations behind Balthasar's work, namely, the insistence that some of the analogies to be employed in the systematic exposition of the mysteries of faith can and preferably will be drawn from aesthetic theory and dramatic theory, not from metaphysics. Balthasar is not anti-metaphysical, as is clear from the two volumes on metaphysics in his *Aesthetics.* Ultimately, however, those volumes make it clear that only the metaphysics of Aquinas passes muster for him, because only this metaphysics can be said to be completely in harmony with the biblical emphasis on the glory of God.[30] Thus for Balthasar the theological criterion for passing judgment even on a metaphysics is aesthetic, in the sense of a theological aesthetics whose prime analogate is divine glory. Again, for Balthasar fidelity to what we are calling the elemental meaning of some of the mysteries of faith will demand that some of the categories employed in systematics be drawn from dramatic and aesthetic theory. With that insistence I am in agreement, but I am also seeking to ground that insistence in a manner analogous to Lonergan's grounding of metaphysical categories in intentionality analysis. With such a grounding it will be possible to speak *in an explanatory fashion* about those elements that are best left in the realm of elemental meaning.

If that is the case, then what is at stake here is what we must regard as an expansion of the normative source of meaning beyond what is generally regarded as Lonergan's view on the issue. In fact, something of an expansion of his own usual view can be found in Lonergan's own later writings, and especially in the wonderful paper 'Natural Right and Historical-Mindedness.' This expanded normative source of meaning will enable us to answer the questions, How is mystery preserved in systematic theology? and What are the grounds that will enable systematic theology to remain in touch with the mystery that it is attempting to speak of?

In 'Natural Right and Historical Mindedness,' then, Lonergan states that there is a *normative* source of meaning in history, as well as a total and dialectical source. The normative source is twofold. It consists, first, of the operators of conscious intentionality: questions for intelligence, questions for reflection, questions for deliberation.[31] These operators are what would usually be considered Lonergan's normative source of meaning. But in 'Natural Right and Historical Mindedness' these several principles of integrity and authenticity are 'but aspects of a deeper and more comprehensive principle,' and it is this deeper and more comprehensive principle that is the normative source: 'a tidal movement that begins before consciousness, unfolds through sensitivity, intelligence, rational reflection, responsible deliberation, only to find its rest beyond all of these,' in 'being-in-love.'[32] This tidal movement is an ongoing process of self-transcendence that in another paper from roughly the same post-*Method* period, 'Mission and the Spirit,' is called 'the passionateness of being.'[33]

The tidal movement or, again, the passionateness of being has a dimension all its own, distinct from but intimately related to the operators and operations of intentional consciousness, a dimension that underpins, accompanies, and reaches beyond the operations of intelligent, rational, and responsible intentionality. As underpinning intentional consciousness, the passionateness of being is an operator that presides over the transition from the neural to the psychic, the unconscious to the conscious. As accompanying intentional consciousness it is the mass and momentum, the colour and tone and power of feeling. As reaching beyond or overarching intentional consciousness it is the operator of community.

My own addition, perhaps, to what Lonergan says consists in the affirmation that in its totality this tidal movement is a series of operators that I will call aesthetic-dramatic. These join with the intentional operators (questions for intelligence, questions for reflection, and questions for deliberation) to yield the normative source of meaning in history. Furthermore, what I call psychic conversion establishes the link, through a turning of intentional consciousness to its aesthetic-dramatic counterpart. It is from the ongoing clarification and appropriation of the aesthetic-dramatic operators that the explanatory use of aesthetic and dramatic categories will be possible in systematic theology. It is psychic conversion that will keep systematic theology in touch with the mystery that it is attempting to understand.

4

Theological Doctrines

1 The Position

While systematics is centred in an understanding of the mysteries of faith, it is not limited to such mysteries, even when 'mysteries of faith' is taken to include more than dogmas, even when it includes the elemental meanings that, as I will argue below, are closest to the form of divine revelation itself. Systematics is an understanding of mysteries, yes, but there are also doctrines, both theological and ecclesial, that do not directly express mysteries of faith but that systematic theologians attempt to work into a synthetic construction. I am especially concerned here, not so much with ecclesial doctrines that are not dogmas as with the *theological* doctrines that one receives from the tradition or from one's contemporaries, or in some cases that one has developed on one's own. These often emerge from attempting to understand scriptural doctrines or church doctrines or dogmas or mysteries of faith, but even if they do not directly transpose any of these, they are among the doctrines that the systematic theologian will attempt to understand, for they have been received as either entering into or explicating the meaning constitutive of the community. Moreover, these appropriated theological doctrines themselves often have systematic implications, and when that happens elements of other *systematic* syntheses are part of the *doctrinal* inventory of a contemporary systematic theologian.

This point can easily be overlooked when one is reading *Method in Theology*. Lonergan is perhaps a bit inconsistent in expressing what the functional specialty 'doctrines' is all about. In his first statement regarding the sixth functional specialty, it is clear that he is referring principally to *theological* doctrines, and it is equally clear that he is not limiting himself to dogmatic formulations of the church.

> Doctrines [meant here as the functional specialty 'doctrines'] express judgments of fact and judgments of value. They are concerned, then, with the affirmations and negations not only of dogmatic theology but also of moral, ascetical, mystical, pastoral, and any similar branch.
>
> Such doctrines stand within the horizon of foundations. They have their precise definition from dialectic, their positive wealth of clarification and development from history, their grounds in the interpretation of the data proper to theology.[1]

It is clear that in this statement Lonergan is thinking of *theological* affirmations, affirmations that include church doctrines and dogmas but that embrace far more as well. But later in the book he writes, 'Doctrines are concerned to state clearly and distinctly the religious community's confession of the mysteries so hidden in God that man could not know them if they had not been revealed by God. Assent to such doctrines is the assent of faith.'[2] In light of the earlier statement, this cannot be taken to mean that the functional specialty 'doctrines' is concerned *only* with the mysteries so hidden in God that they are known only because they are revealed. And perhaps Lonergan's clearest indication of his meaning is found near the beginning of the chapter on doctrines, when he writes that the doctrines 'meant in the title of the present chapter' are 'theological doctrines reached by the application of a method that distinguishes functional specialties and uses the functional specialty, foundations, to select doctrines from among the multiple choices presented by the functional specialty, dialectic.'[3] Theological doctrines thus understood obviously include the mysteries of faith, but they include far more. And their context is the academic discipline called theology. While this context is distinct from the doctrinal context of church confessions, it interacts with it, so that there are clear instances in church history in which theological formulations influenced church doctrines, even while conversely (and obviously) church doctrines provided basic elements to be formulated and reformulated theologically in ever new contexts.[4]

While the expression 'mysteries of faith' names the nonnegotiable elements, whether dogmatic or nondogmatic, that constitute the core of systematic theological meaning, nonetheless no systematic theology begins *simply* from these core meanings. Every systematic theology stands within a history of attempts to understand the Christian faith. Systematic theology itself began within such a history; it was preceded by centuries of theological statements that were not, strictly speaking, systematic, but that, by the questions that emerged from them, gave rise to a theoretical exigence that would find satisfaction only in a more systematic mode of thinking and writing. No systematic theology today, not even a systematic treatment of a single issue, is attempted before one has taken innumerable trips, as it were, through the spiral of the functional specialties, appropriating and making one's own certain elements from a long theological tradition. And if one has made these elements one's own, this means that one speaks them in direct discourse, as one's own word and not simply as the word of another. The doctrines of a contemporary Calvinist are not just the doctrines of Calvin; however much they may be identical with the doctrines of Calvin, they are now also the doctrines of the theologian who believes that he or she is carrying on the Calvinist tradition. Unless one is doing nothing but interpretation and history, one speaks these doctrines in one's own name, not just in the name of Calvin. When one enunciates these doctrines, one is speaking in direct discourse, *in oratione recta* as opposed to *in oratione obliqua*. When one begins to operate in systematics, one has already made decisions, not only regarding the core dogmatic elements constitutive of the church, but also regarding the theological tradition within which one stands. Moreover, every systematic theology is in dialogue with other contemporary efforts to understand the same faith and the same traditions. Systematic theology is inescapably intertextual (though not, as some who would use this contemporary buzzword might want to say, solely intertextual: as Aquinas said, theological understanding terminates not at words, but at realities).

These past and present theologies with which a theologian interacts exhibit genuine achievements of understanding that, once they have been accepted and affirmed as such by a systematic theologian, assume *for that theologian* a certain doctrinal status. This will not be the status of a church teaching. Even less is it the status of a church dogma. But it is the status of theological doctrines that are judged to have passed the tests required if they are to be affirmed *by a theologian* – affirmed, and not simply entertained as interesting hypotheses. It is precisely such *judgment* that constitutes them as among the doctrines that, in systematics, one attempts to understand in a synthetic manner.

We can reinforce the doctrinal status of some systematic achievements by reflecting on what Lonergan has to say about the detrimental effects *for the faith itself* of poorly understanding a genuine systematic achievement. In *De Deo trino*, he outlines the steps that lead from poorly understanding a genuine systematic achievement to rejecting that achievement, and from rejecting a systematic achievement to denying the very facts that are understood in the achievement, that is, mysteries of faith themselves.[5] In our own day we find such a sequence of movements in Trinitarian theology. Karl Rahner's Trinitarian *Grundaxiom* that the immanent Trinity is the economic Trinity *and vice versa* has been variously understood. Rahner, of course, was too good a theologian and too faithful to the Catholic tradition to be the modalist that some would accuse him of being and that others would applaud him for being. But it is clear that he did not understand Thomas's *emanatio intelligibilis,* the basic psychological analogy for the Trinitarian processions. The *Grundaxiom* is built on a misunderstanding of a genuine theological achievement, namely, the notion of *emanatio intelligibilis* and its use in an attempt to understand the divine processions. Misunderstanding the *emanatio intelligibilis* means necessarily that one will not be able to appropriate the relation between divine procession and the divine missions as this relation is expressed in question 43 of the *Prima pars* of the *Summa theologiae.* The *Grundaxiom* is the result of this undifferentiated and regressive move on Rahner's part. From the *Grundaxiom* to the further confusions generated by attempts to collapse the immanent Trinity into the economic Trinity, the steps are short. But they are even shorter from such Trinitarian reductionism to the denial that there is in fact any immanent inner life of a triune God to be understood. Rahner, let me emphasize, would repudiate such conclusions, but they can easily be drawn from his position.

The general movement of Lonergan's method itself, then, as it proceeds from dialectic through foundations to doctrines and systematics, and especially as it does so over and over again, comes to demand the inclusion of certain theological doctrines among the affirmations that systematics would understand. Theology itself provides some of the doctrines that contemporary systematic efforts attempt to understand. This element is often overlooked in the interpretation of what Lonergan means by the 'doctrines' of his sixth functional specialty. Yet, as we have seen, it is clear from Lonergan's own text that this is what he meant. And so we must grant something of a doctrinal status to the systematic framework in which these theological doctrines were expressed.

2 Criteria of Theological Doctrines

We spoke of tests that, if passed, would qualify theological achievements with a certain doctrinal status. What would some of these tests be? What sorts of things transpire in theological study itself to confer on some of its achievements something of a doctrinal status, if not for the church at least for subsequent theologians? Such tests will vary from case to case. The examples of theological doctrines that I will present here manifest different criteria, and I make no claim that this list of criteria is complete. I will speak of three distinct criteria.

The first of these theological doctrines is granted a certain doctrinal status because *it has brought definitive closure to a particular theological debate.* The second has doctrinal status because *it is the only analogy of nature yet discovered and developed that is useful for understanding a particular divine mystery.* The third has doctrinal status because *it is an inescapable practical conclusion of the Gospel of Jesus Christ.* These, then, would be some of the reasons why a particular theological achievement may assume something of a doctrinal status for a given theologian or tradition in theology.[6]

3 Closure: The Example of Operative Grace

The first two examples are drawn from a long theological tradition, and the third from the contemporary theological and ecclesial scene. In considering examples from the tradition, we ask first just what it is to locate oneself within a given theological tradition. For in the sets of operations that Lonergan calls dialectic and foundations, a contemporary systematic theologian determines the particular theological tradition in which he or she stands. Or, perhaps more accurately, when one is making such a crucial determination, one is in effect operating in the functional specialties of dialectic and foundations. To locate oneself within a particular tradition is to decide whom and what one is for and whom and what one is against. But in dialectic and foundations one also articulates the grounds of that decision.

So let us assume that a particular systematic theologian (for example, the present author, who is intended now when I write 'he,' 'him,' or 'his') has determined that the overall theological tradition in which he is working is broadly defined by Lonergan's implementation of the Leonine *vetera novis augere et perficere.* That is, he has determined, with certain qualifications, that he stands in the tradition of Aquinas as this tradition has been made available through the interpretations of Lonergan and advanced by Lonergan's developments and transpositions of some of its essential inspirations.[7] For such a theologian, basic formal-methodological *and doctrinal* components have already been determined, and the affirmation of such components includes content beyond both the mysteries of faith themselves and other church doctrines. Nor is that determination arbitrary: one has considered as best one can the multiple options (dialectic) and discerned as best one can the ground for the determination (foundations).

The doctrines of such a theologian include some of the achievements arrived at in the tradition that one affirms, and so in the previous attempts of other systematic theologians within that tradition to *understand* the mysteries of faith. There are a number of reasons that might lie behind the fact that one grants these achievements a certain doctrinal status. A first reason might be that an achievement is judged to have brought closure to a particular theological debate. If I make such a judgment as a systematic theologian, then the achievement has assumed a certain doctrinal status for me precisely as systematic theologian. It will retain that status for me and for others in my tradition, irrespective of whether it ever attains doctrinal status in the church. Its doctrinal status obtains precisely *for the systematic theologians who judge that in fact this achievement has brought definitive closure to a particular theological debate.*

So, for example, the theological doctrine on operative and cooperative grace, both habitual and actual, that Aquinas expresses very succinctly in the *Prima secundae* of the *Summa theologiae*, q. 111, a. 2, and this theological doctrine precisely as Lonergan has interpreted it,[8] settles previous long-standing, seemingly interminable, and extremely acrimonious theological debates (all of them post-Aquinas) on the relation of divine grace and human freedom. This means that there is no longer any point in revisiting those debates in such a manner as to settle them. They no longer have to be settled. They are already settled. If one agrees, then one has a doctrine in their regard. The doctrine is not church dogma or even, directly, church doctrine. Most likely it never will be either of these. Nor is it originally one's own position. It is the position of Aquinas as interpreted and affirmed by Lonergan with an eye to the post-Aquinas debates. Once one judges that it has brought closure to those debates, it has become a theological doctrine. In itself it is hypothetical, analogical, and obscure: it is after all a piece of systematic theological understanding. Yet in affirming it as settling theological and doctrinal issues, one gives it the status of a theological doctrine. There is nothing to prevent one from revisiting the debates in interpretation and history, and so in indirect discourse, if one so desires. But interpretation and history are not systematics. If one regards those debates as over, if one judges that Lonergan's interpretation of Aquinas has brought closure to the *de auxiliis* controversy (a closure that pronounces a plague on both houses), then that judgment is among the affirmed doctrines that in systematics one would attempt to understand. It may have taken one a number of trips through the loop or spiral of the functional specialties to arrive at the point where one has a theological doctrine of one's own on these issues. But once one has reached that point, the relevant affirmations are doctrinal, not in the sense of assent to scriptural doctrine or to church doctrine or to dogma, but in the sense of assent to a particular theological achievement. They are doctrinal, not in the sense of providing an element of the church's constitutive meaning, but in the sense of being a probable approximation to the correct understanding of that meaning. The achievement is, of course, also judged not to run counter to scriptural doctrine or to church dogma or to other church doctrines. But it is not, as such, included among these forms of doctrine, nor is it likely that it will ever be granted the status of church doctrine. Yet by being affirmed as a genuine theological achievement, it is constituted among the elements that, as a systematic theologian, one would attempt to understand.

There are grounds in Lonergan's own exemplary performance as a theologian for the methodological point I am making. He not only traced the development of Aquinas's thought on operative grace and related it to the tradition that preceded Aquinas. That is, he not only contributed interpretive and historical monographs on the issue. He also included Aquinas's final position on this issue, as he understood it, among the doctrines that his own systematic understanding of grace would comprehend.[9] Aquinas's final theological doctrine on operative and cooperative grace, both habitual and actual, is not itself scriptural doctrine or church doctrine or church dogma. It is the theological doctrine of a particularly authoritative theologian. It is itself the hypothetical result of a systematic effort to understand scriptural, patristic (especially Augustinian), and church doctrine. But especially because one judges that, when correctly understood, it ends a particular theological dispute that resulted largely from a misunderstanding of it on both sides, it assumes a doctrinal status. One can dispute it without denying the faith. Within limits, one might arrive at a different theological understanding of the relation of grace and freedom without denying or compromising the faith. At the very least it may be said that, in all likelihood, neither Molina nor Bañez was a heretic; certainly, neither of them denied either divine grace or human freedom. But if one affirms that Lonergan has demonstrated that neither of them correctly understood either the relation between human freedom and divine grace or what Aquinas eventually came to say about that relation, one has made a theological judgment on a historical matter, a judgment that has doctrinal import. For that historical judgment is linked to the option that Aquinas's position on the issue, precisely as retrieved by Lonergan, closes the debate and so is to be affirmed among one's own doctrines. Thus, it must be among the elements that one would understand in a systematic synthesis. And in attempting to understand it precisely in systematics, and so in theology's phase of direct discourse, one is interpreting it not just as someone else's position but as one's own, as a theological doctrine that one affirms.

4 Analogy: The Example of *Emanatio Intelligibilis*

A second reason for granting a systematic achievement the status of a theological doctrine lies in the judgment that the achievement provides the best or perhaps the only analogy from nature for understanding a supernatural mystery. This is the reason I would affirm the validity of what has been called the psychological analogy for the systematic understanding of the divine processions and would call that affirmation another of my theological doctrines. It is true that this theological-doctrinal status would be contested by others, and that I must be prepared to defend it; but that does not change the fact that my assent to it makes it for me a theological doctrine.

There are three major moments in the history of this analogy. The first is the working out of the analogy in the *via inventionis* over the fifteen books of Augustine's *De trinitate.* The second is Aquinas's metaphysical promotion and deepening of essentially the same analogy and his presentation of it in the *ordo doctrinae,* in the *Summa theologiae, Pars prima,* questions 27–43 (with greater detail on certain points in various chapters of book 4 of the *Summa contra Gentiles*). The third is Lonergan's further advance on the same analogy in the *pars systematica* of his *De Deo trino.* Aquinas offers an advance on Augustine in that he adds metaphysics to psychology and inverts the order of exposition from the *via inventionis* to the *ordo doctrinae.* Thomas begins where Augustine ends. And several reasons may be assigned for judging that Lonergan offers an advance on Aquinas. While he is attempting to understand Aquinas's doctrine, he also grounds his categories in the interiorly differentiated consciousness that *Insight* would bring forth in its readers. Thus he is able to appeal more explicitly, with greater precision than is found in Aquinas, and with greater explanatory power than is found in Augustine, to the *experiences* of the processions of word and love in human consciousness (especially the procession of the word). But he also makes important (and often overlooked) contributions by focusing on the existential (rather than speculative or merely practical) character of the proper analogy for the divine processions and by emphasizing that the proper analogue for the divine Word is not just any inner word proceeding from just any act of understanding but the judgment of existential value proceeding from a grasp of evidence bearing upon one's self-constitution. The theological potential inherent in such emphases has not yet been tapped. It is especially important given some contemporary questions in Trinitarian theology, including stress on intersubjectivity and history.

At any rate, my present point is simply that, if Aquinas is 'advancing a position' found in Augustine, Lonergan is 'advancing positions' found in both Augustine and Aquinas.[10]

The potential for a fourth major moment in the history of the psychological analogy appears in a late work of Lonergan's, where he expresses a further promotion or advancement of the analogy, one whose implications have yet to be explored. He proposes an analogy that would move, as it were, 'from above' in human consciousness rather than 'from below.'

> The psychological analogy ... has its starting point in that higher synthesis of intellectual, rational, and moral consciousness that is the dynamic state of being in love. Such love manifests itself in its judgments of value. And the judgments are carried out in decisions that are acts of loving. Such is the analogy found in the creature.
>
> Now in God the origin is the Father, in the New Testament named *ho Theos*, who is identified with *agapê* ... Such love expresses itself in its Word, its Logos, its *verbum spirans amorem*, which is a judgment of value. The judgment of value is sincere, and so it grounds the Proceeding Love that is identified with the Holy Spirit.
>
> There are then two processions that may be conceived in God; they are not unconscious processes but intellectually, rationally, morally conscious, as are judgments of value based on the evidence perceived by a lover, and the acts of loving grounded on judgments of value. The two processions ground four real relations of which three are really distinct from one another; and these three are not just relations as relations, and so modes of being, but also subsistent, and so not just paternity and filiation [and passive spiration] but also Father and Son [and Holy Spirit]. Finally, Father and Son and Spirit are eternal; their consciousness is not in time but timeless; their subjectivity is not becoming but ever itself; and each in his own distinct manner is subject of the infinite act that God is, the Father as originating love, the Son as judgment of value expressing that love, and the Spirit as originated loving.[11]

The psychological analogy has fallen on hard times in theology. The major twentieth-century contribution to understanding Thomas's own position is, I believe, found in Lonergan's treatment of *verbum* in Aquinas. To this may be added Frederick Crowe's study of points in Aquinas related to the procession of the Holy Spirit.[12] These works have yet to receive the attention that they deserve.[13] A great deal of attention has been paid to Lonergan, of course, but how many people really understand his work on Aquinas? Very few have taken the time to study it, and Wittgensteinian presuppositions have prevented others from even considering its basic framework: acts of understanding grounding inner words, inner words grounding outer words. Lonergan's work on *verbum* in Aquinas shows in intricate detail how Aquinas understood the procession of the eternal Word by analogy with the procession in human consciousness of inner word from understanding. In human consciousness there are two distinct inner words (concept and judgment) proceeding from two quite distinct acts of understanding (direct and reflective). Lonergan's *Insight* promotes the same two processions in human consciousness to a new level of reflective exactness. His *De Deo trino* calls attention to the existential context of self-constitution in which some inner words emerge. The focus is shifted to the judgment of value as the inner word on which an analogy to the procession of the divine Word can be constructed. Again, Crowe's work on complacency and concern focuses on the procession of Love in God and the analogy in human consciousness of the procession of love from inner word. Lonergan's systematics of the Trinity advances the Thomist analogy into the explicit realm of meaning governed and dictated by interiorly differentiated consciousness. And his late work on the relation of love and knowledge, where he insists on a particular relation of the two that, it seems, neither Augustine nor Aquinas grasped,[14] opens the possibility of an analogy 'from above.' Its implications, which have yet to be explored, will link the psychological analogy in immensely fruitful ways to a number of contemporary concerns in Trinitarian theology. But first that analogy must once again be understood; the basic reason that it has been passed by is that it has not been understood.[15]

Why has the analogy not been understood? The answer is complex, and any suggestions I can give are just hints.

First, the lack of understanding is not something peculiar to the present age in theology. Thomas's analogy has rarely been understood in the last seven hundred years. Lonergan once asked, 'Why is it, if I am right in saying that insight is fundamental in Aristotle and St Thomas, that in the course of seven hundred years only seven Scholastics advert to the possibility, and only some of those accept it?'[16] Without the recognition of insight, of the original meaningfulness of human acts of understanding, there is no grasp of the procession of the inner word, and so *no analogy from nature for the procession of the divine Word.* But the problem, Lonergan insists (even while raising the question in the manner just cited), is more than an intellectual problem: it is existential. First, there is the difficulty that one will have in epistemology if one admits insight. '[W]hy is it that insight has been neglected? It is because, if you frankly acknowledge that intellect is intelligence, you discover that you have terrific problems in epistemology. It is much simpler to soft-pedal the fact that intellect is intelligence than to face out the solution to the epistemological problem.'[17] But the existential problem is deeper, and Lonergan devotes many of the pages of *Insight* to analysing it. There are specifically existential and psychic biases that force us to resist insight, to flee understanding, and to refuse to acknowledge the centrality of the act of understanding in human living and human knowing. The contemporary British theologian John Webster writes, 'There is no single thing called "understanding."'[18] Later I will argue that Heidegger's *Verstehen* is distinct from Lonergan's 'insight,' that we must distinguish minor and major formal and actual intelligibility. If I am correct, then so too is Webster. Still, we can ask, Is there or is there not a distinct act that we can locate in the data of consciousness, an act in which we grasp the point, catch on, 'get it,' see the connections, or, again, in which we grasp that the conditions for a prospective judgment of value are or are not fulfilled? That is 'understanding' in its major sense, as originating meaningfulness.

There is also an enormous resistance among theologians, even systematic theologians, to make the move to theory, the move from description to explanation, the move that acknowledges the systematic or theoretic exigence. Moreover, there is an equally strong resistance, even among some who do not disparage theory, to take the further step to interiority, to acknowledge the critical and methodical exigencies that would move one from a stage of meaning expressed in a theory governed by logic to a stage of meaning expressed in a post-theoretical appropriation of intentional operations and their concomitant states or dispositions. Interiority is not an end in itself. It is a region of withdrawal, but for the sake of a return. The return, in the limit, would be a return to a post-critical naiveté, a second immediacy, in the world mediated by meaning.[19] But the resistance to the required withdrawal is as strong as was the resistance of the Athenians to Socrates as he tried to move them beyond ordinary language and into the type of theory represented in *omni et soli* definitions, or the resistance of medieval Augustinians to the appropriation of the metaphysics and psychology of Aristotle into the doing of theology.

Finally, all of this is pointing to the heart of the difficulty: the psychological analogy puts the subject himself or herself at stake, and it calls for a conversion. And this is the merit of Lonergan's emphasis in *De Deo trino*, according to which the precise mode of intelligible emanation that he will use to build the analogy has to do with the subject's self-constitution. The analogy appeals to the integrity of cognitional performance in the realm of the knowledge of facts and in the realm of the knowledge of values. And, whether the analogy is working from below or from above, it appeals to the self-transcendence of love as the ground and basis and also as the ultimate flowering of human authenticity. The subject has become part of the object, and wherever that happens, the subject is on the line. Nor will contemporary toasts to 'spirituality' suffice, if they are less than theoretical and critical. What is required in contemporary efforts in spirituality is a *theology* that promotes syntheses of spiritual reality that not only are explanatory but also include an account of inquiry, understanding, conceptualization, formulation, reflection, grasp of evidence, and reasonable judgment. These too are spiritual, and any account of spirituality that neglects them will prove inadequate at least in the long run and as theology.

At any rate, the affirmations made in the preceding few paragraphs reflect a set of theological doctrines. A renewal and advancement or promotion of the psychological analogy represents the way forward, not backward, in Trinitarian theology, precisely because it is not only the best analogy of nature yet discovered and elaborated, but also the only one that really does what an analogy should do in systematic theology: isolate the mystery, argue persuasively for the absence of contradiction, and allow the possibility of an interconnection of this mystery with others. Its power in generating systematic interconnection is shown in Lonergan's four-point hypothesis, which we will take as part of the unified field structure for systematic theology.

The judgment that the analogy has these characteristics qualifies it as a theological doctrine, just as the judgment that Lonergan's interpretation of Aquinas on operative grace closes a long debate qualifies that position also as such a doctrine. If indeed it is the proper analogy, then it may be assumed that it will provide the resources to integrate important issues being raised in contemporary Trinitarian systematics, and especially the relation of the 'immanent Trinity' to history and to the Paschal mystery. In fact, if one judges as I do that it is the only satisfactory analogy, then one must wager that it will successfully negotiate these contemporary issues, and one must set oneself the task of showing that this indeed is the case. To affirm it as a theological doctrine implies a wager that a truly synthetic systematic statement cannot successfully negotiate the new issues that are being raised in Trinitarian systematics unless it is rooted in an understanding and development of the psychological analogy. I believe this wager will hold up, and so I grant the achievement itself a doctrinal status. My systematic theology would begin by attempting to understand precisely this doctrine. It is not a dogma, but a theological understanding of a dogma, an understanding that has already been offered in the theological tradition in which I have chosen to stand. But because I judge that this particular understanding provides the only analogy from nature that will really do the job, it has assumed for me the status of a theological doctrine. Again, the psychological analogy is not church dogma or church doctrine. The term 'psychological analogy' refers to a genetic sequence of more or less systematic efforts (Aquinas and Lonergan are far more systematic than Augustine) to appeal to operations and *operata* in human interiority in order to reach some imperfect, analogical, obscure, but developing and fruitful understanding of the Trinitarian processions. It provides a perfect example of what I will mean in speaking of a genetic sequence of systematic-theological statements.[20] The analogy becomes a theological doctrine when it is judged to be the best, and perhaps the only, analogy from nature that will yield theological understanding in the sense of Vatican I. It synthesizes past achievements in Trinitarian theology and, I believe, grounds the possibility of genuinely systematic renditions of current and future developments.

5 Practical Consequences: The Example of Preferential Option

My third example of a theological doctrine will be presented more briefly, not because it is less important but because it is probably more familiar to most contemporary readers. It rests on yet another criterion for establishing a theological doctrine, that of praxis. Theologies of liberation have developed a theological doctrine that affirms both a preferential option for the disenfranchised in the church's ministry and a hermeneutically privileged position of the marginalized in the church's interpretation at least of contemporary situations. These theologies, and theologies influenced by them, are also at least moving to theological doctrines that would extend that hermeneutic privilege to the church's retrieval of its own tradition. The preferential option for the poor has become part of official church teaching. Some of the contemporary official church apologies for past mistakes are in effect promoting the movement to make the hermeneutic appropriation of the experience of the oppressed a part not only of our reading of contemporary situations but also of the critical retrieval of the history of our faith community. None of this has achieved the status of dogma. Probably it never will. In fact, if dogma is limited to mysteries hidden in God that we could not know unless they were revealed, then definitely this will never be dogma, even though it reflects an assent to the mysteries of faith and an acceptance of their practical and moral consequences. In this sense, then, it is doctrine. In fact it is both theological and ecclesial doctrine. And more specifically, it is doctrine as a praxis consequence of the gospel of God in Christ Jesus. As such it must be included in any authentic synthetic understanding of the community's constitutive meaning, and so in any contemporary Catholic systematic theology. My own attempt to understand it has employed Lonergan's notion of the scale of values coupled with a development of his notion of dialectic.[21]

I have presented three examples of what I mean by 'theological doctrines' that are not dogmas – in fact, the first two are not even church doctrines – and that express directly not revealed mysteries themselves but either theological efforts to understand the mysteries, as in the first two examples, or theological consequences of the mysteries, as in the third. My principal point in highlighting these examples is that they manifest one kind of affirmation that qualifies as 'doctrine' in the sense of the sixth functional specialty, and so as material to be included in the systematic synthesis that the seventh functional specialty would promote.

But we must face the question, Just what is the relation of such theological doctrines to the mysteries of faith that it is the principal function of systematics to understand? These theological doctrines are themselves the result of systematic attempts to understand the mysteries of faith, either in themselves or in their consequences. But once the contemporary systematic theologian affirms them, they assume the status of doctrines whose further understanding one would pursue in systematics. How are such doctrines to be related as doctrines to the central mysteries that one is attempting to understand? The question opens onto the issue of the ontology of meaning, that is, to the question of the place in systematics itself of an explanatory history of genetically and dialectically related systematic witnesses to the faith of the church. The ontology of meaning will receive more extensive treatment later.[22]

5

Categories

A third area where Lonergan's reflections on systematics can be developed or at least filled out has to do with the transposition of categories. A fourth area concerns the integration of categories transposed from past contexts with categories developed today. And a fifth area concerns the correct way to conceive the relation of the general categories to the special categories. These three points may be covered in one chapter on categories. As my first two points, so these three are rooted in Lonergan's own statements, and I am doing little more than heightening their importance.

1 Transposition

In my discussion of the transposition of categories, I will stay with the same examples that I used in the previous chapter to speak of theological doctrines.

Lonergan's systematic understanding of the doctrine of grace is probably most fully expressed in the schematic supplement *De ente supernaturali* that he wrote for a seminary course in 1946.[1] Still, no matter to what extent one agrees with the positions there put forth, it will not do simply to translate that supplement into a contemporary vernacular and offer it as a satisfactory systematics of grace. While the metaphysical categories in which the systematic understanding of that treatise is expressed are not to be jettisoned or rejected, they must be grounded in terms and relations derived from interiorly and religiously differentiated consciousness. '[F]or every term and relation there will exist a corresponding element in intentional consciousness.'[2]

Thus, for example, the first thesis of *De ente supernaturali* affirms that there exists a created communication of the divine nature through which operations are elicited in us whereby we reach the very being of God. And the second thesis affirms that this created communication of the divine nature is absolutely supernatural. We can agree with both of these affirmations, and in systematics we can attempt to explain what they mean. But there must be a difference between the way we would explain their meaning in a methodically based theology and the way Lonergan adopted in *De ente supernaturali*, and this on Lonergan's own insistence. For we now have to answer a question that, in that supplement, Lonergan did not face. The question is, What, *in terms of interiorly and religiously differentiated consciousness*, is an absolutely supernatural 'created communication of the divine nature'? What are the referents, in interiorly and religiously differentiated consciousness, of the metaphysical terms and relations that Lonergan employs to speak about sanctifying grace? In Scholastic metaphysical terms we are talking about an entitative habit rooted in the essence of the soul. But one can accept that Scholastic metaphysical analysis in its entirety and still not have fulfilled the contemporary exigence, for that exigence calls not only for theory but also for some foundation of theory in corresponding elements in intentional consciousness and/or religious experience. It is the task of systematic theology to answer on the level of one's own time the question, What in the world do these doctrines mean?

Let me stress the difficulty of this exigence. Lonergan writes in the first chapter of his doctoral dissertation that nothing is more difficult than the initial discovery of the proper analogies to be employed in systematic theology.[3] Well, if anything is indeed more difficult, it is the resolution of at least some of the categories of a metaphysical theology into the grounding categories of a methodical theology. On precisely the question under discussion, I have made three successive attempts at an approximation to adequate formulation, mindful that further development is required.[4] The issue is in part one of finding terms and relations in religious experience that correspond to the distinction of sanctifying grace and charity that Lonergan in *De ente supernaturali* takes from Aquinas and that in *De Deo trino* he employs in the basic four-point hypothesis regarding the created participations in the four divine relations. Lonergan's own expressions in terms of an exegesis of Romans 5.5 do not quite do the job, as is clear from the fact that they do not manage to convince some of his students that the phrase 'of God' in the verse 'The love of God is poured out in our hearts through the Holy Spirit who is given us' is a subjective genitive. That meaning is clear in Lonergan's writings, but it has been missed by many of his readers. It is *divine* love that has been poured into our hearts. It is with divine love that we love God with all our hearts and all our minds and all our strength. It is with divine love that we love our neighbours as ourselves. Romans 5.5 is not talking about our love for God, except insofar as God's own love is given to us to be our love as well. Ultimately, only an explicit connection with the Trinitarian processions, such as appears in Lonergan's four-point hypothesis that we will speak of below in more detail, will provide the satisfactory conceptualization. That hypothesis gives us an articulation that allows us to speak of sanctifying grace, however haltingly but also, as Lonergan writes, *sine inconvenientia*, not inappropriately, as the created external participation in the actively spirating love of Father and Son. That created participation in God's own love is what medieval systematic theology conceived as the entitative habit, rooted in the essence of the soul, known as sanctifying grace. The four-point hypothesis goes on to conceive the habit of charity as what is breathed forth in us from sanctifying grace, and so as a created participation in the passive spiration that is the Holy Spirit. As the Holy Spirit is the uncreated internal term of the actively spirating love of Father and Son, so the habit of charity is the created external term of the actively spirating *being*-in-love that is sanctifying grace. This is fundamentally what it means to be *recipients* of the mission of the Holy Spirit. But it is also what it means to say that, when the Holy Spirit is given to us, the Father and the Son come with the Spirit to dwell with us. The mission of the Holy Spirit *is* the eternal procession of the Spirit within the divinity, joined to a created external term, the habit of charity. But the habit of charity flows from the new *being* that is a being in love, and that being in love is a created participation in active spiration, in Father and Son together breathing the Holy Spirit. The dynamic state of being in love gives rise in a habitual fashion to acts of love of God and neighbour, as the agape of the Father and the judgment of value that is the Son together breathe the proceeding Love that is the Holy Spirit. Something of this gift enters into religious experience, but it has seldom been articulated with any sufficient clarity precisely as gift, and so as received. Upon reflection we should be able to understand some of the elements of our own religious experience in this way, and so locate something in consciousness (precisely as experience) that corresponds to that mystery. The mystery is that we are given the capacity to love as a created participation in the proceeding love in God. In us that created participation in God's own proceeding love is breathed forth from the created participation in God's actively spirating love, the entitative change in our being that is sanctifying grace. Clearly, of course, if the mystery of sanctifying grace has to do with an entitative habit, it extends beyond consciousness. But it also must have some implications that can be specified in terms of religious *experience.* Such specifications provide the grounding categories for a theology of grace, the terms and relations that express an understanding of the doctrine of grace.

The relevance of interiority to the second example, the psychological analogy, is obvious. Such an understanding of the Trinitarian mystery clearly must turn to interiorly and religiously differentiated consciousness for its basic terms and relations. The statement is analytic: the relevance occurs by definition. Lonergan has added a technical precision to the fruit of the introspection that was already manifest descriptively in Augustine and in metaphysical terms in Aquinas.

What about the third example? What are the grounds in interiorly and religiously differentiated consciousness for the theological, and now ecclesial, doctrine of the preferential option for the poor and for its systematic understanding? Such a question must be faced when one is engaged in explicit synthetic understanding of the church's constitutive meaning. I have attempted to answer this question by appealing to Lonergan's notion of a normative scale of values. As we will see below,[5] this notion is rooted in Lonergan's intentionality analysis, and so appealing to it satisfies the demands we are making in this third point, namely, that the categories of a systematic theology must be derived from interiorly and religiously differentiated consciousness.[6]

The three examples combined also make it clear that the categories with which we are concerned are both special and general. Special categories are proper to theology, and their ground is religious experience properly appropriated. General categories are shared with other disciplines, and their ground lies in interiorly differentiated consciousness. In particular, let me emphasize here that if systematics shies away from employing the categories that are provided to it by other disciplines, it is also reneging on its responsibility to provide for the realities affirmed in doctrines the witness of contemporary understanding. A systematic theologian who is wary of employing general categories supplied by the best scientific opinions of his or her own time is not accepting proper theological responsibility. While we must not deny or minimize the need to guard against correlations that would reduce the realities named in special categories to those named in general categories, we must insist that the danger is not to be avoided by taking refuge in special categories alone. Because systematic understanding is at its core an understanding of divine mystery, it must remain permanently imperfect, hypothetical, analogical, and open to development. But because it is hypothetical, it *can* employ categories derived from contemporary world views without compromising the faith affirmed in the doctrines whose truth it would understand.[7] And because it is a witness to the truth, it *must* employ at least some of these categories, even while at times refining their meaning;[8] for it is an attempt to understand that truth *on the level of one's own time.* We will see below in this chapter, in section 3, how the general and special categories are to be related to one another.

2 Integration with Contemporary Developments

My fourth point can be stated quite briefly. Categories that are transposed from the theological tradition in which one stands must be integrated with contemporary developments, whether the developments are the work of others or of oneself. The only way to assure such integration, of course, is through the grounding of both traditional and contemporary categories in interiorly and religiously differentiated consciousness. Moreover, the integration will itself entail a development, and in fact one that goes both ways: the transposed traditional emphases will deepen the appropriation of the contemporary developments, frequently making possible a discovery of their metaphysical equivalents, while contemporary developments will affect the expressions adopted in the transpositions. There will take place not so much a correlation as a mutual self-mediation between tradition and contemporary situation.

As the example from liberation theology shows, contemporary theologians propose new theological doctrines, and some of these new theological doctrines are among the doctrines that one attempts in systematics to understand. The same example shows that some of these new theological doctrines become part of the teaching of the church, while others remain affirmations that one may or may not hold without being in conflict with the church's official teaching. History shows as well that, in nondogmatic matters, some of these theological doctrines may eventually persuade the church to change its own teaching. The systematic theologian will accept some of these doctrines among those that he or she tries to understand; and in fact, in some cases the systematic theologian will even propose some such doctrines for the first time. But all of that is purely descriptive. My present question is, How are these doctrines to be integrated with the doctrines that one accepts from the tradition? What are the grounds of such an integration?

To stay with and expand on the examples we have employed, we can ask, How are the liberation emphases to be integrated with dogmas, church doctrines, and past theological doctrines regarding grace and the Trinity? Operative and cooperative grace, both habitual and actual, obviously can be integrated with the psychological analogy for understanding Trinitarian processions. But what do operative and cooperative grace, both habitual and actual, and the psychological analogy have to do with the preferential option for the poor? As we saw in a more general context in chapter 4, theology is in effect today developing a social doctrine and systematics of grace, a theology of grace that would correspond to earlier developments regarding the social constitution of sin. Theology today is also highlighting the social and historical dimensions of the Trinitarian doctrines. Theology must integrate the affirmations it accepts from the tradition with developments such as these. A contemporary systematics that would reach a synthetic statement of the community's constitutive meaning must contribute to that development. But such a synthetic integration is impossible unless the theologies of grace and Trinity, on the one hand, and the contemporary preferential option for the poor, on the other, are grounded in interiorly and religiously differentiated consciousness.[9]

3 Relation of General and Special Categories

On 13 November 2003 Daniel Monsour of the Lonergan Research Institute, Toronto, presented a major paper to the Institute Seminar, entitled 'Harmonious Continuation of the Actual Order of This Universe in God's Self-communication.' The paper addressed a number of issues, but one of its central questions was the relation of the general categories to the special categories. Monsour finds the solution to that question to lie in a theological position on the natural and the supernatural that Lonergan had worked out decades ago. I wish to represent here Monsour's position on the question of the relation of the general and special categories, affirming that I have made his position my own. After years of wrestling with this question in the context of wanting to find an alternative to the method of correlation that was so fashionable in theology until recent years, I found the solution in Monsour's paper.[10]

The paper begins with the distinction between transcendental and categorial intending. Categorial intending regards what at first is a limited, partial, or elementary object, something for inquiring into being, and elevates it to something actually understood, something actually real, something actually worthwhile affecting oneself as originating value. Transcendental intending of the intelligible, the true and real, and the good underpins and penetrates categorial intending.

Next, then, the categories that Lonergan discusses in *Method in Theology* issue from the categorial intending that is underpinned and penetrated by transcendental intending. At least these categories, general and special, have some relation to that categorial intending and to its underpinning and penetrating transcendental intending. They are interlocking sets of terms and relations with limited denotations, and they cluster into groups or sets distinct from other sets. They may be just models, but theologians may come to view them as more than models, and if so then the relations are no longer merely conceptual relations, and the terms are no longer merely objects of thought but terms of real relations.

The general categories are categories that theology shares with other disciplines. The base for deriving them or for appropriating them from other disciplines or for transposing them from those other disciplines is the normative pattern of recurrent and related operations employed in every cognitional enterprise expressly intended to yield cumulative and progressive results: the conscious subject attending, inquiring, reflecting, and deliberating, and the structure of relations among these operations as given in consciousness, and specifically in one's own consciousness as an authentic or unauthentic person, as attentive or inattentive, intelligent or resistant to insight, reasonable or silly, responsible or irresponsible.

The special categories are the categories that are peculiar to theology. The base for deriving special theological categories or for appropriating them from the religious tradition or for transposing them from the tradition is the conscious, dynamic state of being in love in an unrestricted manner, the actualization of the utmost in self-transcendence, as conscious content, or again more specifically the authentic or unauthentic Christian, genuinely in love with God or failing in that love, with a consequent Christian or unchristian outlook and style of living. Being-in-love, as it is achieved, and to the extent that it is achieved in a particular theologian, is the effective base for the theologian's derivation, appropriation, transposition, and development of special theological categories.

The derivation of the categories takes place by way of expanding and enriching the respective bases. Monsour distinguishes two kinds of expansion and enrichment of the respective bases of the categories: one, insofar as the bases function consciously and spontaneously *in actu exercito* as nuclei and origins for an initial expansion and enrichment, and a second insofar as they function thematically, as objects of inquiry in a reflective turn, and so as nuclei and originating references for a second kind of expansion and enrichment. The second kind of expansion and enrichment is mediated by the human and Christian subject effecting self-appropriation and employing this heightened consciousness both as a basis for methodical control in doing theology and as an a priori whence one can understand others, their social relations, their history, their religion, their ritual, their destiny.

The derivation is not logical derivation according to rules of inference, but a recapitulation in objectification of the base realities and of the virtualities inherent in them, as well as (it must be added) the appropriation and transposition on their basis of categories already bestowed by the tradition, by other disciplines, and by other sources.

Lonergan's own account in *Method* regarding the derivation of general theological categories is basically a recapitulation of many points from

Insight and *Method in Theology*. Monsour gives his own spin on this, suggesting that we divide the general categories into sets that might somehow correspond with Lonergan's explicit division of the special categories into sets. He ends his account of this derivation of the general categories with the suggestion, with which I am in complete agreement, that what are most needed are the terms and relations for a general theory of development and a general theory of history.

The basic nest of terms and relations for the special theological categories lies in a formulation of the conscious dynamic state of unrestricted being-in-love that results from God's gift of God's love as an expanded quality of our consciousness, as an experienced fulfilment of our thrust to self-transcendence. This formulation is not some simple thing, but demands a new theology of spiritual formation that would aid one in appropriating one's spiritual self-consciousness. That basic nest is common to many, and potentially to all, and so we have the second set of special theological categories that express togetherness in community and service, witness, a history of salvation, and so on. A third set has to do with the source of our love, the Trinity, the processions of the Word and the Spirit, the missions of the Word and the Spirit. A fourth set is concerned with being-in-love and falling short in such an achievement. And a fifth set places all the preceding categories within the dynamic context of history. 'Authenticity provides the vectorial principle of social progress; unauthenticity provides the vectorial principle of social decline. The divine missions, ordered to each other, both as regards their constitution, their consequent term, and their prolongation through cooperative human agency, provide the third vectorial principle of redemption, in which there is a graced "intussusception of human personalities" and "a leavening of human history" to the undoing of the mischief of evil and decline.'[11] Again, the significance of the theory of history is highlighted with an important quotation from *Insight* regarding the completion of the formal element in a treatise on the mystical body of Christ.[12] Monsour concludes,

> [A] theory of history would be a theory couched in general categories. Taken over in theology, they would become general theological categories and belong to the fifth set of such categories. Include consideration of the divine missions ordered to each other and their constitution and consequent term, of the historical causality exercised by Christ, of the prolongation of the divine missions through cooperative human agency, and you have at least some of the core elements that constitute the vectorial principle of redemption in human history. Formulate these in nests of terms and relations, and you have special theological categories belonging to the fifth set of

> such categories and a theology of history enhancing a general theory of history and making that general theory more concrete by the addition of the third vectorial principle.'[13]

To this I would add only an explicit reference to the need for consideration of the mission of the Holy Spirit, highlighting the need for development in the area of pneumatology.

The issue of the relation between general and special theological categories is of great importance. '[T]he root issue at stake in the question of the proper relation between general and special theological categories is a recurring *aporia* underlying and penetrating much current theological thought, and especially evident in the twists and turns of theological thought fraternizing or succumbing to rationalism, on the one hand, and theological thought fraternizing or succumbing to fideism, on the other.'[14] The tendency to rationalism is found in methods of correlation, while the tendency to fideism is found in theologies that neglect or downplay the importance of the general categories.

Three questions ought to be considered: (1) the relation of the bases for general and special categories, (2) the relation of the spontaneous expansions and enrichments from these respective bases, and (3) the relation of the reflective, explicit expansions and enrichments from these respective bases. The answer to the first question is largely determinative of the answer to the second and third questions, and so Monsour concentrates on that first question. The relation of the base for the general categories to the base for the special categories is a relation of that remote essential passive potency that is capable of being moved to receive a form by the omnipotent power of God alone, and so of obediential potency. '[T]he base of general theological categories, the transcendental notions as the unrestricted core of our capacity for self-transcendence, stands to the base of special theological categories, the state of being-in-love in an unrestricted manner, in the relation of obediential potency.'[15] Because the potency is a real orientation or order, being-in-love in an unrestricted manner is a real, intrinsic, proper, supernatural fulfilment of our natural capacity for self-transcendence. The fulfilment occurs in accord with the actual order of this universe that mirrors forth the glory of God. The missions of the Son and the Spirit are in harmonious continuation with the actual order of this universe and were so from the beginning. In ways we hardly understand, this universe and everything in it were from the beginning oriented, ordered, configured to the missions of the Son and the Spirit.

Monsour suggests that *the key to the solution of the problem of the relation of the general and the special theological categories lies in the relation of their respective bases to one another.* The problem itself is perhaps the single most-to-be-worked-out question left to us by Bernard Lonergan. It is a question that he did not answer in *Method in Theology*. It is the contemporary rendition of the problem that split Catholic theology in the medieval period into the Aristotelians and the Augustinians. Today it plays itself out in various forms of correlationism, where the danger is always one of reducing the special to the general, and in the positions that do not give sufficient grounding to the incorporation of the general categories. As I argued in an article in *Theological Studies* on Lonergan and von Balthasar, the same problem threatens to divide theology again today.[16] In *Theology and the Dialectics of History* I attempted to go to the heart of the problem that I think resides in the method of correlation, and at the same time to defend the use of general categories in theology. But I have never been completely satisfied with my presentation of the issue there, and I think Monsour goes to the heart of the matter in a way that had not occurred to me before reading his paper.

What needs to be done now, it seems to me, is to make an explicit attempt at grouping the general categories into sets, as Monsour suggests, and then to go to work on the interrelation of what in this paper are called the fifth sets in each of the divisions, so as to elaborate a theology of history. On that score, I would ask whether and to what extent my attempts in *Theology and the Dialectics of History* to amplify Lonergan's theological theory of history in terms of the scale of values contributes to the task. In that book history is understood in terms of the interrelations of the levels of value (vital, social, cultural, personal, and religious), the lower or more basic levels are conceived as being in a relation of passive potency to the higher levels (although it is not worked out precisely in those terms), and the relation of personal value to religious value is that kind of passive potency that is called obediential (and that is explicit there).

The implications of this position for the construction of a systematics of grace and an account of collective responsibility will be seen later, in a section on 'Complicating the Structure' in chapter 10.[17]

4 Summary to This Point

We may summarize our first five points (chapters 3 through 5) as follows. Systematics attempts to understand, not only church dogmas — this particular function Lonergan explains better than anyone else I have read — but also (1) the mysteries of faith that are not expressed in dogmatic pronouncements; (2) ecclesial and theological doctrines from the tradition that one affirms but that are not included among the mysteries of faith, whether dogmatic or not; and (3) new theological doctrines that have been developed in one's own time, whether by contemporaries or by oneself, irrespective of whether these doctrines have or will become church doctrine. (4) Systematics attempts as well to integrate all of these affirmations with one another, by deriving the appropriate categories from the basic terms and relations provided by interiorly and religiously differentiated consciousness. (5) The categories will be general and special, and the relation of the general to the special categories will parallel, and be grounded in, the relation of their respective bases to one another, a relation of obediential potency. This becomes most clear in a theological theory of history, where the full intelligibility of history is a function not only of progress and decline but also of redemptive grace.

6

Mediation

Next we must consider the function of mediation. The issue is intimately related to what we have just said about systematic theological understanding. And more will be said on the topic below, in the context of a discussion of praxis and of theology itself as the praxis of constitutive meaning.[1]

Lonergan writes in an often-quoted sentence at the beginning of *Method in Theology*, 'A theology mediates between a cultural matrix and the significance and role of a religion within that matrix.'[2] But seldom has the question been faced, What kind of mediation is performed by theology, and especially by systematic theology? In a posthumously published paper entitled 'The Mediation of Christ in Prayer,' Lonergan distinguishes four kinds of mediation: simple mediation, self-mediation, mutual mediation, and mutual self-mediation.[3] Which of these best fits the sort of mediation between a religion and a cultural matrix performed by the functional specialty 'systematics'? Lonergan does not tell us. Let me suggest that the answer is mutual self-mediation.

A brief examination of the four types of mediation is in order. Before differentiating the types, Lonergan presents the general notion of mediation. '[W]e can say of any factor, quality, property, feature, aspect that has, on the one hand, a source, origin, ground, basis, and on the other hand, consequences, effects, derivatives, a field of influence, of radiation, of expansion, or that has an expression, manifestation, revelation, outcome – we can say that this factor, quality, property, feature, or aspect is immediate in the source, origin, ground, or basis, and on the other hand is mediated in the consequences, effects, derivatives, outcome, in the field of influence, radiation, expansion, in the expression, manifestation, revelation.'[4] The notion is Aristotelian, not Hegelian, at least in inspiration: certitude is immediate in first principles, and mediated in the conclusion of a syllogism. 'Our assumption ... shall be that the usage of the words "immediate" and "mediate" or "mediated" in Aristotle can be generalized. For example, in Aristotelian logic the first principles are necessary, evident, true – necessarily true, and of their nature evident. In them necessity, evidence, and truth are immediate. And while in the conclusions you have necessity and evidence and truth, still it is a mediated necessity, a mediated evidence, a mediated truth.' The general notion of mediation arises from generalizing the Aristotelian notion of the immediate and the mediated.[5]

The general notion is then differentiated into four distinct types of mediation.

First, there is simple mediation. Four examples are given. In a watch, movement is immediate in the mainspring and mediated by the mainspring in the other parts; and control is immediate in the balance wheel and mediated by the balance wheel in the other parts. Again, the supply of oxygen to our bodies is immediate in the respiratory system and mediated by the respiratory system to the other parts of the body. Within consciousness, anger is immediate in the release of aggressivity by some stimulus and mediated in the eyes, the look, the voice, the jutting jaw, the up-raised hand. Finally, truth, evidence, and necessity are immediate in first principles and mediated in the conclusions drawn from these principles.

Second, however, the same examples can be complicated to yield the notion of mutual mediation. There is mutual mediation when a functional whole is constituted by mutually mediating parts. Four examples are given. (1) The balance wheel of the watch controls itself and all the other moving parts, including the mainspring; and the mainspring moves itself and all the other parts, including the balance wheel. The balance wheel and the mainspring are different centres of immediacy, and the mediations of different immediate centres overlap, precisely as mediations. A watch is a functional whole. (2) The respiratory system supplies fresh oxygen not merely to the lungs but to the whole body. The digestive system supplies nutrition not merely to the digestive tract but to the whole body. The nervous system supplies control not merely to the nervous system but to the whole body. The muscles supply locomotion not merely to the muscles but to the whole body. The result is a functional whole. There are a number of immediate centres, from each of which there flow over the whole the consequences of that centre. (3) Within consciousness there is a mutual mediation or feedback from, say, the results of anger into the causes of anger, until the 'functional whole' heads for an explosion. (4) In empirical science, what is empirical is immediate in attention to data, and what is scientific is immediate in scientific method. There are two principles of immediacy, and the result is the compound functional whole called empirical science.

Third, there is self-mediation. A whole has consequences that change the whole. Three forms are distinguished. There is self-mediation by physical parts, self-mediation by consciousness, and self-mediation by self-consciousness.

The growth of an organism is a self-mediation by physical parts, through what is figuratively called a 'displacement upwards.' It entails a process of division in which growth originates itself by giving rise to physical parts within itself. At any stage of growth the organism is alive and preparing later stages. The transitional developments account for a self-mediation. Anticipatory developments prepare for future self-mediation; for example, the size of the infant's brain is out of proportion to the size of its body but preparing for future self-mediation. There is a structuring that accounts for both present and future functioning. The analysis can go on from growth to differentiation, and from the individual to the species. The species may be said to mediate itself by its individuals. 'What lives does not live alone, and what grows also dies. But the species mediates itself by reproduction. Within the genus, the lower species mediate the emergence and sustenance of higher species. Trees do not grow in desert sand but in soil; herbivorous animals presuppose vegetative life; and carnivorous animals presuppose herbivorous animals.'[6]

If the self-mediation of the organism can be considered to take place by reason of a 'displacement upwards,' the self-mediation of the animal by consciousness occurs through a 'displacement inwards.' The animal mediates itself by presence to self, by the learning that this makes possible, by the summations of learning into its living that are manifest in skills, habits, ways of doing things. The intentional order involves a displacement inwards to the subject of consciousness. But it also involves an extension outwards. 'The tree can respond only to things that act upon it, but the animal can respond to anything it perceives, to anything it apprehends. Finally, the displacement inwards gives rise to the group, to the "we."'[7]

Again, the human being also mediates itself by self-consciousness, by doing things for oneself, deciding for oneself, finding out for oneself, finding out that one has to decide what one is to be and executing that decision, and doing this in the community of family, church, and state (thus setting up mutual self-mediation). Human development is the mediation of autonomy, and it occurs in the two stages or times of the subject, a first time when one is preoccupied with objects and a second time when one takes the turn brought about by the existential moment at which one discovers that it is up to oneself to decide for oneself what one is to make of oneself.[8] This is done in the fundamental communities of the family, the state, and the church. And these communities mediate themselves in history, by common meaning, common commitments, common values.

And so, finally, there is mutual self-mediation. One reveals one's self-discovery and commitment to another, and receives the self-revelation of the other. One opens oneself to be influenced at the depth of one's being, and others open themselves to be influenced by us. I quote:

> [W]e remarked of existential decision that it occurs in community, in love, in loyalty, in faith. Just as there is a self-mediation towards autonomy, and a mutual mediation illustrated by the organism or the functional whole that is not just a machine, so there is a mutual self-mediation. One's self-discovery and self-commitment is one's own secret. It is not a natural property that you can predicate of all the individuals in a class. It is an idea conceived, gestated, born, within one. It is known by others if and when one chooses to reveal it, and revealing it is an act of confidence, of intimacy, of letting down one's defenses, of entrusting oneself to another. In the process from extroversion, from being poured out on objects, to existential self-commitment, to fidelity, to a destiny, we are not Leibnizian monads with neither doors nor windows. We are open to the influence of others, and others are open to influence from us.
>
> Mutual self-mediation occurs in a variety of contexts and to a greater or less extent. Meeting, falling in love, getting married is a mutual self-mediation ... There is a mutual self-mediation in the education of children, of the infant, the child, the boy or girl, the adolescent, the young man or woman. There is a mutual self-mediation in the relationships of mother and child, father and son, and brothers and sisters. And there is mutual self-mediation between equals, between brothers and sisters, between father and mother, husband and wife; and between superiors and subjects, parents and children, teachers and pupils, professors and students, professors and staff, fellow students. There are matrices of personal relations in the neighborhood, in industry and commerce, in the professions, in local, national, and international politics.
>
> To explore this field of mutual self-mediation is perhaps the work of the novelist ... Mutual self-mediation provides the inexhaustible theme of dramatists and novelists. It is also the imponderable in education that does not show up in charts and statistics, that lies in the immediate interpersonal situation which vanishes when communication becomes indirect through books, through television programs, through teaching by mail.[9]

Now my present point has to do with the mediation that theology performs with respect to religion and culture. Later, we will inquire also about mediations that are internal to theology, mediations that enable us to speak of a mediating phase and a mediated phase. For the moment, however, I am concerned solely with the mediation that is meant in the statement 'A theology mediates between a cultural matrix and the significance and role of a religion in that matrix.' At the end of his discussion of self-mediation Lonergan says that communities perform self-mediation in history. I am suggesting that a similar comment be added to the discussion of mutual self-mediation. The mediation of religion and culture that theology performs is not simply a self-mediation of Christian constitutive meaning, *from* the data on revelation *through* their ongoing consequences in history *to* the contemporary faith of the church. For the ongoing consequences of the data on revelation are a function of the *exchange* that takes place between the community grounded in those data and various cultural matrices. The very constitutive meaning of the church in its historical development is a function of that exchange. Theology *does* perform the self-mediating function, but this function does not adequately exhaust the role of theology as mediating *faith and culture*. Rather, as theology performs the latter role, its self-mediating function is sublated into the mutual self-mediation of the church's constitutive meaning with the meanings and values constitutive of a given way of life. Theology is a contribution to the mutual self-mediation of the constitutive meaning of the church with the meanings and values constitutive of contemporary cultural matrices.

What is perhaps Lonergan's most complete definition of 'a culture' can be found in his 1957 lectures on existentialism: '[T]he current effective totality of immanently produced and symbolically communicated contents of imagination, emotion, and sentiment; of inquiry, insight, and conception; of reflection, judgment, and valuation; of decision and implementation.'[10] Theology in its entirety exercises a mutual self-mediation between that 'current effective totality' and the meanings constitutive of the Christian church. It is not simply a self-mediation of traditional ecclesial contents of the various levels of consciousness. That self-mediation is but the beginning of theology's work. Nor is it the simple mediation of Christian constitutive meaning to the culture. The church is, or should be, and willy-nilly has always been, a learning church, a church whose own constitutive meaning is, within the limits imposed by truly dogmatic meanings, changed by interaction with various cultural matrices.

I am emphasizing this role of theology in a mutual self-mediation because I think it is easily overlooked, and also because it provides an alternative and preferable way of speaking to the talk of a 'method of correlation.' Lonergan's very treatment of mediation provides a basis for the first type of mediation performed by theology, that is, for the self-mediation of Christian constitutive meaning from the past into the present. For he extends the notion of self-mediation to the historical development of communities. But his treatment of mutual self-mediation does not mention the mutual self-mediation of communities, and that is what I am trying to open up in asking the question about the kind of mediation performed by systematic theology.

Again, the functional specialty 'communications' (that is, the operations of theologians vis-à-vis pastoral situations, dialogue with other sciences, communication with other world religions, ecumenical contacts within Christianity itself, use of the diverse media of communication) entails a process of mutual self-mediation that takes theology back through the functional specialties, at times to the articulation of new doctrines and their understanding in systematics, and at times to the modification and even abandonment of former items that the church had been teaching. The mediation of faith and culture that characterizes theology in its entirety is a mutual self-mediation. It is not simply an intramural self-mediation of Christian constitutive meaning from revelation to the contemporary faith of the church (as, for instance, is by and large the case in the theology of Karl Barth). It is also a mutually illuminating dialogue between the contemporary faith of the church and the contemporary cultural matrices within which the faith community lives and operates. And in its function of memory (research, interpretation, history, and dialectic) it is a mutually illuminating dialogue not only between the contemporary faith of the church and the cultural elements that were appropriated by the church but also between the contemporary faith of the church and elements in previous cultural matrices that may have been overlooked, bypassed, or neglected by the church or by theology. So today theology helps the church apologize for past mistakes, both doctrinal and pastoral. So too, at least in the future if not now, theology will be invited to help the church apologize for the mistakes it is making today.

Still, despite the opening sentence of *Method in Theology*, which speaks of what in fact is a mutual self-mediation, the mediation that Lonergan actually explicates in the book, at least until the final chapter, Communications, is rather a self-mediation from the data on revelation to the contemporary faith of the church. That is, it is a mediation *within the religion* rather than a mutual self-mediation that contributes, however remotely, to the constitutive meaning of both the faith community and the contemporary cultural matrix. It is for this reason, I believe, that Lonergan only hints at some of the other operations of systematic theologians to which I am attempting to draw attention. Mutual self-mediation entails a set of theological operations that, unless I am mistaken, are indeed prefigured but not thoroughly accounted for in *Method in Theology*. I am trying to call attention to such operations.

If I may give one concrete instance, I do not believe that *Method in Theology* provides explicit materials for an operational, methodological understanding of the kind of development that John Courtney Murray achieved in the church's teaching on religious liberty. Murray was working as a systematic theologian in dialogue with his culture, and his work entailed a mutual self-mediation between that religiously pluralistic cultural matrix and the significance and role of his own religious community within that matrix. His work involved more than the operations that Lonergan would include in the functional specialty 'communications.' For out of that dialogue he developed a new *doctrine* regarding religious liberty, and he attempted to express an *understanding* of this new doctrine in a fashion that certainly could be called systematic. His new doctrine called for a change in the church's official teaching. After some severe opposition from church authorities, his doctrine became, at the Second Vatican Council, the official teaching of the church. It is not dogma, and in all likelihood it never will be or can be, if dogma is limited to divine mystery. But it is doctrine. It is no longer simply the theological doctrine of a particular theologian; it is now part of the doctrine (though not the dogma) of the church. Yet even before it became church doctrine it was a theological doctrine that Murray not only put forth but also laboured to explain, to understand, and to communicate to his contemporaries. In all of this, I suggest, he was doing the work of the systematic theologian. But I do not believe that this particular type of set of operations is adequately accounted for or at least sufficiently stressed in Lonergan's work. And the reason may have something to do with the difference between, on the one hand, theology's function in the self-mediation of the church's constitutive meaning from the past into the present and, on the other hand, its function in the mutual self-mediation between that constitutive meaning and the meanings and values that one discovers and affirms in one's contemporary cultural matrix, a mutual self-mediation that contributes to the meanings and values of both the church and the cultural matrix. *Method in Theology* accounts for self-mediation in theology; perhaps more is needed to account for the mutual self-mediation of cultural matrices and religious traditions.[11]

There is a doctrinal component to this insistence on mutual self-mediation. Systematic theology is not only de facto a mutual self-mediation between the accumulated wisdom of the community and the cultural matrix. It is this type of mediation *in principle, de iure.* Why? Because there is such a thing as the universal mission of the Holy Spirit. The universal mission of the Holy Spirit, and in fact even the invisible dimension of the mission of the Word in whom all things were created, prompt the believing community at its best to *expect* to find meanings and values that are operative in the cultural matrix in ways that have yet to be realized in the church itself. Needless to say, this position is, when correctly understood, anything but accommodationism, which would not be mutual self-mediation at all but simply an abdication of responsibility. There are times when mutual self-mediation is explicit dialectic, where dialectic involves saying no because one's own position is and must be simply and irrevocably contradictory to the prevailing values. But the initial attitude of the genuine Christian individual or community is not one of suspicion but one of a readiness to learn. The Ignatian presupposition for the director of the Spiritual Exercises says it well and can and should be generalized: '[E]very good Christian is to be more ready to save his neighbour's proposition than to condemn it.'[12]

How can theologians determine which cultural meanings are indeed authentic and which are not? The beginnings of an answer to that question will be discussed below in the discussions of the scale of values.[13]

7

Structure

Next, there is the question, What determines the overall structure of a systematic theology? How would one go about a synthetic organization of the meaning constitutive of the Christian church? Where would one begin? In particular, is there a set of theorems and/or hypotheses that can serve, however inchoately at the present time, as what we might call a unified field structure for the entire discipline or functional specialty 'systematics'?

In attempting to provide an answer to these questions, I will build on several quite explicit affirmations that appear in very different places in Lonergan's writings.

First, as we have seen, in his major pre-*Method* statement of methodological considerations regarding systematics, Lonergan proposes that the systematic theologian does best to look to the dogmas themselves for the central problems to be addressed in a systematic theology.[1] That is, the systematic theologian should make his or her central problem the issue, What do the dogmas mean? Other considerations, such as those that we have already outlined, should be addressed around this central core, and be subsidiary to it.

Second, in attempting to understand what the dogmas mean, the systematic theologian should proceed, as much as possible, in the *ordo doctrinae*, 'from above' as it were. One should begin with that element or those elements the understanding of which does not entail understanding anything else but is rather the basis of understanding everything else. As chemistry texts begin with the periodic table, which itself is the result of an entire history of work in the *via inventionis*, the way of discovery, and proceed from there to compose the chemical elements of the table into compounds, so systematic theological treatises should begin with achievements that themselves may have taken centuries to develop, but which, once understood, provide the key to understanding other elements. The question of a unified field structure is the question, What might such a set of achievements be? What might be the fundamental set of conceptions with which a systematics might begin?

Here I wish to review an important discussion that has been going forward for some time at the Lonergan Research Institute, Toronto, in classrooms at Regis College, Toronto, and at the Lonergan Workshop at Boston College, and to renew my own contribution to that discussion.

1 The Thesis

My fundamental thesis is that there is at hand an initial, heuristic unified field structure for the functional specialty or theological discipline 'systematics,' an initial 'upper blade.'[2] While it does not yet have the concreteness of content that can be elaborated only by filling out the heuristic structure that it provides, it is enough to get us started. A subsidiary thesis is that previous attempts, including my own, to state what that structure is have not quite hit it off correctly, even as they have made contributions to its accurate presentation. In the course of the discussion I will try to summarize some of these previous attempts.

But first, we must face the question, What is meant by a unified field structure? The expression 'unified field structure' is not mine, but Daniel Monsour's, and Monsour is adapting the phrase made popular (and subsequently criticized) by physicist Stephen Hawking, 'unified field theory.'[3] However, I have developed, or at least am developing, my own way of expressing what I mean by speaking this way. The unified field structure would be not some finished system but an open and heuristic set of conceptions that embraces the field of issues presently to be accounted for and presently foreseeable in that discipline or functional specialty of theology whose task it is to give a synthetic understanding of the realities that are and ought to be providing the meaning constitutive of the community called the church. The unified field structure would be found in a statement, perhaps a quite lengthy one, perhaps even one taking up several large volumes, capable of guiding for the present and the foreseeable future the ongoing genetic development of the entire synthetic understanding of the mysteries of faith and of the other elements that enter into systematic theology. It would guide all work at bringing these elements into a synthetic unity. It would stand in continuity with the implicit unified field structure of the *Summa theologiae* of Thomas Aquinas, which marks what we might call the first great plateau in the unfolding of systematic theology, and it will leave itself open to further enrichments, differentiations, and transformations analogous to those that it itself adds to the Thomist conception.

To draw on one of Monsour's articulations, the unified field structure would stand to a contemporary systematics as the periodic table stands to contemporary chemistry. But its relation to systematics is also different from that of the periodic table to chemistry, in that it remains heuristic for future elaborations that can be developed only as theologians tackle the relevant issues one by one. Again, in my own somewhat different articulation, it would be a summation and integration of what Lonergan once called the dogmatic-theological context[4] as that context stands at the present time, given both the development of theology to this point and an intelligent, faith-filled anticipation of where theology must go from here. Again, it would stand to a contemporary systematics as the theorem of the supernatural joined to Aristotle's metaphysics stood to the emergent systematics of the Middle Ages as this systematics came to its first great synthesis in Aquinas, and in fact it will be a genetic development upon that unified field structure. The conjunction of the theorem of the supernatural with Aristotle's metaphysics provided perhaps the first great unified field structure for a systematic theology, and any future structure must build on that synthesis even as it shows itself capable of addressing issues which that framework could not handle. Thus, an adequate contemporary field structure would make systematics historically conscious and would place it in tune with modern scientific methods and achievements, with exegetical methods, and with historical scholarship. A contemporary systematics has to be able to address problems and relate to theological functional specialties that had not emerged at all at the time that Thomas did his work. Thomas knew nothing of what we have come to call scientific historical-critical exegesis, nothing of critical history, nothing of modern science whether natural or human. That is not to say that he has nothing to contribute to these, but only that the methods and results of these disciplines as we know them were simply beyond his horizon. A theology that mediates between a cultural matrix and the significance and role of a religion within that matrix cannot simply repeat even the permanent achievements of another age but must carry them forward in the same spirit as the one Lonergan embodied when he took as a central inspiration for so much of his work Pope Leo XIII's injunction *vetera novis augere et perficere*, to augment and complete the old with the new.

So the two principal components of the structure that I will suggest are sublations of the two components of Thomas's structure, that is, of the theorem of the supernatural and of Aristotle's metaphysics. Lonergan's notion of sublation (in German *Aufhebung*) is taken not from Hegel but from Karl Rahner. '[W]hat sublates goes beyond what is sublated, introduces something new and distinct, puts everything on a new basis, yet so far from interfering with the sublated or destroying it, on the contrary needs it, includes it, preserves all its proper features and properties, and carries them forward to a fuller realization within a richer context.'[5] Thus, like the medieval organizing conception, the unified field structure that I am going to suggest combines a specifically theological element with a more general set of categories. The theorem of the supernatural was discovered around the year 1230 by Philip, the Chancellor of the University of Paris. And it is precisely a theorem: it no more changes the data on the experience of our spiritual life than the scientific notion of acceleration as d^2s/dt^2 changes our experience of going faster or slower. A theorem is a scientific elaboration of a common notion. As Lonergan says, the theorem of the supernatural 'completed a discovery that in the next forty years released a whole series of developments. The discovery was a distinction between two entitatively disproportionate orders: grace was above nature; faith was above reason; charity was above human good will; merit before God was above the good opinion of one's neighbors.' As these two orders are disproportionate, so they are related to one another in the most intimate fashion. And as Lonergan has shown in his great work *Grace and Freedom,* based on his own doctoral dissertation, the discovery and the distinction and organization that it brought about 'made it possible (1) to discuss the nature of grace without discussing liberty, (2) to discuss the nature of liberty without discussing grace, and (3) to work out the relations between grace and liberty.'[6] But, it may be argued, it did more than this. It grounded the specifically theological component of Thomas's entire conception, while Aristotle's metaphysics provided its general categories, the categories that dealt not with the supernatural but with nature.

The principal specifically theological element in the unified field structure now at hand is a four-point hypothesis proposed in Lonergan's systematics of the Trinity. The hypothesis differentiates the theorem of the supernatural into a set of connections between the four real divine relations – what the tradition calls paternity, filiation, active spiration, and passive spiration – and created supernatural participations in those relations. Thus, (1) the secondary act of existence of the Incarnation, the assumed humanity of the Incarnate Word, is a created participation in paternity. 'Whoever has seen me has seen the Father' (John 14.9). In the immanent Trinitarian relations, the Word does not speak; the Word is spoken by the Father. But the Incarnate Word speaks. However, he speaks only what he has heard from the Father. Again, (2) sanctifying grace as the dynamic state of being in love is a created participation in the active spiration *by* the Father and the Son *of* the Holy Spirit, so that as the Father and the Son together breathe

the Holy Spirit as uncreated term, sanctifying grace as created participation in the active spiration of Father and Son – that active spiration that is really identical with paternity and filiation taken together as one principle – 'breathes' some created participation in the same Holy Spirit. (3) The habit of charity is that created participation in the passive spiration that *is* the Holy Spirit, a created participation in the third person of the Blessed Trinity. And (4) the light of glory that is the consequent created contingent condition of the beatific vision is a created participation in the Sonship of the divine Word. And so the hypothesis enables a synthetic understanding of the four mysteries of the Trinity, the Incarnation, grace, and the last things.[7] The hypothesis is beyond anything explicit in Aquinas, even though it may be argued that the seeds of much of it are present in question 43 of the *Prima pars* of the *Summa theologiae*, where Thomas discusses the missions of the Son and of the Holy Spirit. There is in Lonergan's hypothesis a coordination of the divine processions with the processions of word and love in authentic human performance, a coordination that, in Lonergan's beautiful words, almost brings God too close to us.[8] And this coordination, I believe, like many other things in Lonergan's work, is only potential in Aquinas; it is spelled out perhaps for the first time in the hypothesis of Lonergan's from which I am taking my lead.

The set of general categories that would represent a sublation of the Aristotelian metaphysics that provided Aquinas with his own general categories will be provided, I am arguing, by what Lonergan calls a 'basic and total science.' That basic and total science is to be found in the cognitional theory, epistemology, and metaphysics of Lonergan's great book *Insight* and in the existential ethics of both *Insight* and *Method in Theology*, but principally as these are brought to bear on the development of a theory of history. And I hope that I have been able to provide some developments on that theory of history in my own work *Theology and the Dialectics of History*, so that the basic structure of that work would contribute to the constitution of the unified field theory for systematic theology.

2 The Four-point Hypothesis

Lonergan's four-point hypothesis, which we have already seen, reads as follows.

> [T]here are four real divine relations, really identical with the divine substance, and so four special ways of grounding an imitation or participation *ad extra* of God's own life. And there are four absolutely supernatural created realities. They are never found in an

> unformed or indeterminate state. They are: the secondary act of existence of the Incarnation, sanctifying grace, the habit of charity, and the light of glory.
>
> Thus it can appropriately be maintained that the secondary act of existence of the Incarnation is a created participation of paternity, and so that it has a special relation to the Son; that sanctifying grace is a [created] participation of active spiration, and so that it bears a special relation to the Holy Spirit; that the habit of charity is a [created] participation of passive spiration, and so that it has a special relation to the Father and the Son; and that the light of glory is a [created] participation of filiation that leads perfectly the children of adoption back to the Father.[9]

This passage explicitly embraces the doctrines of the triune God, of the Incarnate Word, of the inhabitation of the Holy Spirit, and of the last things, and it does so in such a way that the mysteries affirmed in these doctrines are related systematically or synthetically to one another. Thus it presents in a systematic order some of the principal realities named by the special categories, the categories peculiar to theology.

3 Previous Discussion on the Issue

Now, over the past few years there has developed a discussion at the Lonergan Research Institute, Toronto, in some of the graduate seminars sponsored by the Institute, in some of the systematic courses at Regis College, Toronto, and at the Lonergan Workshop at Boston College, as to whether this four-point hypothesis is adequate to function on its own as a unified field structure for systematics. The discussion of these issues has been clearly focused in the two papers by Daniel Monsour mentioned above in note 3. The terms of the question are adequately displayed, I believe, in these two papers. The second repeats many of the general points made in the first, but goes on to develop a much more complete argument in favour of an antecedent likelihood that the four-point hypothesis will in fact provide the integrating principle, the unified field structure.

The first paper frames the question in terms of a problem raised by Henri Rondet in his book *The Grace of Christ.*[10] Rondet states that Western Catholic thought on grace has been one-sided. The questions of grace and freedom, grace and merit, justification and predestination are divorced from the emphases of the Greek Fathers on divinization, adoption, union with Christ, and the Indwelling of the Holy Spirit. There is in Western Catholic theology a split between the tract on grace and the treatise on the Trinity, which discusses the mission of the Holy Spirit. Created grace has been in the foreground of Western Scholastic theology, while the gift of the Holy Spirit has been severely underemphasized. But, Monsour claims, the final chapter of *De Deo trino, Pars systematica,* overcomes this trend. Some earlier attempts to overcome the 'error in perspective' in the dominant trend, notably those of M.J. Scheeben in the nineteenth century[11] and Karl Rahner in the twentieth,[12] despite their grasp of the problem, proved inadequate because of their use of formal causality or quasi-formal causality as a way of understanding God's self-communication and so the relation between the gift of the uncreated Holy Spirit and the created grace on which the Western paradigm placed its emphasis. The integration of the two emphases is achieved in principle, it would seem, in Lonergan's treatment of the divine missions, and perhaps to date – this is my addition – only there.

But Monsour's question goes further than simply seeking a more satisfactory theory on this precise issue. He asks whether there can be found in Lonergan's writings, and especially in his theology of the divine missions, 'a more comprehensive perspective ... that would not only successfully overcome the split ... but ... also weigh against *any* such split or disconnection and systematically favor and promote ... the systematic understanding of the mysteries of faith' (3).[13] If there is such a conception to be found or developed, he says, 'it would be the conception that expresses an understanding of the organizing and integrating principle that is virtually sufficient for the resolution of all questions in the functional specialty Systematics,' that is, in every tract in systematic theology (5–6), not because of some logical deduction but rather in the way in which the periodic table is virtually sufficient for the resolution of the major questions currently being asked or anticipated in chemistry. Like the periodic table for chemistry, the unified field structure would mediate the relation of *every* less comprehensive conception in the whole of systematics to *every other* less comprehensive conception in the whole of systematics. But as the periodic table is open to further development and even transposition, even while what it has enabled chemists to understand will remain permanently valid, so the unified field structure of a systematic theology would be open to further development and transposition, even while some of its achievements must be regarded as permanent. It will be the secure basis of an ongoing genetic sequence of ever more comprehensive systematic syntheses, even as it is itself transposed in the light of new questions and exigencies to something that may look very different from the present conception. Thus the conception that I will offer is in continuity with the medieval structure, even as it goes far beyond it, and any development on the present conception will be in continuity with it even as it extends the parameters of the field structure to limits that presently belong at best to the known unknown that comes within our horizon only as a set of questions, and at worst to the unknown unknown that has not even begun to emerge as a question.

Monsour argues that an appropriate name for such an organizing conception would be a 'unified field structure' for systematics. He chooses this name in preference to 'axiom,' as in Karl Rahner's term *Grundaxiom*, and again in preference to 'unified field theory,' the term used in physics. 'Axiom' suggests, he says, something self-evident, or perhaps a fundamental proposition from which one can draw conclusions logically; and neither of these characterizations applies to the four-point hypothesis. And the unified field theory that, at least until recently, physicists desired to achieve would bring classical theoretical physics, at least in its present phase, to a close, whereas the four-point hypothesis or for that matter any unified field structure in theology, if accepted, would do anything but bring systematics to a close; in a sense, it would enable it to begin, by providing its fundamental organizing and integrating principle. It would enable the construction of a systematics that to date remains, for all practical purposes, not yet assembled. Again, 'just as metaphysics is the whole *in* knowledge, but not the whole *of* knowledge, so,' suggests Monsour, 'the hypothesis [or any other unified field structure] might be considered the whole *in* Systematics but not the whole *of* Systematics.' Thus the question is whether the four-point hypothesis on its own may be 'virtually sufficient for the resolution of all questions in the functional specialty Systematics' (8), where 'virtually sufficient' does not have a logical meaning but a heuristic one. Still, a caveat is added: '[T]hough it would certainly function heuristically in Systematics, the hypothesis is not purely heuristic, for it contains theological content' (8).[14] That, however, implies no contradiction, since the periodic table may be said to function heuristically for chemistry, and differential calculus for classical physics. Heuristic structures are not some permanent feature of the human mind. They develop in the course of history, and they are modified and transformed by accumulated discoveries and by corrections of past mistakes. Today's unified field structure in systematic theology will be greatly refined and differentiated as the theological community follows its lead in constructing an actual systematics.

After discussing some of the difficulties presented by the hypothesis and relating them in a very creative way to what Lonergan says in the third part of *The Ontological and Psychological Constitution of Christ* about the classification and resolution of the truths we know about God,[15] Monsour proposes in the first of his two papers a test of the viability of the four-point hypothesis as a unified field structure for systematics: 'Take some or all of the five sets of special theological categories enumerated by Lonergan in Foundations and actually attempt to work out tentatively the categories belonging to each set. Then transfer whatever categories one has derived in Foundations into Systematics and try to map them onto the proposed unified field structure … If it is truly a unified field structure for Systematics, it would … provide the organizing principle integrating all the categories of all the five sets. To the extent that one continues to succeed in mapping the categories onto the hypothesis, to that extent one continues to confirm the hypothesis as indeed a unified field structure for Systematics' (16).[16] In this regard, Monsour speaks of some categories being 'mapped onto the structure through their connection with the four absolutely supernatural [realities] understood as participations in the four real subsistent relations' (17). Furthermore, 'if one supposes that the categories in each of the five sets are intrinsically irreducible to the categories of any of the other sets, then not only will there be a permanent diversity in Systematics, that no proposed unified field structure will abolish, but also with each successful transfer and mapping of categories onto the unified field structure, the structure itself, while retaining its identity as an organizing and integrating principle, will be enriched and rendered more complex' (17).

So much for the initial framing of the question. In his second paper, Monsour begins the test. He begins to attempt to map the five sets of categories onto the four-point hypothesis. He insists that he has 'no intention of adopting a definitive position as to whether it is possible and theologically sound and fruitful to bring together Lonergan's four-point hypothesis and the set of five special theological categories.' '[A]ll I propose to offer here,' he says, 'is a set of inchoate considerations that perhaps may incline one to regard the attempt to bring the four-point hypothesis and the special theological categories together as a worthwhile and promising line for subsequent investigation' (19).

Those considerations, however inchoate they may be, are nonetheless quite complex. I will not summarize his arguments here. It is sufficient for my present purposes to say that Monsour begins by asserting an antecedent likelihood that the four-point hypothesis will provide the integrating principle for the five sets of special categories, and that the rest of his points build on this initial assertion.

4 A Proposal

Is the four-point hypothesis adequate to function on its own as a unified field structure for systematics? Is it sufficient to point us in the direction of doing for systematic theology something analogous to what the periodic table does for chemistry? Is it enough to enable us to sum up and integrate the dogmatic-theological context of the church as that context has developed up to the present time? Does it suffice, if we want something that will do for a contemporary systematics what the theorem of the supernatural combined with a transformed Aristotelian metaphysics did for the theology of the *Summa theologiae*? I propose that, however synthetic the four-point hypothesis may be, and however much it may provide those core categories to which all other categories must be referred, still it does not stand on its own; it is not enough to unify a synthetic contemporary theological understanding. There are two reasons for this. One has to do with the special categories, those that are peculiar to theology, and the other with the general categories, those that theology shares with other disciplines.

First, while the four-point hypothesis does provide a specifically theological element in the unified field structure, still there are other specifically theological realities, and so other special theological categories, that a unified field structure must integrate, and they cannot be mapped adequately onto the four-point hypothesis or reduced to it. They are related to it, and must be configured to it in some way, so that theological reflection that employs them must be enlivened and informed by the hypothesis. But they have a theological reality of their own that is not simply reducible to the realities named in the hypothesis. I have in mind categories regarding creation, revelation, redemption, the church, the sacraments, and Christian praxis in the world. While all of these are intimately related to the elements expressed in the four-point hypothesis, still they are not organized by that hypothesis alone. Part of the specifically theological reality is reality on the move, reality in development, reality as history, and that part is not accounted for by the hypothesis alone.

Second, and consequently, the integration of these further theological realities with the four-point hypothesis, their configuration to the hypothesis, will entail locating the divine missions, which are at the heart of the hypothesis, in creation and especially in the history whose dynamics of progress, decline, and redemption are part of the reason for the missions in the first place. If possible, the missions must be located in creation and in history, not vaguely but precisely. And I believe this can be done through the scale of values, which, as a key to the theory of history, will form an additional component in the unified field structure. But this means that these theological realities must be integrated not only with one another but also with the heuristic account of the order of the universe (what Lonergan calls emergent probability) and with other realities constitutive of human history, that is to say, with realities that are known by sciences and scholarly disciplines other than theology. An additional set of sets of categories beyond those rooted in the four-point hypothesis and beyond the other special categories is required for such a theological synthesis to take place. *General* theological categories are required even for the adequate theological understanding of specifically theological realities. As the medieval theorem of the supernatural needed a metaphysical system, in the theology of

Thomas Aquinas, if it was to mediate religion and the cultural matrix influenced by Aristotle, so the four-point hypothesis requires general categories shared with other disciplines if the divine missions that are at the core of the hypothesis are to be located in relation to their historical occasions and effects. More precisely, a mission is for a purpose, and the divine missions are for the purpose of establishing and confirming interpersonal relations, first between God and us, and then among ourselves; and interpersonal relations are also the core element in the structure of the human good that is coincident with the immanent intelligibility of history. Thus understanding the divine missions entails understanding the history that the Word was sent to redeem from the alternating cycles of progress and decline and that the Holy Spirit is sent to renew with the outpouring of self-sacrificing love.

Where, then, are the general categories to be located, or at least grounded? My thesis is that the set of sets of general categories will be based in the cognitional theory, epistemology, and metaphysics of *Insight,* in the existential ethics of *Insight* and *Method in Theology,* and in the theory of history proposed by Lonergan over the span of his writings and complemented by the contributions that I have tried to offer in *Theology and the Dialectics of History.* My thesis, then, is that, taken together, these two elements – a four-point theological hypothesis and what Lonergan calls the basic and total science, the *Grund- und Gesamtwissenschaft,* especially as the latter issues in a theory of history – provide the basic framework, the set of terms and relations, of a unified field structure for systematic theology. The combination of the four-point hypothesis with the grounding base of the general categories will be required even for the discussion of the other *special* theological realities: creation, revelation, redemption, church, sacraments, and Christian praxis. None of these can be understood solely in the terms provided by the special categories. But with the four-point hypothesis and the philosophical positions that are for the most part already in place in *Insight* and that are complemented where necessary by later developments, we have everything we need to begin constructing a systematic theology. And that 'everything we need to begin constructing a systematic theology' is precisely what I mean by a unified field structure. It is true that no systematic theology will be complete until we enjoy the systematic theology that is coincident with the beatific vision. There is no possibility of a closed system in theology any more than there is in mathematics or empirical science. Eventually, every system will give rise to questions that cannot be answered on the basis of the resources provided by that system. Every system is an open system, that is, one in which it is anticipated that questions will arise from within the system itself that the system is not able to answer, that will demand the move to a higher viewpoint, perhaps a paradigm shift, before satisfactory hypotheses can be provided. Any system that claims not to be open in this way is an idol. Still, we must begin somewhere, and we must begin with the anticipation that the further categories that emerge will be validated by their connection with the categories that frame this unified field structure. Lonergan says as much, I believe, in section 3.121 of his response to a 'Questionnaire on Philosophy' sent to him in preparation for a symposium on philosophical studies for Jesuits. In brief, '[T]he Christian religion as lived is the sublation of the whole of human living. It follows at once that to thematize the sublation of the whole of human living is a task beyond the competence of theology as a particular science or particular discipline, that theology can perform that task only by broadening its horizon by uniting itself with philosophy as the basic and total science.' Moreover, 'theology is the sublation of philosophy. For philosophy is the basic and total science of human living. The Christian religion as lived is the sublation of the whole of human living. Hence the Christian religion as thematized is the sublation of the basic and total science of human living.'[17] At one point that sublation yields a theologically transformed theory of history, and here is where the principal though not the sole general categories of systematics will be applied.

5 History and the Special Categories

If I am going to back up my proposal with an argument that meets the exigencies of the conversation in which the proposal arose, I must turn to the test that Daniel Monsour proposed. In the chapter on Foundations in *Method in Theology*, Lonergan spells out five sets of special theological categories. The test lies in the question, Can these five sets be mapped without remainder onto the four-point hypothesis? I will argue that the four-point hypothesis will not be able to integrate the second, fourth, and fifth of these sets into an overall systematic exposition unless there is added to it the theory of history that issues from the *Grund- und Gesamtwissenschaft*, the basic and total science, of *Insight*, *Method in Theology*, and the developments offered in *Theology and the Dialectics of History*.

The first set of special categories, then, is derived from religious experience. These categories will emerge from 'studies of religious interiority: historical, phenomenological, psychological, sociological. There is needed in the theologian the spiritual development that will enable [one] both to enter into the experience of others and to frame the terms and relations that will express that experience.'[18]

A second set has to do, not with the subject but with 'subjects, their togetherness in community, service, and witness, *the history of the salvation that is rooted in a being-in-love*, and the *function of this history* in promoting' the reign of God in the world.[19]

A third set 'moves from our loving to the loving source of our love. The Christian tradition makes explicit our implicit intending of God in all our intending by speaking of the Spirit that is given to us, of the Son who redeemed us, of the Father who sent the Son and with the Son sends the Spirit, and of our future destiny when we shall know, not as in a glass darkly, but face to face.'[20]

A fourth set differentiates authentic and inauthentic humanity and authentic and inauthentic Christianity. '[T]o the unauthentic [person] or Christian, what appears authentic is the unauthentic. Here, then, is the root of division, opposition, controversy, denunciation, bitterness, hatred, violence.'[21]

And a fifth set 'regards progress, decline, and redemption. As human authenticity promotes progress, and human unauthenticity generates decline, so Christian authenticity – which is a love of others that does not shrink from self-sacrifice and suffering – is the sovereign means for overcoming evil. Christians bring about the kingdom of God in the world not only by doing good but also by overcoming evil with good ... Not only is there the progress of [humankind] but also there is development and progress within Christianity itself; and as there is development, so too there is decline; and as there is decline, there also is the problem of undoing it, of overcoming evil with good not only in the world but also in the church.'[22]

In my view only the third set of special categories can be adequately mapped onto the four-point hypothesis. The mapping of the third set will resolve the initial problem with which Monsour began, namely, the divorce between Trinitarian theology and the theology of grace and the imbalance and loss of perspective in the relations between the theological conceptions of uncreated and created grace. But, I propose, any attempt to map the other sets onto the four-point hypothesis is really an attempt to reduce the other sets to the third set. And if the other sets cannot be mapped without remainder onto the four-point hypothesis, then clearly more is needed if we are to arrive at a unified field structure for the functional specialty 'systematics,' and this on Monsour's test itself. Not even all the *special* categories can be adequately mapped onto the four-point hypothesis. Now, obviously, the third set matches the four-point hypothesis almost point by point, so that it can safely be said that this set can be mapped without remainder onto the hypothesis. Moreover, I believe the hypothesis provides a key to clarifying religious experience as receiving the love of God and being in love with precisely that love, and so it is relevant to elements of the first set of special categories. But mapping the other three sets onto the hypothesis is not only more difficult; in the last analysis, it is, I believe, impossible. One can relate the other three sets to the third set, and so to the hypothesis, but any attempt to go further would be an attempt to reduce the other three sets to the third. The other three sets demand a framework that locates within, or in relation to, the dialectical dynamics of history the four created supernatural realities that are the created consequent conditions either of the divine missions (the *esse secundarium* of the Incarnation, sanctifying grace, and the habit of charity) or of the beatific vision (the light of glory). The categories that detail the relation of these created supernatural realities to history are required if we are to have a systematics of creation, revelation (which, as Lonergan says, introduces a new meaning into *history*), redemption, the church, the sacraments, and Christian praxis. And I have already suggested, following Monsour himself, that the basic relation of general to special categories parallels the obediential potency by which nature and history stand ready to be elevated and transformed by grace.

The four-point hypothesis, then, has to be placed in history. Speaking as it does of the divine missions certainly does locate it in history, but it has to function within a conception of history that will enable the integration of the second, fourth, and fifth sets of special categories into the overall systematic conception. The created contingent external terms that make possible that there are divine missions are not enough to allow for this integration. The divine missions have to be related in a thematic and explicit manner to the dynamics of history, and the dynamics of history have to be configured in a thematic and explicit manner to the divine missions. That can be done only by developing a theological theory of history. The four-point hypothesis does not in itself tell us anything about what the Incarnation and the Indwelling of the Holy Spirit have to do with historical progress and decline, whereas creation, revelation, redemption, the church, the sacraments, and Christian praxis cannot be understood theologically apart from historical progress and decline.[23] As Lonergan himself wrote at the time of his breakthrough to the notion of functional specialization, a contemporary systematic theology in its entirety must be a theological theory of history; or again, the mediated object of systematics is *Geschichte*. We may conclude, then, that the basic organizing systematic conception must contain, in addition to the four-point hypothesis, the fundamental elements of a theological theory of history. And I would propose that those fundamental elements are provided at least in an incipient fashion in Lonergan's analysis of the dialectic of history in terms of progress, decline, and redemption and in the complementary suggestions that I offer in *Theology and the Dialectics of History*. While there is no doubt that further work (for example, in social theory and economics) will uncover other elements and so other categories, these give us enough to get started and provide the basic map or grid for locating the elements that further work will discover. And, I repeat, that is all we can hope for, and it is all that I mean by speaking of a unified field structure.

6 A Distinction

I would like to support my contention with an important distinction, one that explicitly introduces another element into the discussion. It is one thing to integrate the special categories, and it is something further to integrate the functional specialty 'systematics.' Systematics is more than the special categories, however integrated and synthetic may be their presentation. Let me elaborate.

Lonergan's method and the emphases that I have highlighted in several articles on the method of systematic theology[24] impose on our use of the four-point hypothesis a twofold requirement. First, *the objects intended in this statement must be spoken of in categories based in interiorly and religiously differentiated consciousness.* The categories employed to frame the hypothesis itself are derived, not basic. In Lonergan's words, 'general basic terms name conscious and intentional operations. General basic relations name elements in the dynamic structure linking operations and generating states. Special basic terms name God's gift of his love and Christian witness. Derived terms and relations name the objects known in operations and correlative to states ... For every term and relation there will exist a corresponding element in intentional consciousness.'[25] More specifically, since the four-point hypothesis speaks of realities that are named in special categories, the base of these categories in religiously differentiated consciousness must be specified as carefully as possible. But general categories will be important even in unpacking the hypothesis in its own terms, since (1) the divine relations are based in the divine processions, (2) the processions are understood by analogy with intelligible emanations of word and love in human consciousness, and (3) the categories that express such emanations are not peculiar to theology but are fundamental to the *Grund- und Gesamtwissenschaft* whose fundamental components Lonergan has put forth in *Insight.* But a differentiation in terms of religious experience is also required, and this is particularly true for the second and third points of the hypothesis, those having to do with sanctifying grace and the habit of charity as created participations, respectively, of active and passive spiration.

The second requirement builds on an argument that I have offered elsewhere, which is in harmony with elements that appear in Lonergan's papers at the time of his breakthrough to functional specialization. The argument was to the effect that systematics is to assume the general form of a theology of history. And building on it means that the primary general categories must be those that enable us to formulate a theory of the complex dialectical process of human history. These categories include pre-eminently those that Lonergan has employed to speak of progress, decline, and redemption as constituting the basic structure of history, and the structure of the human good that he has proposed most clearly in *Method in Theology*. But complementing these are other categories that can be found in Lonergan's work and added to his analysis of history: principally, the scale of values as explaining the intelligible ongoing relations among three complex dialectical processes – in the subject, culture, and community – and so as providing further details of the dynamics of progress and decline in history. This mediation of general and special categories in a theology of history is required if we are to relate the doctrines of Trinity, Incarnation, grace, and eschatology concretely to the processes of history and to add to the core systematic spheres of Trinity, Incarnation, grace, and eschatology the understanding of doctrines regarding creation, revelation, redemption, the church, the sacraments, and the praxis of religious persons, of Christians, of Catholics, and of the Christian churches. The doctrines of creation, revelation, redemption, church, sacraments, and praxis are not explicitly included in the core 'focal meanings' contained in the four-point hypothesis, but positions in their regard are obviously demanded in a systematic theology. And those positions cannot be developed without a theory of history. Even the four-point hypothesis contains a demand for expansion into a theory of history, since at the core of the hypothesis is the theology, not only of the immanent Trinity – there are four real divine relations (three of them really distinct), and these relations are really identical with divine being – but also and especially of the divine missions; and the divine missions are the Trinity in history, for the missions are identical with the divine processions linked to created external terms that are the consequent created conditions of the fact that the processions are also missions.

7 Glimpsing Some Implications

Perhaps we can already glimpse the enormous theological implications of the twofold methodological insistence on basing everything in interiority and on locating everything in relation to history. It is one thing to transpose, for example, Trinitarian theology into categories dictated by interiorly and religiously differentiated consciousness. We are already familiar with the historical antecedents of such a transposition in the psychological analogies first of Augustine and then of Aquinas. Lonergan in *Divinarum personarum* and then in *De Deo trino* transposes the psychological analogy into categories explicitly derived from interiorly differentiated consciousness. But to add to this requirement the additional demand that all of this material must be formulated in terms of a theory of history adds a new dimension. The direct impact, of course, is on that portion of Trinitarian theology that treats the divine missions, and particularly the mission of the Holy Spirit. But the implications are more far-reaching.

The theory of history based on the interrelations of the levels of value – from above, religious, personal, cultural, social, vital – proposes that the recurrent intelligent emanation of the word of authentic value judgments and of acts of love in human consciousness (personal value) is due to the grace of the mission of the Holy Spirit (religious value) and is also the source of the making of history, of historical progress through schemes of recurrence in the realms of cultural, social, and vital values. But the mission of the Holy Spirit *is* the eternal procession of the Holy Spirit linked to a created, contingent external term that is the consequent condition of the procession being also a mission, or of the proceeding Holy Spirit being also sent. Thus the intelligent emanation in God of the Holy Spirit, the eternal procession in God of the Holy Spirit, joined to the created, contingent, consequent external terms that are sanctifying grace and the habit of charity (as well as to the operative movements that are known as *auxilium divinum* or actual grace), the eternal intelligent emanation of the Spirit in God as also Gift in history, is the ultimate condition of possibility of any consistent or recurrent intelligent emanation of authentic judgments of value and schemes of recurrence rooted in acts of love in human beings. This collaboration of intelligent processions, divine and human, is, then, the condition of the possibility of the consistent authentic performance of what Lonergan calls the normative source of meaning in history.[26] And if such personal value conditions the possibility of functioning schemes of recurrence in the realms of cultural, and then social, and then vital values, if that normative source, functioning communally, is the origin of progress in history, then the mission of the Holy Spirit, which is identical with the eternal procession of the Spirit linked to the created, contingent, consequent term of charity, and so the Spirit as Gift, is the very source of progress in history. Conversely, wherever genuine progress (measured by fidelity to the scale of values) takes place, the Spirit is present and active. The combination of the four-point hypothesis with the theory of history thus enables us to relate Trinitarian theology, and even the theology of the immanent Trinity, directly to the processes not only of individual sanctification but also of human historical unfolding. The discernment of the mission of the Holy Spirit thus becomes the most important ingredient in humankind's taking responsibility for the guidance of history.[27]

These implications will be repeated and spelled out in greater detail below in chapter 10.

8

Anticipations

The level of our own time, which demands thinking on the plane of history, and the related issue of adequate categories impose at least three demands on a systematic theology, three expectations that someone beginning such a theology must anticipate meeting. More will be mentioned later about these expectations,[1] but it is well to call attention to them now before proceeding further.

1 An Open but Continuous Future

First, the ground is now available to enable a contemporary systematic theology to anticipate an ongoing genetic sequence of interrelated systematic positions. Systems are inevitably open. Every system eventually will give rise to questions that the resources of the system cannot answer. Nonetheless, the inevitable sequence of systems can be what I am calling an ongoing genetic sequence, where each later effort builds on those that have preceded and preserves all that is lasting in them.

The ground of this possibility is, radically, the integration in Lonergan's work of historical consciousness and foundational methodology.[2] 'Foundations' and 'ground' are, of course, loaded words in contemporary theology. I do not find it necessary to engage in rigorous dialectical argument with proponents of non-foundationalism, for I share their critique and rejection of what they call foundationalism, and I do not believe that what they mean by 'foundations' is what I mean or what Lonergan means. Genuine foundational reality is simply *inevitable pragmatic engagement* in certain operations and certain states or dispositions, along with the discovery that there are *norms* for authentic performance of the relevant operations, and *criteria* for discerning authentic and inauthentic states and dispositions. The criticisms of anti-foundationalists do not apply to such a notion of foundations, for this notion does not imply any attempt to provide rigorous conceptual or indubitable propositional grounds for intellectual activities.

Pragmatic engagement in the operations of inquiry, understanding, reflection, judgment, deliberation, and decision has always been operative in theology, for theology is a human enterprise. But it has been operative for the most part *in actu exercito,* as the Scholastics might say, and only seldom *in actu signato.* That is to say, theologians have minds, and they use them more often than they explicate what they are doing when they are using them. With few exceptions, the foundational reality to which Lonergan appeals has enjoyed only more or less coincidental appropriation on the part of theologians. Making it explicit is what enables us to anticipate an ongoing genetic sequence of systematic theologies, a collaboration over time that, in principle, would never cease. For it provides an ever-developing account of the sources of such a sequence. The anticipation is one of successive systematic expressions of theological understanding, with the later building on and transposing the earlier, and with all of them building on the same engagement in the operations constitutive of cognitive, moral, religious, and affective integrity, and so of the *imago Dei* that we are. The articulation of those operations and of their concomitant states can itself be expected to be constantly unfolding and developing. 'Foundations' as a functional specialty in theology is itself no more immune to development than is systematics itself.

2 The Ontology of Meaning

A second anticipation is intimately related to the first, and in fact has the same ground. It has to do with what we may expect the content of such an ongoing sequence to include. It is reflected in a little-known passage in Lonergan's work: 'today's scholars resemble twelfth-century compilers more than they do thirteenth-century theologians.'[3] This means that the accomplishments of exegetes and historians stand to what is coming in theology as the Lombard's *Sentences* stood to the *Summa theologiae.*

The second anticipation, then, is an expectation of a new step in understanding, a new step in theology's comprehension of the meaning of dogmatic statements (and of Christian constitutive meaning in general). This step is analogous to, but also goes beyond and sublates, the systematic leap that was prepared by twelfth-century compilers but that occurred only in the thirteenth century.

We might call this new step in understanding something like 'explanatory history,' that is, a systematic 'take' on the history of salvation, the history of the church, and the history of theology itself, and all of these in relation to 'general history.' Explanatory history would exhibit all the concreteness that we find in ordinary historical narrative. Yet it also would be governed by a set of heuristic notions that, when applied to data, could establish the *genetic and dialectical relations* that obtain among various stages in the evolution of Christian constitutive meaning. It is explanatory: it relates these stages to one another. The theology that emerges from such an advance will not be systematic theology in the traditional sense of that term. It is, Lonergan says, *praeter theologiam systematicam.*[4] It will include such systematic theology, of course, because it will understand the genetic and dialectical relations among various systematic theologies. But in itself it will be something new. Not only will it anticipate an indefinite *future* series of genetically related synthetic statements, as the first anticipation does; it also will comprehend the historical economy of revelation and salvation itself, as well as the past history of theology, in a synthetic and explanatory manner. As twelfth-century collections of theological materials laid the groundwork for thirteenth-century systematic speculation, so contemporary scriptural, religious, and historical scholarship, when its results are joined to the appropriate 'upper blade' of method, will yield a more concrete explanatory presentation of the emergent meanings that have come to constitute not only the Christian community but also the entire religious history of humankind. Thus, if the first anticipation regards foundations that render possible a way of directing the process of further developments, both doctrinal and theological, the second anticipation appeals to what we might call the ontology of meaning to enable as well an explanatory recapturing of the past. The notion that I am presenting here is in effect a development of the notion of the functional specialty 'dialectic' in *Method in Theology*. But I am concerned with its further effects as the wheel of theological operations continues and moves to systematics. At that point it yields, I believe, a systematic theology *of theologies.*

The emphasis that Lonergan is stressing in his statement relating today's scholars to twelfth-century compilers and tomorrow's theology to the *Summa* calls to mind the methodical and scientific hermeneutics of philosophical statements that he proposed in chapter 17 of *Insight.* Unless I am mistaken, it is an emphasis that remained important to him, but also, if not tentative, at least undeveloped. The section of *Divinarum personarum* where the theological reminder of this hermeneutics appears was dropped from the 1964 edition of the same material, *De Deo trino: Pars systematica.*[5] *Method in Theology* gives only vague and somewhat uncertain references to such a hermeneutics and explanatory history. It has always been something of a surprise to me, in light of chapter 17 of *Insight,* that the chapter on interpretation in

Method in Theology mentions these emphases only at the end. Here is what Lonergan says there.

> What is needed is not mere description but explanation. If people were shown how to find in their own experience elements of meaning, how these elements can be assembled into ancient modes of meaning, why in antiquity the elements were assembled in that manner, then they would find themselves in possession of a very precise tool, they would know it in all its suppositions and implications, they would form for themselves an exact notion and they could check just how well it accounted for the foreign, strange, archaic things presented by the exegetes.[6]

The paragraph in *Method in Theology* that follows these remarks asks whether such a project is possible, but then offers barely more than a few suggestions as to how it might be carried off. These suggestions point back explicitly to the section on the stages of meaning in chapter 3 of *Method in Theology*, and they probably also implicitly anticipate the chapter on dialectic. But the precision of chapter 17 of *Insight* must not be lost in the developments that make possible the further differentiations of *Method in Theology*.

My suggestion assumes that such a project is indeed possible. I envision it in the form of an ontology of meaning, and I ask about its relation to systematic theology. While it is different from systematics as traditionally conceived, is it also different from systematics as that discipline or 'functional specialty' is emerging, that is, from a systematics that emerges from a fully conscious and deliberate engagement in the functional specialty 'dialectic,' as Lonergan presents that specialty? Or would it be part of that new, post-dialectical systematics? If one were to say that it constitutes the entirety of systematics as that discipline is emerging, one would be courting an idealism of a Hegelian sort. But does this mean that such an explanatory history belongs only to the phase of theology in which theology mediates the past? Does it belong only to indirect discourse? Or is it *part* of what is mediated into the present as theological direct discourse? My option will be to include it in the latter phase, as a systematic theology of theological witness itself.

In many ways this option speaks to and transcends so-called postmodern appeals to intertextuality. It speaks to them insofar as it relates to one another both texts and other expressions or concrete carriers of meaning. It transcends them insofar as it is a theology of witness, where witness is not to words but to realities meant by the words. Ultimately, appeal to 'mere intertextuality' lacks, if not good judgment itself, at least a good theory of judgment.

3 Anticipations of Content

Third, if Lonergan has called attention to an analogy of *method* between our theological situation and the one that prevailed at the end of the twelfth century, there are also similarities between the two situations that have to do with the very *content* of systematic theology. I can mention at least three. Taken together, they constitute my third anticipation.

First, as at the end of the twelfth century, so today in Catholic systematic theology there are several strands of inquiry and argument that will be seen to have validity and perhaps even permanent significance, but that still are related to one another in a purely coincidental fashion. In a moment I will speak of three of these.

Second, unless a way can be found to relate these currents systematically to one another, there is a danger that they will confront each other in a conflictual manner that, at least in principle, is entirely avoidable.

Third, even the emergence of what in principle is a coherent ordering cannot guarantee its own acceptance on the part of the theological community. Eventually, the issue will be 'pushed back,' as it were, to the level of foundations and method.

First I mention the twelfth-century analogues.

Regarding the first point, Yves Congar has shown that, by the end of the twelfth century, there had arisen at least the potential for a significant alternative to monastic and contemplative theology. For there had emerged in theology the logical, dialectical, and methodological techniques that could give rise to the sort of speculative synthesis that was soon to be found in the work of Aquinas. Yet these two strands or currents of theological thought went their own way, without integration. And this did not have to happen.

With regard to the second point, in fact over time the new techniques came to be strenuously opposed by the representatives of monastic and contemplative theology.[7]

With regard to the third point, while Aquinas actually went a long way in integrating Augustinian and Aristotelian influences on his own thought,[8] he was not able to forestall the unfortunate divisions between these two traditions in theology. Rather, his own work became for a time (in some ways, for seven centuries) a victim of these conflicts.[9]

Lonergan has argued that the integration of the various currents came in principle around 1230 with the discovery by Philip, Chancellor of the

University of Paris, of the theorem of the supernatural. At the end of the twelfth century and in fact down to about 1230, the theology of grace (to take the clearest example, and in fact the issue that catalysed the major development that I am referring to) was standing particularly poised for a clarification that would, at least in principle, settle problems that had been building for about eight centuries.[10] But the issues had not yet settled into place. Two things were required. First, Philip's discovery of the theorem of the supernatural settled in principle problems that previous positions and emphases had not been able to address in a satisfactory fashion. But second, Philip's discovery had to be integrated with the previous insights. The synthesis in the area of the theology of grace comes, Lonergan says, only in the *Prima secundae* of Thomas's *Summa theologiae.* Moreover, the theology of grace was not the only domain of theology that exhibited a coincidental manifold of tendencies, views, and doctrines that could be systematically ordered only after a breakthrough to a specifically theological principle. There can be found, Lonergan writes, 'in the writings of Anselm and of the twelfth-century theologians a nest of antinomies that center round the couplets "grace and freedom," "faith and reason," to make the very conception of these terms paradoxical and to render an attempt at formulating the theological enterprise either heretical or incoherent.'[11] Lonergan consistently emphasized that the dividing line that enabled theology to move to some kind of systematic consolidation came with Philip's discovery.

Now, as I said above, the discovery of a theorem is not the uncovering of further data. A theological theorem no more adds to the data than the concept of temperature changes our sensations of hot and cold or the notion of acceleration changes our experience of going faster or slower. The theorem of the supernatural named what it is that makes a question and a discussion distinctly theological. It gave theology access to what Lonergan would later call its special categories, those categories that are proper to theology.[12] At the same time it freed human speculation to investigate what is not supernatural, what belongs to the domain of 'nature' – to investigate it in its own right, and to relate it to the realities that could be included under the rubric of the supernatural. Thus it freed theology to employ general categories as well, that is, those categories that theology would share with other disciplines, and especially (at that time) with philosophy. Some of these categories would be employed in the analogies that theology would rely on in order to reach some imperfect understanding of the mysteries. But the derivation of these categories is essential for a further reason: the realities named by the special categories must be related in theology to the realities named by the general categories. The real dividing line in the Aristotelian-Augustinian split in medieval theology was over the issue of whether and to what extent what Lonergan calls general categories may be employed *in theology*.

The issue is alive in our own day. This is clear in any dialogue with Barthians, but it also could become a major problem in contemporary Catholic theology, if, for instance, conflicts were to develop between Thomists and representatives of a Bonaventurian tradition. The principal issue between Bonaventure and Thomas is over the legitimacy and importance of employing general categories. 'Where Bonaventure had been content to think of this world and all it contains only as symbols that lead the mind ever up to God, Aquinas took over the physics, biology, psychology, and metaphysics of Aristotle to acknowledge not symbols but natural realities and corresponding departments of natural and human science.'[13] A Bonaventurian will be reluctant to honour the employment and constant development of general categories in theology, and the resultant *development of theology itself.* Of course, even if one comes down in favour of the use of the general categories, the complications of the issue are not yet resolved. For there are methods of correlation that would deny or water down the distinct significance of the special categories. This is not unlike what the Augustinians feared in their own context in the thirteenth century.

It was as the implications of the theorem of the supernatural became clear that a consistent and ordered presentation of an understanding of the Christian faith became possible. The Catholic tradition has regarded the work especially of Aquinas as the principal manifestation of what became possible once theology had discovered the source of its specifically theological categories as well as the source of the general categories that theology shares with other disciplines. It is true that Thomas's synthesis was tenuous, in the sense that his achievements, indeed even some of the central and most important features of his thought, have been correctly understood only quite rarely. Nonetheless, in Lonergan's words,

> Just as Euclidean geometry selects and orders a domain, just as Newtonian mechanics selects and orders a domain, just as the periodic table selects and orders a domain that makes the science a single whole with a clear method, clear criteria, and full awareness of what pertains to it and what does not, similarly theology selects an order that consists in grace which is above nature, in faith which is above reason, in charity which is above ordinary human good will, and in merit for eternal life which is above any human deserts. There is an entitative order of grace, faith, charity, and merit that comes to us through Christ, that is known by faith, that is realized by charity, that is socialized in the mystical body which is the church.[14]

This entitative order is disproportionate to any order natural to created reality, and so it is 'absolutely supernatural.' At root it is a created communication of the divine nature itself, and in fact, as Lonergan's synthetic statement (our 'four-point hypothesis') makes clear, a set of created communications of the divine relations. By discovering it precisely as a distinct order, theology found its proper or formal object or set of formal objects. What in the twelfth century remained a coincidental collection of data reaches systematic and synthetic ordering in the thirteenth century, precisely because of the discovery and articulation of a particular theorem.

My reason for dwelling on this point is not only to call attention to the abiding importance for systematics of the medieval theorem of the supernatural (whatever may be the necessary reformulations) but also to emphasize that in our situation we have yet to find or at least to exploit a principle or set of principles that will make possible the intelligible interrelating of the most significant prevalent *contemporary* emphases in the same way that the theorem of the supernatural enabled medieval synthesis to take place. Something must happen in theology today that has an effect on the entire field similar to that which the theorem of the supernatural had in the thirteenth century. In addition, of course, there is some reason to fear that we may lose hold of the medieval synthetic principle, the theorem of the supernatural itself. Certainly this is what has happened in many instances of what is known as the method of correlation. We may want to come up with another name for the medieval discovery, but the reality that was named 'supernatural' is lost only at the cost of giving theology nothing more to do. But some *further* principle or set of principles is required in order to integrate the major theological achievements of our age. It may be that the principle or principles that would enable an intelligible relationship among the valid theological advances of the twentieth century have yet to be discovered and named. On the other hand, it may be that the core of a synthesis has in fact already been articulated but has yet to be acknowledged as such and exploited for all that it is worth. In either case, there is a similarity to the situation that prevailed at the end of the twelfth century, in that the explicit influence of an ordering principle is required. Moreover, as in the medieval situation, so too today the tendencies that could be united in a higher synthesis can also become antithetical to one another if the higher synthesis is not achieved or if, once achieved, it fails to take root and become fruitful.

I have already indicated, in the preceding chapter, what I think the organizing conceptual framework of a contemporary systematics should be, at least at the present time and in expectation of further development. In the next chapter I will speak further of the grounds or foundations of that framework. But here I will mention the principal contemporary emphases that can be integrated on these grounds and within such a conceptual framework, but that will also, without such a grounded framework, be left to combat one another in a way that ultimately will prove harmful to themselves and to theology. There are at least three permanently valid but still largely unrelated tendencies that emerged in the Catholic theology of the twentieth century and that await the discovery, articulation, or successful application of the principle or principles that will enable them to be intelligibly ordered to one another. The first two of these are similar, respectively, to the Aristotelian and Augustinian emphases that contended so mightily in the medieval period. The third is distinctly contemporary.

We must always wager, of course, when it comes to determining 'what is going forward' in our own time, especially in intellectual and doctrinal movements. Only the hindsight of history will indicate whether such a wager is correct. With this important caveat, then, I present my own wager. It is a wager regarding not only what will survive from contemporary Catholic theology – in fact, a great deal more will survive than the emphases I am highlighting – but also what will prove in the long run to be the most influential Catholic theological achievements of our time.[15] But more than anything else, it is a wager that theology will go forward precisely to the extent that it is able to integrate these achievements with one another.

First, there is a distinct brand of basically Thomist thought that extends, roughly, from Pierre Rousselot through Joseph Maréchal to Karl Rahner and Bernard Lonergan. Often this tradition is called 'transcendental Thomism.' I do not think this is a particularly felicitous designation. There are clear differences and distinct inspirations behind the various accomplishments. A label such as 'transcendental Thomism' tends to flatten out these distinct emphases. Moreover, the label has come to be used in an extremely dismissive manner by reactionary Catholics who mask their fear of subjectivity by claiming that Rahner and Lonergan, for example, are 'Kantian.' Nothing could be further from the truth.[16] But what can be said, I believe, is that there is an effort represented by these and other figures to retrieve basic Thomist insights in the light of *questions* raised by Kant and, at least in the cases of Rahner and Lonergan, also by Hegel. Partly because Lonergan has done more than the others to appropriate the methods and categories of contemporary natural and human science and historical scholarship, and partly because, alone among these Catholic philosophers, he recognizes the central role that is to be attributed to the act of insight, his work is methodologically by far the most important within this tradition. In the long run it will, I believe, have the most impact.

Lonergan uncovered the transcendental aspirations of the human spirit that are so momentously overtaken and overshadowed by divine revelation and grace. As I have previously argued,[17] he did so in a way that does not run the risk of subordinating the divine initiative to human transcendental aspirations; this is clear from his doctoral dissertation right through to his last works. Moreover, he has elucidated the dynamics of human intentional consciousness in a clarification that may be unparalleled in the history of thought. He makes sense of and relocates previous philosophical epochal advances, and he grounds a new stage of philosophical and theological discourse. He provides new basic terms and relations both for direct discourse in these disciplines and for the hermeneutic reappropriation of past achievements, particularly in the realm of the general categories. And he does all this without succumbing to the danger frequently encountered in or suspected of so-called 'transcendental' approaches, the danger, namely, of making the divine initiative a function of human aspiration, subject to the criteria uncovered in intentionality analysis.

Second, there is the *ressourcement* project of *la nouvelle théologie.* It is associated with such names as Henri de Lubac and Hans Urs von Balthasar. In particular, Balthasar's presentation of the aesthetic and dramatic character of many of the specifically theological categories has yet to be exploited by theology in the manner it deserves. Nor will it be properly exploited until it is related to the realities named by the general categories. This Balthasar did not do in any systematic fashion. But his salutary emphasis on the absolutely free initiative of Trinitarian love and of its revelation counters attempts to regard that initiative as simply the fulfilment of human transcendental aspirations and anticipations.[18] And his insistence on and practice of a continual *ressourcement* as intrinsic to and partly foundational of direct discourse in theology fulfils the best intentions of the school of *la nouvelle théologie.*

Third, there is a praxis component, and in particular the insistence emergent in liberation theologies on the preferential option for the poor in church ministry and in our retrieval of the gospel. Despite continued official ecclesial reluctance to acknowledge the theology of liberation by name – while it *is* an ambiguous category, the church has nothing to fear and much to learn from the work of, for example, Gustavo Guttierez – this particular insistence has in fact already become part of the Catholic Church's official teaching. But it has yet to be integrated with the most significant theological achievements of the Catholic tradition past and present, including the recapturing and updating of those achievements that have occurred in the work of Balthasar and Lonergan.

Theology, at least Catholic theology, will be able to go forward confidently into the future, with some hope of generating a sequence of interrelated systematic positions, to the extent that some principle or set of principles can be expressed that will relate these three emphases to one another and integrate them. On the other hand, no Catholic systematic statement of Christian constitutive meaning on the level of our own time and in harmony with the principal theological achievements of the twentieth century will be possible until such an integrating focus is discovered and exploited. This is my wager, and I believe that the organizing conceptual framework offered in the previous chapter and the grounds that will be discussed in the next chapter will enable the integration of which I am speaking to take place.

Balthasar's emphasis, by and large, uncovers the grounds of those categories that are specific to theology. It renames the ground that Philip the Chancellor discovered in a metaphysical context when he articulated what has come to be called the theorem of the supernatural. It points to and begins to clear a field that is aesthetic and dramatic. A genuine Christian rendition of 'religiously differentiated consciousness' will employ categories that are, in great part, aesthetic and dramatic in nature.

Lonergan's emphasis, on the other hand, uncovers the grounds of the categories shared by theology with other sciences and disciplines. It does in our day for the development of systematic meaning in philosophy and theology what Aristotle was able to do for Aquinas once the theorem of the supernatural freed theologians to study 'nature' on its own terms.

The legitimate emphases of liberation theology name a new and lasting insight into a dimension of the distinctive praxis component that must permeate any contemporary Catholic systematics.

But as yet these three developments have not been consistently and intelligibly related to one another. Until they are, theology will remain in a position that bears some resemblance to the state of the discipline at the end of the twelfth century, with all the promise and all the danger inherent in such an unfinished position. The integration of Lonergan, Balthasar, and central liberation insights is the way forward for Catholic systematic theology, the most fruitful way to proceed at the current juncture in the history of Catholic systematics. There is, in fact, a certain urgency for the sake of the church that exists around the tasks (1) of integrating what Lonergan and Balthasar stand for and represent, (2) of drawing out the implications of their respective emphases for the concerns of liberation theology, and (3) of highlighting the balance that the latter concerns bring to the work of these two great theologians. These three major twentieth-century developments must be allowed to complement and, where necessary, correct one another. It is in this mutual reciprocity and correction that Catholic systematic theology will find its way forward.

9

The Question of Ground

1 The Issue

Our first anticipation named one important manner in which the situation today is remarkably *unlike* the medieval scene. For in our time we know in a quite explicit manner the limits of possible achievement. We know that we may ambition, not some grand synthesis that will stand secure forever, but only an ongoing set of genetically related successive syntheses, all of them incomplete, with the totality residing at a given time not in the mind of any single theologian, but in a collaborative community. Thus a methodological statement that clarifies the objective – What is systematic theology? – and the open heuristic procedures of moving toward it – How is systematic theology to be constructed? – might increase the probabilities, not that a collaboration would come to rest in a completed *Summa,* but that it will become an ongoing enterprise, part of a movement in history, and indeed of a movement that in principle would continue developing indefinitely. In that case what will result will be, not some single system but an ongoing succession of systems genetically related to one another. The present work is intended to be programmatic for just such a sequence of systems in theology.

Needless to say, a major concern of anyone who would anticipate such an ongoing development of Catholic systematics is to identify and state the grounds of authentic development itself, indeed the grounds of a genetically related sequence of systematic orderings of Christian constitutive meaning. It is in the clearing of the grounds that there will be found the principle or principles that will enable the synthesis or integration to happen in the first place.

The grounds, of course, must be invariant, for if there are not invariant grounds of authentic development, or if we cannot locate them and state something true about them, then any ongoing set of syntheses will necessarily remain, as a set, no more than coincidental. This statement is analytic. As my own proposal to add 'psychic conversion' to Lonergan's work indicates, even method and the foundations that it disengages constitute ongoing tasks.[1] Still, it is only in reflection on method and foundations that the permanently valid grounds of permanently valid content in systematic theology can be located, and there *is* something of a pragmatic foundation on which that reflection can build, a foundation on which even the proposal regarding psychic conversion is based. That ground receives its first articulation in chapter 11 of *Insight*, 'The Self-affirmation of the Knower.' Over the course of time Lonergan expanded the articulation by speaking first of a fourth level of consciousness, then of a movement 'from above' as well as 'from below,' then of a fifth level of consciousness, and finally of the possibility that the subject as subject may consist of six levels of consciousness, two of which (the 'lowest' and the 'highest') are not spoken of explicitly as intentional.[2] Only on that basis does 'foundations,' as elaboration of foundational reality, have the resources to include and articulate what I have called psychic conversion. Within foundations itself, the position on spirit and intentionality, which is the position on intelligent, rational, and moral consciousness, is more radical than the position on empirical consciousness, which is what I was after in speaking of the sensitive psyche of an incarnate spirit.

We will revisit the notion of psychic conversion later. My present point, however, is that the result of uncovering foundational reality is that theological synthesis from this point on in history should be able to be self-consciously cumulative and progressive. It will be cumulative when there is effected 'a synthesis of each new insight with all previous, valid insights.' It will be progressive when there is 'a sustained succession of discoveries.'[3] But it will be possible at all only because of Lonergan's methodological efforts at clearing a permanently valid ground.

Now, talk of a permanently valid ground is not popular in the postmodern context, with its talk, at times quite informed and persuasive, of anti-foundationalism. Here I would appeal to Lonergan's distinction, just alluded to, between 'foundational reality' and 'foundations' as the objectification of that reality.[4] Foundational reality, we have said, is *pragmatic* engagement in knowing, deciding, loving, acting. It is the *vécu* rather than the *thématique*. The foundational question is, Does such engagement have a formal structure of self-transcendence that it must satisfy if it is to be authentic, or does it not? If it does, then 'foundations' is the ever incomplete, ever to-be-qualified objectification or thematization of that formal structure. If 'anti-foundationalism' is in fact insisting that all such articulations are incomplete and further to be qualified, then we have no argument. If 'anti-foundationalism' maintains that the integrity that we would name in speaking of a normative structure of such pragmatic engagement is never realized in practice in a fully untainted way, again we have no argument. Authenticity, as Lonergan insists, is ever a withdrawal from inauthenticity; it is ever precarious.[5] But if 'anti-foundationalism' wishes to dispute that there are formal structures of human integrity that can be incrementally articulated and that must be and, with God's grace, can be at least asymptotically satisfied, and satisfied with greater regularity as one develops affectively, intellectually, morally, and religiously, then there is no point to argument, since argument will not correct such a mistake. To argue would be to presume that conceptualization is more basic than pragmatic engagement. That is the real 'foundationalist' mistake. But at least some anti-foundationalist literature is ill equipped to correct it, because it is not grounded in the reality from which praxis and conceptualization emerge. More precisely, any legitimate argument would be a retortion, and retortion arguments, however valid they may be, seem to convince only those who have already become convinced on other grounds, while only angering those who will not allow themselves to be convinced.

The question of the ground or foundation, then, is essential. Lonergan points to what is required. He has uncovered in a heuristic fashion the radical formal constituents of the grounding structure of human integrity. But if there are still serious methodological questions facing systematic theology, if the explicit conception of systematics itself that Lonergan entertains in *Method in Theology* is still a bit narrow, if it shortchanges the dynamic movement that his articulation of theological method has already released, one reason may be that the renewed foundation that he proposes for a renewed systematic theology does not quite anticipate the full range of the permanently valid ground of systematic theology. To put the issue in another way, the principle or principles needed to integrate the three permanent theological achievements of twentieth-century Catholic theology to which I have called attention may not be completely articulated in Lonergan's work. The addition that will complete the range is what I have called psychic conversion. This addition not only will provide the needed complement. It will offer as well as the key to integrating Lonergan's emphases with those of both von Balthasar and liberation theology, the key to correcting von Balthasar at times with Lonergan's emphases and at other times with the social insistence of liberation theology,[6] and the key to presenting the lasting insights of liberation theology in a manner that frees them from the alienation and ideology to which they are so easily subject.

The theorem of psychic conversion names a dimension of foundational reality that is additional to those explicitly mentioned by Lonergan. The objectification of what I call psychic conversion entails an appropriation of an aesthetic-dramatic operator of human authenticity, an operator that accompanies, but also precedes and goes beyond, the intentional operators that Lonergan identifies with the three basic forms of questions: questions for intelligence, questions for reflection, and questions for deliberation. Psychic conversion enables a person, among other things, to approach some understanding of the aesthetic form of God's revelation in Christ Jesus and of the dramatic exchange of freedoms that it demands. It allows one to relate this form and this drama to other forms and other dramas. It allows one to gain some analogical understanding of the *divine* 'drama' in which eternal Trinitarian love chose to manifest itself in the lamb slain from the foundation of the world. From this aesthetic and dramatic element of foundations, the transition to the praxis component of Christian constitutive meaning is easy and readily available. And finally, as we will see, the notion of psychic conversion may also integrate Lonergan's philosophical analysis with some of the emphases to be found in the work of both Martin Heidegger and Ludwig Wittgenstein.

It is, then, only by overcoming a certain restriction in Lonergan's notion of foundations that there can occur the integration needed to move Catholic systematic theology forward. We can integrate Lonergan's work with von Balthasar's and with the permanently valid points made by liberation theology only, I believe, if we are willing to add to Lonergan's foundations what I have called psychic conversion. With this completed heuristic structure of foundations, the principles are available to ground the ongoing genetic sequence of systematic theologies that the present work anticipates.

2 Lonergan on Foundations

The problem of foundations was always a central concern for Lonergan. In *Insight* the issue is resolved in one area, namely, the cognitive; it is resolved principally in chapter 11, where the term 'foundation' appears in the context of the discussion of self-affirmation as immanent law, that is, as something incontrovertible.[7] The deepest foundation one can find is one's own pragmatic engagement in the activities that constitute human knowing, for to attempt to refute or radically revise the account of these activities involves one precisely in that pragmatic engagement, so that the attempt entails a performative self-contradiction. In chapter 14 of *Insight*, the term used is not 'foundation' but 'basis,'[8] and this term is used precisely of cognitional theory, which, it is said, has two aspects: it is determined by an appeal to the data of consciousness and to the historical development of human knowledge, and its formulation necessarily entails taking some stand on 'basic issues in philosophy,' namely, the real, knowing, and objectivity. If cognitional theory is the basis, then metaphysics, ethics, and theology are the 'expansion.' The relation between the basis and the expansion is complex, and we can see it developed principally in the derivation of the elements of metaphysics. There is a very strict logical component to this derivation, since 'in its general form, the transition [from latent to explicit metaphysics] is a deduction' with a major premise in the isomorphism between the structure of knowing and the structure of the known, a set of primary minor premises in 'a series of affirmations of concrete and recurring structures in the knowing of the self-affirming subject,' and a set of secondary minor premises supplied by 'reorientated science and common sense' providing the materials to be integrated in a metaphysics that would be the conception, affirmation, and implementation of the integral heuristic structure of proportionate being.[9] And yet never is the logical component a function of a static deductivism, which in fact is a position explicitly ruled out in the same chapter. Rather, the entire exercise is a matter of pedagogy, of self-pedagogy, of the self-affirming subject issuing to himself or herself a set of dictates that involves and calls upon the fundamental integrity of the person precisely as a knower.

As Lonergan says in *Philosophy of God, and Theology*, the room is open in *Insight* for a discussion of the foundational role of moral and religious as well as of intellectual conversion, but that room is not very well furnished.[10] In Latin notes on a course that Lonergan presented at the Gregorian University in 1959, *De intellectu et methodo*, the problem of foundations emerged as a major issue that, it would seem, was at that time not yet completely resolved in Lonergan's mind.[11] Appeal is made to wisdom, and with that appeal there are resonances (though not yet explicit affirmations) of components to foundations that are over and above the cognitional, that in a way ground even the cognitional. With the breakthrough to functional specialization, the ground is cleared for a much more thorough discussion of these components, and with *Method in Theology* the three dimensions of conversion that Lonergan affirmed are reciprocally related to two differentiations of consciousness that provide theology with its foundations, namely, interiorly differentiated consciousness and religiously differentiated consciousness.

I want to discuss Lonergan's understanding of these dimensions of foundations precisely in their relation to systematics. We have seen several consistent emphases in Lonergan's writings on systematics. First, there is his position regarding the relation of systematics to doctrines. His position on this particular issue remains consistent from the period when theology in its entirety, as he conceived it, consisted of dogmatics, systematics, and positive theology, right into the period where theology is conceived far more expansively in terms of eight functional specialties. The affirmation of doctrines precedes an attempt to understand them in systematics, and the attempt to understand the doctrines is to be carried out in the spirit of Vatican I's recommendation of an imperfect, analogical, gradually deepening and increasing, and highly fruitful understanding of what remain mysteries, that is, realities so hidden in God that we would not know them at all were they not revealed by God.

Second, for Lonergan the central doctrines to be submitted to such understanding are the defined dogmas that express such mysteries of faith; the principal function of systematics is to understand these dogmas, that is, to attempt some understanding of the realities affirmed in these dogmas. This, too, is a constant element in his thinking.

Third, throughout his writings on systematics there is a recognition of other mysteries of faith that are not included in dogmas, for example, the redemption, to which Lonergan devotes three systematic theses at the end of his *De Verbo incarnato*, and also of other doctrines that do not express mysteries of faith at all but that do name something of the constitutive meaning of the Christian community.

Fourth, there is some acknowledgment of the non-technical, symbolic expression of many of these realities, particularly in the scriptures, though I do not think there is ever a satisfactory position expressed on the relation between such symbolic expression and systematics.

And fifth, there is a clear acknowledgment of new problems that arise from new situations and that force a deeper understanding of some mysteries and a development in general of systematic theology. Here again, I do not think Lonergan ever reaches the 'two-way street' notion of the relation of systematics and situation, the application to that relation of the notion of mutual self-mediation, that I believe is essential to a full position on what systematic theology is.

Now, with functional specialization we have seen a distinction of the 'doctrines' affirmed in a functional specialty that bears that name from the church doctrines and theological doctrines that are known in the functional specialty 'history.' In terms of content, of course, there is an identity between some of the doctrines known in history and some of the doctrines affirmed in the sixth functional specialty. But the orientation of the knowing subject is quite different in each case. The doctrines that are affirmed in the functional specialty 'doctrines' are *selected* by the theologian as his or her own positions, selected from dialectic *on the basis of foundations*. The ground of the selection is variously named intellectual, moral, and religious conversion or, more precisely, interiorly and religiously differentiated consciousness, that is, the differentiations that are reached when one objectifies the three conversions.

Interiorly and religiously differentiated consciousness are appealed to as well in systematics, when one attempts to understand the doctrines. Not only are these differentiations the source of the categories, general and special, that a systematics will employ. Even more important for our present discussion, these differentiations answer a basic need, namely, to find *an invariant basis for ongoing systems.*

Thus Lonergan writes of interiorly differentiated consciousness that it 'identifies in personal experience one's *conscious and intentional acts* and the *dynamic relations* that link them to one another. It offers *an invariant basis for ongoing systems* and a standpoint from which all the differentiations of human consciousness can be explored.'[12] Interiorly differentiated consciousness is the base from which are derived *general theological categories,* that is, the categories that 'regard objects that come within the purview of other disciplines as well as theology.'[13] 'The base of general theological categories is the attending, inquiring, reflecting, deliberating subject along with the operations that result from attending, inquiring, reflecting, deliberating and with the structure within which the operations occur.'[14] It is clear from what Lonergan writes about the general categories in *Method in Theology* that he believes that many of these categories have already been provided, at least in their general form, in *Insight.*

Religiously differentiated consciousness is basically a matter of familiarity with God's gift of God's own love as this gift 'gives human living an orientation to what is transcendent in lovableness.'[15] Religiously differentiated consciousness is the base from which are derived *special theological categories,* that is, the categories that 'regard the objects proper to theology.'[16] The dynamic state of being in love in an otherworldly fashion, as this state is manifested in inner and outer acts, 'provides the base out of which special theological categories are set up.'[17] Thus the first set of these special categories will objectify that religious experience itself.[18]

It is in categories derived proximately or remotely from these two differentiations that a theologian working in direct discourse will state his or her theological doctrines and his or her systematic understanding of these doctrines. The transposition of doctrines selected from dialectic into such categories or the grounding of these doctrines in such categories is part of what distinguishes them as the doctrines that Lonergan intends in his chapter on the functional specialty 'doctrines,' and so precisely as the doctrines to be understood in systematics. As I have said, they will often be identical in their meaning with church doctrines or earlier theological doctrines, and they will always be informed by and continuous with some of these earlier doctrines. But they will be expressed in categories derived explicitly from interiorly and religiously differentiated consciousness. The basic rule governing the formulation of such categories is stated in *Method in Theology*: 'For every term and relation there will exist a corresponding element in intentional consciousness.'[19] The theologian working in the second phase must be prepared to specify just what that element is, whether it be remote or proximate; and when one turns to that precise task, one is operating in the functional specialty 'foundations.'

Again, the categories, as words, need not be different from the words that were used in the original doctrinal affirmations of the church. The issue is not the word but the subject who uses the word. The church may have reached intellectual conversion at the Council of Nicea, precisely in relation to its use of the term *homoousios*, but it did so, to use a Scholastic expression, *in actu exercito* rather than *in actu signato*, that is, in fact but without appropriation. The same is true (perhaps even more so) of Athanasius when he formulated his rule for the interpretation of the Nicene dogma: The same things are to be said of the Son as are said of the Father, except that the Son is Son and the Father is Father. But such unappropriated intellectual conversion is not enough for second-phase theology. Here, if the term 'consubstantial' is retained, its base in interiorly differentiated consciousness has to be made explicit. The 'corresponding element in intentional consciousness' has to be named: in this case, what is affirmed in true judgments.

Now it seems to me that such prescriptions already determine the structure of certain areas of systematic theology. This option on categories determines that Trinitarian theology, for example, will start by understanding the divine processions from an analogy with the intelligible or spiritual emanations that can be discovered in the intelligent, reasonable, and existential consciousness of the self-affirming and self-constituting subject. And the theology of grace is already determined to take its basic categories from the experienced fulfilment and transformation, by God's gift of love, of the natural dynamisms of intentional and psychic awareness. Whatever else may be added to systematic theologies of the Trinity and of grace, these basic (precisely as basic) elements must be preserved. For example, there is much insistence today on an approach to Trinitarian theology that emphasizes history, and on a social doctrine of grace. I agree with these emphases, but I will take very sharp issue with any theology of the Trinity that tries to argue that such emphases call for us to negate the psychological analogy or to relegate it to secondary status, and with any theology of grace that neglects the foundational position in the experience of God's gift of love. Only the transposition of these permanent achievements into a contemporary key will promote the historical and social emphases.[20]

Why can one build on these grounds in a methodical fashion? Partly because they are grounds to which one can always return for further support, but mostly because of the 'exceptional validity'[21] to be found in these basic terms and relations. That validity is due to the fact that these terms and relations 'refer to transcultural components in human living and operation.'[22] On their basis the theologian working in foundations constructs a set of interlocking terms and relations that at least have the utility of models and that may be discovered, as one is doing doctrines and systematics, to be more than models. What one must do is keep one's further terms and relations grounded in the transcultural core provided by interiorly and religiously differentiated consciousness. '[G]eneral basic terms name conscious and intentional operations. General basic relations name elements in the dynamic structure linking operations and generating states. Special basic terms name God's gift of his love and Christian witness. Derived terms and relations name the objects known in operations and correlative to states.'[23]

Some of the derived general categories will be metaphysical, in the sense of the metaphysics proposed by Lonergan in *Insight,* where metaphysical categories are derived from cognitional theory and epistemology, and so are claimed to be critically grounded and able to integrate the 'diverse heuristic structures within which operations accumulate towards the attainment of goals.'[24] The critically grounding cognitional theory differentiates what one is doing when one is knowing, and the critically grounding epistemology clarifies (1) the meaning of being as the objective of the desire to know, and (2) the meaning of objectivity as the fruit of authentic subjectivity. Thus categories such as potency, form, and act are rehabilitated in a new context, where they and other metaphysical categories are no longer primary or basic but can be traced to 'a corresponding element in intentional consciousness.'

> 'Potency' denotes the component of proportionate being to be known in fully explanatory knowledge by an intellectually patterned experience of the empirical residue.
>
> 'Form' denotes the component of proportionate being to be known, not by understanding the names of things, nor by understanding their relations to us, but by understanding them fully in their relations to one another.
>
> 'Act' denotes the component of proportionate being to be known by uttering the virtually unconditioned yes of reasonable judgment.[25]

Such a critically grounded metaphysics presents an integral heuristic structure on the basis of which one is able to reorient and integrate scientific and commonsense knowledge. The theologian who has uncovered and identified in his or her own operating what experience, understanding, and judgment are and how they are related to one another thus has a critical ground for understanding and employing not only metaphysical categories but also their embellishments, derivatives, and scientific correlatives. In this manner, Lonergan further develops the ground of the general categories, to yield a summary statement of much of *Insight* and of much of the first four chapters of *Method in Theology*. In fact, it is clear from Lonergan's treatment of general categories in *Method in Theology* that *Insight* would contribute not only a great portion of the general categories themselves but also the basic framework for generating all of these categories. Lonergan implies (correctly, I believe) that on this basis one is prepared to transform, transpose, and employ in theology categories provided by other disciplines (as well as to contribute to the reorientation of those disciplines themselves).[26]

3 Categories

The interplay of the general and special categories is a matter of particular complexity. I have stated above, at the end of chapter 5, my position that the overall relation of the general to the special categories parallels the obediential potency of nature to grace. But there are other issues still to be addressed. Even the issue of obediential potency calls for further comment, but that is reserved for a later section.[27] Here I will simply cover a few items that have not been mentioned yet.

First, then, *Method in Theology*'s treatment of 'the question of God, of religious experience, its expressions, its dialectical development' is listed among the terms and relations that constitute *general*, not special, categories;[28] and elsewhere Lonergan states that he regards his description of religious experience in terms of 'being in love in an unqualified fashion' as *philosophical*, not theological, language.[29] This means that the treatment even of the objects specific to theology will employ not only the special categories but also general categories derived from intentionality analysis and integrated in a metaphysics of proportionate, that is, intraworldly, being.

Again, the philosophy of God proposed in chapter 19 of *Insight* is later relocated as a part of systematic theology. While this transposition of the philosophy of God implies that the horizon required even for a *philosophic* and so 'natural' affirmation of God is a function not only of the intellectual conversion that leads to the basic positions on knowing, being, and objectivity on which the argument for God's existence builds, and of the moral conversion that rises above the influence of bias, but also of religious conversion, philosophic knowledge of God remains 'natural.' Even though the appropriate context for a philosophy of God is a theological context, even though the horizon within which philosophical knowledge of God is attained includes a supernatural element, the argument for God's existence and the categories that it employs remain philosophical. The requisite horizon is broader than that afforded by *Insight*'s basic positions on knowing, being, and objectivity; only in the abstract are these positions sufficient to ground an affirmation of God's existence: if being is intrinsically intelligible, complete intelligibility must exist; but complete intelligibility does not exist in a world whose every existent and every event is contingent; such sheer contingence is transcended only if there exists an unrestricted act of understanding not contingent in any respect and capable of causally grounding contingent existence and occurrence. Such an argument is natural, and it is purely philosophic. Yet it will not function successfully in any horizon devoid of the religious dimension of conversion. The very horizon of natural knowledge is a function in part of a supernatural element. Yet the knowledge remains natural.

Again, many of the categories to be employed in a systematics of the Trinity are derived, not from religiously differentiated consciousness but from intentionality analysis. The entire psychological analogy employed by Lonergan in the systematic portion of his *De Deo trino* moves from the emanations of word and love in human intentional consciousness, as these are appropriated as it were 'from below upwards,' to the divine processions that are the very first topic or theme of the systematics of the Trinity. The principal foundational function of *religiously* differentiated consciousness is to serve as the basis for the derivation of those categories that depend on religious conversion, but the examples I have just cited serve to show that the general and special categories operate together in the generation of a systematics. Even when the analogy for the Trinity shifts, as it does in Lonergan's later writings, to a starting point in 'that higher synthesis of intellectual, rational, and moral consciousness that is the dynamic state of being in love,' and so that is sanctifying grace, still, because the language used is philosophical, general categories continue to be employed. In Lonergan's later psychological analogy,[30] the created analogue is actually not nature but created *grace*. But the categories that are employed to describe it and to explain it are by and large general categories. Conversion – intellectual, moral, and religious – 'transforms the concrete individual to make [one] capable of grasping not merely conclusions but principles as well.'[31] And so a systematics based on conversion and its objectification will 'present a single unified whole'[32] of philosophical and theological affirmations.

To summarize: systematics has the task of constructing a coherent understanding of what the theologian judges to be the constitutive meaning of Christian existence, and so of providing the proximate basis for the multiple tasks of communication in the various contemporary contexts in which the self-constituting community process that is the church finds itself. Its function is 'to work out appropriate systems of conceptualization, to remove apparent inconsistencies, to move toward some grasp of spiritual matters both from their own inner coherence and from the analogies offered by more familiar human experience.'[33] 'Its task is to take over the facts, established in doctrines, and to attempt to work them into an assimilable whole.'[34] It is grounded in the radically concrete foundation of conversion events and processes and in their objectification in (1) 'an intentionality analysis that distinguishes four levels of conscious and intentional operations, where each successive level sublates previous levels by going beyond them, by setting up a higher principle, by introducing new operations, and by preserving the integrity of previous levels, while extending enormously their range and their significance,'[35] and (2) a differentiation of our orientation to transcendent mystery and of the inchoate satisfaction of that orientation in religious love. Since the orientation provides 'the primary and fundamental meaning of the name, God,'[36] systematic theology's treatment even of specifically theological themes will contain a philosophic component expressed in the general categories. Such a concrete foundation will enable the generation of basic terms and relations that are both *trans*cultural, in that they express the bond that unites people despite cultural differences, and *cross*cultural, in that they enable communication across cultures on the basis of an appropriation of this common bond. These basic terms and relations articulate human interiority in the dimensions of both nature and grace, and the objects known or valued in the operations and states thus objectified will be expressed in categories derived from the interior and religious differentiations. Ultimately, again, for every term and relation there will exist, proximately or remotely, a corresponding element in intentional (or, as the case may be, nonintentional) consciousness.

4 Conversion and Foundations

More will be said on categories later.[37] Now let us discuss in more detail the three conversion processes specified by Lonergan as well as the fourth that I have suggested.

4.1 Intellectual Conversion

There is an explicit variety of *intellectual conversion* that occurs as the subject comes to something like the following affirmations.

(1) Fully human knowing occurs in a world mediated and constituted by meaning and motivated by values, not in the world of immediacy. It is a

cumulative compound of operations occurring on the three distinct levels of (a) reception of data, (b) understanding of data (insight) grounding the procession or emanation of an inner word of conceptualization (definition, hypothesis, supposition) and leading to formulations, and (c) reflective grasp of the sufficiency of the evidence, the fulfilment of conditions for affirming one's understanding and conceptual synthesis, and so of a 'virtually unconditioned' that grounds the procession or emanation of a second inner word, the yes or no of rational judgment.

The first level (reception, experience)[38] is not to be understood as confrontation and duality of subject and object but, with Aristotle, as an identity in act of subject and object: the sense in act is the sensible in act. The second level proceeds from insight into the presentations of sense and imagination, where the identity of subject and object is maintained (the intellect in act is the intelligible in act), to concepts or inner words grounded in insight, where meaning and meant are distinguished, and so where objectification occurs, and to formulations or outer words that directly mean the inner words and only through the latter the 'thing' understood. The third level culminates in reasonable judgment, which occurs not before understanding but only consequent upon both the direct understanding of the data and the reflective understanding that grasps the sufficiency of the evidence. If the evidence is grasped as sufficient, then in the affirmative judgment that proceeds as a second inner word upon this reflective insight, the conceptual synthesis formulated at the second level is posited as knowledge of what is, of the real, of being.

(2) Being, then, is the objective of the desire to know that sustains and permeates the entire process from reception of data through understanding to judgment. Being is whatever can be intelligently grasped and reasonably affirmed. It is what would be known completely in the totality of true judgments, and what is known incrementally with each single true judgment. And so being is intrinsically intelligible, and since apart from being there is nothing, being is the real. Since the real is thus intelligible, it is not known as real in any other way than through the process or series of processions or emanations affirmed in the knower's self-affirmation: from experience and image through inquiry to understanding (procession of an operation, from potency to act), from understanding to conceptualization (procession of a product, from act to act), from reflection to reflective insight (procession of an operation, from potency to act), and from reflective insight to judgment (procession of a product, from act to act).[39]

(3) Objectivity is the consequence or fruit of intelligent inquiry and critical reflection, of authentic subjectivity. There is the experiential objectivity of the givenness of data, the normative objectivity of fidelity to the desire to know, and the absolute objectivity of true judgment grounded in

the grasp of the virtually unconditioned. But the notion of objectivity is found principally in a patterned set of judgments, of the type '*A* is, *B* is, *A* is not *B*, I am *A*.'

There seems to be a development in Lonergan's thought regarding the foundational adequacy of intellectual conversion. In *Insight*, it seems, he judged that these three basic positions could ground not only a metaphysics but also an ethics and, it would appear from the last two chapters and from explicit statements at the beginning of chapter 14, both a philosophical theology or philosophy of God and something at least of what was then called fundamental theology. He would subsequently change his mind on the foundations of ethics and of all forms of theology in direct discourse, introducing for ethics a foundational account of moral conversion, and for theology an account of religious experience and conversion that is to be added to the accounts of moral and intellectual conversion to form the foundations of direct theological discourse. Religious conversion, in fact, normally precedes moral conversion, and religious and moral conversion normally precede intellectual conversion, so that there is ultimately a religious or theological grounding even of sciences and disciplines other than theology.[40] For the moment, however, our affirmation is that even the realities discussed in the last three chapters of *Insight* would seem to demand for their objectification a foundation more generous than *Insight* provides them.

4.2 Moral Conversion

The *moral* dimensions of conversion are spoken of in two ways by Lonergan, the first in *Insight* (chapter 18, though without explicit mention of a moral conversion) and the second in *Method in Theology*, chapter 2. Lonergan seems to have regarded the presentation in *Method* as something of a corrective to that found in *Insight*, for he writes:

> In *Insight* the good was the intelligent and reasonable. In *Method* the good is a distinct notion. It is intended in questions for deliberation: Is this worthwhile? Is it truly or only apparently good? It is aspired to in the intentional response of feeling to values. It is known in judgments of value made by a virtuous or authentic person with a good conscience. It is brought about by deciding and living up to one's decisions. Just as intelligence sublates sense, just as reasonableness sublates intelligence, so deliberation sublates and thereby unifies knowing and feeling.[41]

Central to the development, of course, was Lonergan's recognition shortly after he finished writing *Insight* that there is a distinct fourth level of consciousness concerned with decision, and that its operations cannot be reduced to those of intelligence and rationality.

I wish to suggest that both of Lonergan's expressions of moral conversion have validity and that they complement one another. In fact, it can probably be argued that they are elements in distinct but complementary approaches to a 'psychological analogy' for a systematic understanding of Trinitarian processions and relations, and that they are especially pertinent to that dimension of Trinitarian theology that treats the procession of the Holy Spirit, just as Lonergan's position on intellectual conversion is particularly pertinent to one of the analogical understandings of the procession of the Word. (Note, however, that even Lonergan's earlier psychological analogy for the procession of the eternal Word is from the procession in our consciousness of a judgment of *value*, and so it depends on his earlier account of *moral* integrity as well as on his understanding of intellectual conversion.)

On my interpretation, the two approaches can be related to St Ignatius Loyola's 'times of election' as the latter are proposed in the *Spiritual Exercises*. Actually, St Ignatius proposes 'Three Times, In Each of Which a Sound and Good Election May Be Made.'

> The first time is when God our Lord so moves and attracts the will, that, without doubt or the power of doubting, such a devoted soul follows what has been pointed out to it, as St Paul and St Matthew did when they followed Christ our Lord.
>
> The second time is when much light and knowledge is obtained by experiencing consolations and desolations, and by experience of the discernment of various spirits.
>
> The third time is one of tranquility: when one considers, first, for what one is born, that is, to praise God our Lord, and to save one's soul; and when, desiring this, one chooses as the means to this end a kind or state of life within the bounds of the Church, in order that one may thereby be helped to serve God our Lord, and to save one's soul. I said a time of tranquility; that is, when the soul is not agitated by divers spirits, but enjoys the use of its natural powers freely and quietly.[42]

Ignatius goes on to specify in some detail two methods of making a decision in this third time, when one is not agitated by various 'pulls and counterpulls' (to use Eric Voegelin's expression)[43] but enjoys the use of one's natural powers (that is, presumably, something like experience, understanding, judgment, and decision) freely and quietly. In each case, the criterion is found in the constituents of *rational* choice, within the overall horizon provided by faith. And in another and major section of the *Exercises* he proposes 'Rules for the Discernment of Spirits' to be employed in part (but only in part) when one is in the second time of election: 'only in part' because these rules for negotiating pulls and counterpulls do not apply only to times of election; they may be used in what has come to be called the examination of consciousness.

I suggest the following considerations.

First, the times of decision that Ignatius lists are exhaustive. There are no other times of decision. Either God has done something to move one in such a way that one has no doubts as to what one is to do, and then one is in the first time, or God has not so moved one, and so one has questions, and then one is in either the second or third time. If one is agitated by various pulls and counterpulls, one is in the second time, and one is not free to exercise one's natural powers of intelligence and reason but must rely on various guidelines for discerning, so as (in Ignatius's words) to admit the good and reject the bad. If one is not agitated by various pulls and counterpulls but still must make a decision, one is in the third time, and then one is free to employ not only the two methods that Ignatius proposes for this time but other methods as well of arriving at judgments of value and decisions that acknowledge particular goods and goods of order as genuine values precisely insofar as they are possible objects of rational choice.

Second, there is a mutual complementarity between the second and third times. The judgment of value and the decision that one arrives at in the second time by discerning pulls and counterpulls must be able to be adjudicated as well by the criteria of intelligence, reason, and responsibility that are explicitly appealed to in the third time; and the judgments of value and decision that are arrived at in the third time must produce the same 'peace of a good conscience' on the part of a virtuous person (note the 'pragmatic engagement' entailed in moral conversion) that would result from the proper discernment of pulls and counterpulls in the second time. And in the first time, there are no further questions, and one *knows* there are no further questions, because the same criteria of self-transcendence have been met, and one knows they have been met. In any and all cases, to quote Lonergan, 'inner conviction is the conviction that the norms of attentiveness, intelligence, reasonableness, responsibility have been satisfied.'[44] While these criteria are met, these norms satisfied, in different ways in different times of decision, ultimately these criteria and their affective correspondences will be relied on in all three moments and appealed to when one gives an account of one's value judgments and decisions, no matter in which time a given value judgment or decision is arrived at.

Third, Lonergan's account of judgments of value and decision in *Insight* presents principal points of the general form of St Ignatius's third time of evaluation and decision. It explicitly prescinds from any discussion of affective involvements, and at least implicitly presupposes that the person confronted with a time of decision and election is not agitated in such a way that one is prevented from employing one's natural powers of experiencing, understanding, judging, and deciding. This would mean, if I am correct, that Lonergan's account in *Insight* would remain valid, but that it would not be the only account, because it names only one of the times, and so only one of the methods, of arriving at a good decision. This also means that this account will continue to provide one form or element of the psychological analogy that we may employ for understanding the mystery of the divine processions of Word and Holy Spirit, so that a systematics of the Trinity will continue to be informed in part by this account of human existential consciousness, or of what in *Insight* Lonergan calls rational self-consciousness.

Fourth, even this general form of the third time of evaluation and decision can be filled out with a consideration of the affective elements that are present even in this third time, when one is in a state of tranquility and is not agitated by various pulls and counterpulls. This self-transcendent affectivity is an affectivity that matches the reach of what in his later work Lonergan calls the transcendental notion of value.

Fifth, this general form of the third time of evaluation and decision (which is also the general form of the psychological analogy for Trinitarian processions presented by Lonergan in his systematics of the Trinity in *De Deo trino*) is a form of human development 'from below upwards.' Furthermore, the second time of election in the *Exercises* is also a movement from below upwards in human consciousness; while the second time can include movements 'from above,' the process toward value judgments and decisions is still essentially from below, precisely because there *are* further questions that must be answered before one can arrive at a judgment of value and a consequent decision.

Sixth, the presentation that Lonergan gives in *Method in Theology* is relevant, not to the third but to the second time of election. For here it is self-transcendent affectivity that provides the criteria for the decision. Which object of choice, which course of action, when considered and reflected upon, leads me to the self-transcendent affectivity that matches the reach of the transcendental notion of value? The answer to that question is what provides the indication as to the direction in which one is to go as one heads towards a judgment of value and a consequent decision. And note that in neither case (nor for that matter in Ignatius's 'first time') is the decision generalizable to others. The good is always concrete. What I am to do, and what you are to do, in very similar circumstances must both be in harmony with the general requirements of self-transcendent affectivity and of rational choice. But the particulars of what I am to do may be very different from the particulars of what you are to do.

Seventh, there is also another time of evaluation and decision, the one that St Ignatius places first. The type of experience that St Ignatius is talking of when he writes of a first time of decision is an experience of a movement that occurs distinctly and, I think, exclusively 'from above downwards' in human consciousness.

The statement of ethical integrity that is offered in chapter 18 of *Insight*, together with Lonergan's cognitional theory, offers the psychological analogy for the Trinitarian processions that Lonergan develops most fully, that presented in the *pars systematica* of his *De Deo trino*. It corresponds to what St Ignatius calls the third time of election, and it also reflects St Thomas Aquinas's developed teaching on freedom and responsibility, transposing that teaching into more contemporary categories. According to this presentation, moral integrity is a matter of *generating decisions and consequent actions that are consistent with what one knows*, that is, that are consistent with the inner words of judgments of fact and judgments of value that one has sufficient reason to hold as true.

Lonergan's second statement of moral integrity is based on the developments that are found in *Method in Theology*, especially in chapter 2, and in later writings. Especially as it is found in post-*Method* writings, where the elements 'from above' are explicitly acknowledged, it grounds a distinct psychological analogy for the Trinitarian processions. The second statement of moral integrity, as it is found in *Method in Theology*, is related to what St Ignatius calls the second moment of election; and in the further development on this second statement that can be found in Lonergan's post-*Method* writings, it is pertinent to the first moment as well. In these later developments in his thinking, Lonergan arrived at a qualified and nuanced position on the respective roles assigned to knowledge and love in the Thomist teaching on freedom and responsibility. In the most fully developed articulation of his statement, moral integrity is a function of generating either the decisions and actions, and even the prior judgments of value, of a person in love in an unqualified way or the decisions, actions, and judgments that will move one closer to that state. Being in love in an unqualified way is, of course, a created participation in the passive spiration that in God is the Holy Spirit. It is the habit of charity. In us it flows, not from our knowledge, but proximately from the entitative habit of sanctifying grace, and remotely from the active spiration in God that is Father and Word as one principle of the Holy Spirit.

Lonergan's second statement on moral conversion, then, is not so much a correction of the statement in *Insight* as a complement to it. As with Ignatius's times of election, so here too any moral decision must stand the test of being judged against the criteria of either procedure. And as with Ignatius's times of election, decisions are generated in distinct manners, not because one manner is better than another, but because the antecedent state of the person deciding determines the method that will be followed in moving to the decision.

As we have seen,[45] after he had come to an even more nuanced presentation of his later position on these issues, Lonergan suggested a somewhat different psychological analogy for the Trinitarian processions from that which he employs in the systematic part of the *De Deo trino.* It is based on the fuller implications of his second statement of moral integrity, implications that become obvious when he distinguishes movements from above and movements from below in consciousness. In this later analogy, the created analogue is in the order of grace or of graced nature, whereas the earlier version of the psychological analogy is strictly drawn from nature alone.

4.3 Religious Conversion

I would like also to make some suggestions regarding religious conversion. Lonergan's understanding of religious conversion, as presented in *Method in Theology* and later writings, rests on his answer to the question, Can something be loved that is unknown? This question vexed Augustine, as he attempted to discover some analogy that would give us some understanding of the Trinitarian processions. But Lonergan's answer in *Method in Theology* is different from Augustine's, and for that matter from Aquinas's and from Lonergan's own earlier position as reflected in *De Deo trino.* Moreover, the issue affects the psychological analogy. Augustine was not able adequately to develop a psychological analogy based on love, and he admitted as much; and one reason may lie in his answer to this prior question. Aquinas's analogy depends on an answer similar to Augustine's, as does the analogy that Lonergan offers in *De Deo trino,* which is a retrieval and development of Aquinas's analogy. There Aquinas's position is explicitly appealed to: 'de ratione amoris est quod non procedit nisi a conceptione intellectus.'[46] It may be that Lonergan's later analogy depends on a quite different answer to this question. That different answer is the following.

> It used to be said, *Nihil amatum nisi praecognitum,* Knowledge precedes love. The truth of this tag is the fact that ordinarily operations on the fourth level of intentional consciousness presuppose and complement corresponding operations on the other three. There is a minor exception to this rule inasmuch as people do fall in love, and that falling in love is something disproportionate to its causes, conditions, occasions, antecedents. For falling in love is a new be-ginning, an exercise of vertical liberty in which one's world undergoes a new organization. But the major excep-

> tion to the Latin tag is God's gift of his love flooding our hearts. Then we are in the dynamic state of being in love. But who it is we love, is neither given nor as yet understood. Our capacity for moral self-transcendence has found a fulfilment that brings deep joy and profound peace. Our love reveals to us values we had not appreciated, values of prayer and worship, or repentance and belief. But if we would know what is going on within us, if we would learn to integrate it with the rest of our living, we have to inquire, investigate, seek counsel. So it is that in religious matters love precedes knowledge and, as that love is God's gift, the very beginning of faith is due to God's grace.[47]

This gift is sanctifying grace. It is a created participation in the active spiration of the Holy Spirit by the Father and the Son. It breathes forth consistent loving acts, a habit of charity that is a created participation in the passive spiration that *is* the Holy Spirit. It has a transcultural aspect. It is offered to all, and while it is manifested more or less authentically in the many religions of humankind and apprehended in as many different manners as there are different cultures, the gift itself as distinct from its manifestations is transcultural. One of the reasons we can make this claim is precisely that the gift is not conditioned by our knowledge or apprehension.

The gift has something to do with our orientation towards an unknown mystery. The gift, as establishing a state, is an inchoate fulfilment of the orientation, which itself is nature. The fulfilment is supernatural, because it exceeds the capacities of the orientation itself. Other manifestations of God's gift may be found, for example, in the awakening of the orientation from the slumber of the triviality or fanaticism of everyday living, but the latter manifestation is best spoken of in terms that would capture the meaning of actual grace rather than sanctifying grace. The gift of God's love is some initial satisfaction of an orientation to mystery that is the pure question that human consciousness by nature is.

What Augustine was seeking in the opening chapters of book 8 of the *De trinitate,* what Lonergan expresses in terms of God's own love flooding our hearts, is what Lonergan elsewhere calls 'the transition from the natural to the supernatural.'[48] It is the greatest discontinuity of all, and the transition over the divide is God's doing, not ours. In order to express what God does to effect this transition, Lonergan reverses the normal priority of knowledge over love and speaks of a 'being in love' that is given to us in complete independence of any knowledge or decision on our part; this articulation marks the beginning of an attempt to translate the obediential potency of a formal ontology into terms of consciousness. The love that is given to us independently of any knowledge on our part is the very love of God. More precisely, sanctifying grace is a created participation in the active spiration of the Spirit by the Father and the Son, and the habit of charity breathed forth from sanctifying grace is a created participation in the passive spiration that *is* the Holy Spirit.

Only such a theological articulation of the matter in explicitly Trinitarian terms will do justice to the reality of which Lonergan speaks. Between sanctifying grace and the habit of charity there is as much a real distinction as there is between active and passive spiration in the Trinity. Active spiration is identical with paternity and filiation, and so with Father and Son, as one principle. Passive spiration is identical with the Holy Spirit. As active and passive spiration are distinct by mutually opposed relations, so sanctifying grace and charity, the created participations in these divine relations, are also distinct by mutually opposed relations, and the tricky point is to try to capture in language the conscious element entailed in these created supernatural relations. Religious experience is, for the most part, well spoken of in terms of the dynamic state of unqualified being in love. But that gift has to be further differentiated into an actively spirating love and the acts of love and habit of love that flow from that spiration.

The corresponding conscious element, however, is not an element exclusively in intentional consciousness, precisely because the experience occurs without there being an *apprehended* object to which it responds. The conscious component of sanctifying grace is an actively spirating love that is *given* to us, that is not a response to an apprehended object, and that is a participation in the active spiration of the Holy Spirit by the Father and the Son as one principle. What proceeds in God is *amor procedens*, the Holy Spirit, and what proceeds in us is charity, the created participation in the passively spirated Holy Spirit. Charity is intentional consciousness, but the conscious component of sanctifying grace is nonintentional, in that it is not a response to an apprehended object.

4.4 *Psychic Conversion*

I am going to suggest here a development or expansion on the notion of psychic conversion. But first, I think, I should summarize what I have said up to now on this topic.

In my work on psychic conversion, I have been concerned with two complementary movements of thought. The first suggests the possibility of a reorientation of depth psychology on the basis of Lonergan's intentionality analysis.[49] The second complements Lonergan's intentionality analysis with the reoriented depth psychology. It is in the latter movement that there arises the claim of an additional dimension to theological foundations, and so of an expanded base for the derivation of the categories.

4.4.1 The Immanent Intelligibility of Psychic Conversion

In *Insight,* at the beginning of a discussion of the genetic and dialectical sequences in which meaning advances to new stages, Lonergan spoke of two distinct sets of *operators in human consciousness,* and at least by implication of two dimensions to that consciousness itself, which we may call spiritual and psychic or sensitive.

> [M]an's concrete being involves (1) a succession of levels of higher integration, and (2) a principle of correspondence between otherwise coincidental manifolds on each lower level and systematizing forms on the next higher level. Moreover, these higher integrations on the organic, psychic, and intellectual levels are not static but dynamic systems; they are systems on the move; the higher integration is not only an integrator but also an operator; and if developments on different levels are not to conflict, there has to be a correspondence between their respective operators.
>
> ... [O]n the intellectual level the operator is concretely the detached and disinterested desire to know. It is this desire, not in contemplation of the already known, but headed towards further knowledge, orientated into the known unknown. The principle of dynamic correspondence calls for a harmonious orientation on the psychic level, and from the nature of the case such an orientation would have to consist in some cosmic dimension, in some intimation of unplumbed depths, that accrued to man's feelings, emotions, sentiments.[50]

The two dimensions of consciousness are, of course, familiar from other contexts in *Insight.* Among other things, they give rise to perplexing problems concerning the nature of human knowledge. But while the position on fully human *knowing* involves breaking the duality of our knowing, and affirming that knowing is experiencing, understanding, and judging, the two dimensions of *consciousness* are never fused into one, without any further distinction.[51] Rather, as the passage just quoted indicates, their concrete unity involves a principle of dynamic correspondence between what remain distinct dimensions.

Psychic conversion affects directly this dynamic correspondence. It effects a habitual *conversio ad phantasmata,* a restoration of a 'natural orientation' of incarnate spirit,[52] just as intellectual conversion effects a restoration of fidelity to the transcendental notions of the intelligible, the true, and the real, as moral conversion effects a restoration of fidelity to the transcendental notion of the good, and as religious conversion effects a restoration of fidelity to the transcendent exigence through an inchoate experience of its satisfaction in the gift of God's love.

In the passages of *Insight* to which we are presently referring, Lonergan is treating the dynamic correspondence of spirit and psyche by speaking of affect-laden images that have to do with 'the sphere of the ulterior unknown, of the unexplored and strange, of the undefined surplus of significance and momentousness,' which constitute the 'primary field' of what he calls mystery and myth;[53] and his purpose in discussing them in *Insight* is to provide some way of discriminating symbolic expressions of positions (mystery) from symbolic expressions of counterpositions (myth). This sphere constitutes a dimension of the total field affected by psychic conversion, but not the only dimension of the field of affect-laden images nor the only dimension of correspondence affected by psychic conversion.

Psychic conversion is a transformation of the censorship exercised with respect to the entire field of what is received in empirical consciousness. The censorship is exercised by dramatically patterned intentional consciousness, by the collaboration of one's habitual accumulation of insights, judgments, and moral spontaneities with one's imagination, by one's 'mentality' or mindset; psychic conversion is a transformation of that censorship from a repressive to a constructive exercise as one engages in the delicate artistry of producing 'the first and only edition' of oneself.[54]

One is initiated into interiorly differentiated consciousness by Lonergan's cognitional analysis, and especially by the 'self-affirmation of the knower' that is the topic of the eleventh chapter of *Insight*. Lonergan later extends self-appropriation beyond cognitional analysis into a generalized intentionality analysis that sublates cognitional analysis into a self-appropriation of the existential subject concerned with the constitution of the human world as a good or evil place in which to live and with the concomitant constitution of oneself as an originating value or disvalue. But I have argued that the process can and must be further extended to include the self-appropriation of those dimensions of consciousness that are properly psychic: in effect, an appropriation (1) of the first, empirical level of consciousness (the psyche) that consists in the sensitive flow of sensations, memories, images, conations, emotions, associations, spontaneous intersubjective responses, bodily movements, and received meanings and values,[55] and, as we will see in a moment, (2) of the potential openness of intentional consciousness to an underpinning transition from the neural or the organic to the psychic. The key to this dimension of self-appropriation is the transformation of what in the sixth chapter of *Insight* Lonergan calls the repressive censorship into a constructive censorship that wants insight, rational judgment, and responsible decision, and so that admits into consciousness the sensitive and imaginal materials and the received meanings and values that will provide the data for insight (the original meaning of *conversio ad phantasmata*). Psychic conversion is to be understood as the transformation especially of the psychic dimension of the censorship, the dimension affected by what Lonergan calls 'dramatic bias.' The transformation occurs through the extension to the level of the sensitive psyche and of the preconscious neural functioning of the organism of the conversion process that promotes the condition of 'universal willingness' or total being-in-love or charity.[56]

4.4.2 Psychic Conversion and the Levels of Consciousness

Another dimension of psychic conversion can be indicated by appealing to the levels of consciousness. In *Insight* Lonergan distinguished the three levels constitutive of the subject as knower: experience, understanding, and judgment. Shortly thereafter he realized that the operations that enter into and culminate in decision require the addition of a fourth level. In *Philosophy of God, and Theology* he offhandedly says of the dynamic state of being in love without restriction, as God's free gift, 'You can say it's on the fifth level.'[57] After reading some of my earliest material on psychic conversion, where I speak of a symbolic operator effecting the entry of neural process into consciousness in the dream,[58] he began to speak of a quasi-operator at this level, but without identifying the dream and other similar experiences as a distinct 'level' of consciousness. At this time, too, he started to talk of an 'upper' quasi-operator that heads into intimacy, interpersonal relations, family, community, and the love of God, but again without specifying a further 'upper' level of consciousness. In a passage that we have already seen, and that will be very important for us again in the next chapter, he writes:

> [The] passionateness [of being] has a dimension of its own: it *underpins* and *accompanies* and *reaches beyond* the subject as experientially, intelligently, rationally, morally conscious.
>
> Its *underpinning* is the quasi-operator that presides over the transition from the neural to the psychic. It ushers into consciousness not only the demands of unconscious vitality but also the exigences of vertical finality. It obtrudes deficiency needs. In the self-actualizing subject it shapes the images that release insight; it recalls evidence that is being overlooked; it may embarrass wakefulness, as it disturbs sleep, with the spectre, the shock, the shame of misdeeds. As it channels into consciousness the feedback of our aberrations and our unfulfilled strivings, so for the Jungians it manifests its archetypes through symbols to preside over the genesis of the ego and to guide the individuation process from the ego to the self.

> As it underpins, so too it *accompanies* the subject's conscious and intentional operations. There it is the mass and momentum of our lives, the color and tone and power of feeling, that fleshes out and gives substance to what otherwise would be no more than a Shakespearian 'pale cast of thought.'
>
> As it underpins and accompanies, so too it *overarches* conscious intentionality. There it is the topmost quasi-operator that by intersubjectivity prepares, by solidarity entices, by falling in love establishes us as members of community. Within each individual vertical finality heads for self-transcendence. In an aggregate of self-transcending individuals there is the significant coincidental manifold in which can emerge a new creation. Possibility yields to fact and fact bears witness to its originality and power in the fidelity that makes families, in the loyalty that makes peoples, in the faith that makes religions.[59]

So too, we read of 'a tidal movement that *begins before* consciousness, *unfolds through* sensitivity, intelligence, rational reflection, responsible deliberation, only to find its *rest beyond* all of these.'[60] Finally, Lonergan's most complete statement on levels of consciousness appears in the posthumously published paper 'Philosophy and the Religious Phenomenon,' where the quasi-operators become (possibly) operators, and so where there is introduced the possibility of *two additional levels of consciousness.*

> Our intentionality analysis distinguished the four levels of experience, understanding, factual judgment, and existential decision. We must now advert to the fact that this structure may prove open at both ends. The intellectual operator that promotes our operations from the level of experience to the level of understanding may well be preceded by a symbolic operator that coordinates neural potentialities and needs with higher goals through its control over the emergence of images and affects. Again, beyond the moral operator that promotes us from judgments of fact to judgments of value with their retinue of decisions and actions, there is a further realm of interpersonal relations and total commitment in which human beings tend to find the immanent goal of their being and with it their fullest joy and deepest peace.
>
> So from an intentionality analysis distinguishing four levels one moves to an analysis that distinguishes six levels.[61]

Again:

> [W]e have introduced two further extensions. First, we mentioned

> the possibility of a symbolic operator that, through image and affect, headed psychic process to its own and to higher ends; and an exploration of this area we felt highly relevant to an account of religious symbolism. Secondly, we adverted to a topmost level of interpersonal relations and total commitments, a level that can be specifically religious, a level that in one of its actuations is easily verified in New Testament doctrine, that conforms to the view of all Scholastic schools that without charity even the infused virtues are unformed, that provides a basis for explicitating the universalism of Christianity and relating it positively to other religions ... [W]hat in a philosophic context I have named being in love in an unrestricted manner, in a theological context could be paralleled with [Karl] Rahner's supernatural existential.[62]

Even in this passage Lonergan's affirmation of a symbolic operator effecting an elemental emergence of image and affect remains tentative, more tentative than his affirmation of a topmost level of total loving commitment. Obviously I wish to be more forthright on the issue: the intellectual or spiritual operators *are* preceded by a symbolic operator, or, better I think, they are *preceded, accompanied, and transcended by an aesthetic-dramatic operator.*

One of the primary areas, of course, in which 'exploration of this area' has occurred is in the therapeutic context established by much modern depth psychology. Of this context, Lonergan writes in *Insight* that the insights that can aid in moving one beyond scotosis and its effects must occur

> ... not in the detached and disinterested intellectual pattern of experience, but in the dramatic pattern in which images are tinged with affects. Otherwise the insights will occur but they will not undo the inhibitions that account for the patient's affective disorders; there will result a development of theoretical intelligence without a change in sensitive spontaneity ... [T]he patient is not to be thought capable of curing himself, for the cure consists precisely in the insights which arise from the schematic images that spontaneously the patient represses; and even if by an extraordinary effort of intellectual detachment the patient succeeded in grasping in part what he was refusing to understand, this grasp would occur in the intellectual pattern of experience and so would prove ineffectual; indeed, the effort would be likely to produce an obsession with analytic notions, and there would be some danger that such merely theoretical insight would tend to inoculate the patient

> against the benefit of a true analytical experience with its dramatic overtones.[63]

Now the context of an affirmation of psychic conversion includes but is not limited to therapy and analysis.[64] It is analogous to therapy at least in this, that, if one is to come to affirm psychic conversion, there must occur 'a re-formation of [one's] mentality.'[65] But von Balthasar, too, has pointed to a pathology of the aesthetic and the dramatic that is extremely difficult to overcome and that is met in culture generally and not just on the analyst's couch. Overcoming it calls for a shift in basic horizon, and, it seems, no argument will effect such a shift. But at least we can point to the area of consciousness that is opened up when the pathology is met at its roots. The pathology is a truncation of that natural orientation that Aquinas called *conversio ad phantasmata.* The truncation is abetted by almost all Western philosophies since Scotus, who denied the fact of insight into images, and so the connection between presentations of the singular (*haecceitas,* in Scotus's strange language) and mental conceptions. The overcoming of conceptualism and its effects at both superstructural and infrastructural levels of culture will entail not only an intellectual, but also a psychic, conversion.

I have already taken a stand regarding at least one dimension of the topmost level of consciousness affirmed by Lonergan in 'Philosophy and the Religious Phenomenon.' I want to affirm this dimension precisely as created grace, as what an interiorly and religiously differentiated consciousness would affirm in transposing the Scholastic notion of a created communication of the divine nature or sanctifying grace. I have distinguished this grace from charity, which it grounds or breathes forth. From what we have just seen in 'Philosophy and the Religious Phenomenon,' two things are clear. First, that topmost level now must be affirmed as, not a fifth, but at least a sixth level; and second, what I am affirming as occurring at this level may be but 'one of its actuations.' Whether it grounds all of the others remains a question that was left open by Lonergan, one that can be answered, I think, only by further foundational and systematic-theological reflection. I think the answer to this question is yes ('God is love, and those who abide in love abide in God, and God abides in them'),[66] but I am not prepared yet to argue this in any detail.

This presentation of psychic conversion in terms of levels of consciousness manifests that, while the core intelligibility of psychic conversion has to do with the censorship that regulates the transition from the neural to the psychic, its effects extend through and beyond the four levels of intentional consciousness. It enables the internal communication that makes possible the identification of the feelings that accompany one's intentional operations,[67] and it involves as well an appropriation of the intersubjectivity, solidarity, and love that affect the topmost level. Its importance throughout intentional consciousness can be estimated by reflection on what Lonergan has written concerning *ressentiment*, which is perhaps, says Lonergan, 'the most notable' aberration of feeling, and so the most intransigent instance of the effects of dramatic or psychic bias.

> [R]essentiment is a re-feeling of a specific clash with someone else's value-qualities. The someone else is one's superior physically or intellectually or morally or spiritually. The re-feeling is not active or aggressive but extends over time, even a life-time. It is a feeling of hostility, anger, indignation that is neither repudiated nor directly expressed. What it attacks is the value-quality that the superior person possessed and the inferior not only lacked but also feels unequal to acquiring. The attack amounts to a continuous belittling of the value in question, and it can extend to hatred and even violence against those that possess that value-quality. But perhaps its worst feature is that its rejection of one value involves a distortion of the whole scale of values and that this distortion can spread through a whole social class, a whole people, a whole epoch.[68]

And, we might add, through a whole intellectual movement, manifesting itself when developments to such a movement are brought forward that some adherents of the movement are unable to follow. '[L]ess differentiated consciousness finds more differentiated consciousness beyond its horizon and, in self-defence, may tend to regard the more differentiated with that pervasive, belittling hostility that Max Scheler named *ressentiment*.'[69]

4.4.3 A Difficulty

For some people, talk of additional levels of consciousness beyond the four that are clearly Lonergan doctrine is problematic, and this for honest methodological reasons that have to be addressed. The eight functional specialties that constitute theology's structure are derived from the four levels of intentional consciousness operating in two phases. Additional levels, it is claimed, would necessitate additional functional specialties, and yet the eight we have seem to account for all theological operations.[70]

This objection, I think, can be answered as follows. The only levels of consciousness that could provide the *objectives* of different theological operations are the four that Lonergan employs to differentiate *intentional* consciousness and to ground the functional specialties. But in the passage that I have just quoted from 'Philosophy and the Religious Phenomenon'

Lonergan is not explicitly ascribing to *intentional* consciousness the two additional levels. Rather, he says, the structure of intentional consciousness, in which his analysis distinguished four levels, *may be open* at both ends. It is the four levels of specifically intentional consciousness that provide theological objectives. Research provides data (experience). Interpretation understands the data provided by research (understanding). History ascertains what was going forward in certain periods at certain places (judgment). Dialectic reduces the really serious conflicts to their roots in conversion and the lack of it, discloses the need for a choice (decision), and helps us live with the more superficial differences. In foundations one articulates the choices one has made on basic issues (decision). In doctrines one states the truth one affirms within that horizon, out of the multiple possibilities offered by dialectic (judgment). In systematics one expresses one's understanding of the truths one has affirmed in doctrines (understanding). And communications produces new data in the present for the future (experience). The lower level to which this structure of intentional consciousness is open, that of affects and images in such events as the dream, does not offer theology any distinct objective (though perhaps it does offer a source!), and the higher level, at least when considered in respect to the supernatural actuation that has been our concern, is to be identified, not with the human nature in which intentional operations are elicited, some of which are theological, but with the created grace that at its roots, as an entitative habit, is the nonintentional reception of God's favour and the ground of our religious, moral, intellectual, and psychic conversion. Furthermore, Lonergan has always insisted that conversion events occur outside theology, however much they may be prepared and occasioned by work in theology, and however much they need to be objectified as theology's foundational reality. And because of the effect that 'secondary-process' objectifications can have on the 'primary process' of life itself,[71] to insist that the only levels of consciousness are the levels around which academic disciplines, however humanistic, are structured is to risk truncating conscious life itself. This is particularly clear in regard to theology, for the created grace that makes conversion possible is a topmost level of consciousness, what happens there is part of foundational reality, and theology is a function of what happens there as these events condition the authenticity of the theological operations that occur, not on this topmost level, but at the four intentional levels constitutive of the structure of the discipline itself.

4.4.4 The Theological Context of Psychic Conversion

We can point as well to the theological significance of the lower additional operator, and so provide another way of highlighting the significance of psychic conversion, especially in this context of establishing its role as foundational for systematics. Here we appeal to chapter 20 of *Insight*, where Lonergan discusses the elements that embody in this world God's response to the mystery of evil in human affairs.

Chapter 20 of *Insight* represents a *via analytica* or 'way of discovery' approach to the question of grace, as opposed to the *via synthetica* or 'way of teaching' approach characteristic of systematic theology. Thus chapter 20 *ends* with the hint of an absolutely supernatural participation in divine life, which is precisely where in *De ente supernaturali* the systematic treatment of grace *begins*. Chapter 19 of *Insight* arrived at an affirmation of an absolutely transcendent ground of contingent being, but the God thus affirmed is not a datum within this world. However, in chapter 20 Lonergan affirms that, since there exists an all-knowing, all-good, and all-powerful God, there also exists in this universe a set of created formal intelligibilities beyond those realities grasped in the physical, chemical, biological, psychological, and human sciences and in a philosophy that has methodically restricted itself to proportionate being, that is, to the *virtually* unconditioned. This something more provides theology, as a distinct discipline, with what Lonergan would later call its special categories. If there is something more in this world, something that has to do with transcendent being, it must be something that God is doing in this world, some created reality that enables us to transcend the mystery of evil by responding with something better.[72] Discussing it will not only set a context for understanding psychic conversion, but also add to what we have already seen regarding religious conversion.

The 'more' that God is doing consists fundamentally of created habits or (in *Insight*'s metaphysical terms) conjugate forms that are supernatural operators in human consciousness (thus the term 'operative grace'). If that is the case, then we may presume that the supernatural operators introduced into human consciousness by grace will affect both dimensions of consciousness (spiritual and psychic), and that is precisely what Lonergan affirms when he turns in chapter 20 to the question of the divinely originated solution to the problem of evil. Within the context of the graced existential that is the topic of *Insight*'s chapter 20, psychic conversion will bring about a correspondence of the operators and processes occurring on the respective conscious levels of spirit (the levels of insight, judgment, decision) and psyche, when all those operators have acquiesced as obediential potency to the reception of a set of habits created as free gift and have allowed those habits to become operative throughout living. Within a strictly theological context, where religious conversion is primary, psychic conversion enables the acquiescence of the sensitive operator of psychic development to be obediential potency for the penetration of grace to the sensitive and primordially intersubjective levels of consciousness. With that acquiescence there are released requisite and appropriate images that are laden with affect oriented to God. There is released precisely the *mystery* that is at once symbol of an ever inexhaustible and uncomprehended absolute intelligence and love, sign of the fragments of complete intelligibility that have been grasped, and psychic force empowering living human bodies to a collaborative, joyful, courageous, wholehearted, intelligent adoption of the dialectical attitude that meets evil with a greater good.[73]

Perhaps only this theological context of 'special transcendent knowledge' can adequately illuminate the significance of what I have called psychic conversion. Let us examine this context more closely.

In *Insight* the supernatural habits are correlated with faculties, but we can speak of them better in accord with Lonergan's later language of intentionality analysis, and as far as possible that is what I will try to do here. I will speak of conjugate forms that directly affect the spiritual dimensions of intentional consciousness (charity, hope, and faith) and of the extension of these to a habitual openness that directly affects the psychic dimensions of the same consciousness (the images and affects that emerge as the divine solution penetrates as mystery to the sensitive level).

First, then, the basis of all the other conjugate forms created in grace and universally accessible and permanent in human situations is *charity*. Charity is a love, a universal willingness, whose measure is God. Whether explicitly or anonymously, it is a love of God, because it is unrestricted and unqualified. And it is prompted by the goodness of what one is in love with. It constitutes persons of 'good will' who, like the universe itself, are in love with God. Because of it, one wills every other good, and the order of the universe itself, because of what one is radically in love with, and since that order includes pre-eminently the good that *persons* are, enjoy, and possess, one loves, wills the good of, all persons because of the love of God. This love of the universe and of all persons is a willing of the emergent probability that is the immanent intelligibility of universal order; and so it is realistic, expecting and willing that things and persons develop. Moreover, 'it is not to exclude from man's world the possibility of the social surd, nor to ignore it (for it is a fact), nor to mistake it for an intelligibility and so systematize and perpetuate it, but to acknowledge it as a problem and to embrace its solution.'[74]

Embracing the solution to the social surd is a matter of adopting a dialectical attitude in its regard. 'The dialectical method of intellect consists in grasping that the social surd neither is intelligible nor is to be treated as intelligible. The corresponding dialectical attitude of will is to return good for evil. For it is only inasmuch as men are willing to meet evil with good, to love their enemies, to pray for those that persecute and calumniate them, that the social surd is a potential good.'[75]

Second, being in love grounds *hope*, the second of the conjugate forms discussed as a created 'something more.' Hope keeps alive and maintains or restores the desire for God. It is a habitual determination that motivates deliberate decisions against self-interest, group bias, rationalization, and the instrumentalization of intelligence and reason that Lonergan calls general bias. At its roots, hope (in *Insight*'s formulation) is a confidence 'that God will bring man's intellect to a knowledge, participation, possession of the unrestricted act of understanding' that *is* God.[76] But its objective is not only otherworldly. The social significance of hope is clear from what has just been said about its relation to bias, and in the intellectual order itself, hope prompts 'a decision against ... despair, ... the deeper hopelessness that allows man's spirit to surrender the legitimate aspirations of the unrestricted desire and to seek comfort in the all too human ambitions of the Kantian and the positivist.'[77] It prompts as well a decision against the presumption that forgets that the fulfilment of the conditions for attaining knowledge of God lies with God and not with us.

Third, love and hope ground a knowledge that could not be had without them, a knowledge better expressed in Lonergan's later depiction of *faith* as the knowledge born of religious love and in the distinction drawn in *Method in Theology* between faith and beliefs. Faith is the knowledge born of love when that love is God's love flooding our hearts. It apprehends transcendent value, places all other value in the light and shadow of transcendent value, absorbs the human good in an all-encompassing good, and relates us not only to one another and nature, but, with one another and nature, to God and to God's world. It brings us together not only to settle human affairs but also to worship, involves us in a new development in holiness, and extends the limit of our expectation beyond the grave.[78]

Fourth, in addition to the conjugate forms of charity, hope, and faith, which are introduced into the spiritual dimensions of human consciousness, there is a *penetration of God's action to the level of our sensitivity and spontaneous intersubjectivity and even physiology*. It is here that the discussion of psychic conversion is relevant. Psychic conversion is not so much this penetration itself – I distinguish psychic conversion from affective conversion[79] – but a release, perhaps effected ultimately by the penetration of grace, that enables a *sensitive* and *organic* appropriation of the other effects of grace (and of many other things as well). Permit me a quotation from *Insight* on the reaching of grace to sensitivity and intersubjectivity.

> [A]ll exercise of human intelligence presupposes a suitable flow of sensitive and imaginative presentations, and again, inasmuch as intelligence and reasonableness and will issue into human words matched with deeds, they need at their disposal images so charged

> with affects that they succeed both in guiding and in propelling action. Again, besides the image that is a sign of intelligible and rational contents and the image that is a psychic force, there is the image that symbolizes man's orientation into the known unknown; and since faith gives more truth than understanding comprehends, since hope reinforces the detached, disinterested, unrestricted desire to know, man's sensitivity needs symbols that unlock its transforming dynamism and bring it into harmony with the vast but impalpable pressures of the pure desire, of hope, and of self-sacrificing charity.
>
> It follows that the solution will be not only a renovation of will that matches intellectual detachment and aspiration, not only a new and higher collaboration of intellects through faith in God, but also a *mystery* that is at once symbol of the uncomprehended and sign of what is grasped and psychic force that sweeps living human bodies, linked in charity, to the joyful, courageous, wholehearted, yet intelligently controlled performance of the tasks set by a world order in which the problem of evil is not suppressed but transcended.[80]

Again, '[i]t is to be noted that this transformation of sensitivity and intersubjectivity penetrates to the physiological level though the clear instances appear only in the intensity of mystical experience.'[81]

Fifth, what God would effect by creating the 'something more' in this world that theology has called created grace can be impeded to the extent that there is opposition between the operators on the intellectual and the psychic levels. With grace the spiritual operator is transformed by developing charity, hope, and faith because it reaches by them, as it were, a proleptic fulfilment. But there is a corresponding sensitive operator that, if it can interfere with the desire to know unless there have occurred appropriate 'adaptations of human sensibility' through the discovery of adequate dynamic images,[82] all the more can oppose the acquiescence of the total subject to the requirements of transcendently measured living. When psychic conversion occurs in this context, it effects the correspondence of the sensitive operator with a spirit that has acquiesced as obediential potency to the created grace that makes of one's living a conscious partnership with God. And it is reasonable to expect that, when this occurs, dynamic images will be released in one's own sensitive process, images that are pertinent to the circumstances of one's own conscious living, that embody the graced response, and that are invested with the same potential intelligibility as are the dynamic images that for centuries have enlivened and empowered the religious community in which one stands. Psychic conversion enables the appropriation of these dynamic images as telling the story of what God has been doing in one's own life. And it enables one to relate these images, and so God's actions in one's own life, to the images that constitute the community's living memory of God's actions in history.

4.4.5 Hermeneutical and Systematic Implications

Psychic conversion and the elements that are relevant to it also stand as reminders that the subject whose transcendental intentional structure Lonergan has disengaged is a historically situated, culturally conditioned, hermeneutic subject. I do not think there is any difficulty affirming the reconciliation of the transcendental and the hermeneutical in Lonergan's work.[83] But to add psychic conversion, and its appropriation of the historically effected character of one's own symbolic system, to Lonergan's religious, moral, and intellectual conversion, settles the issue, I think, once and for all.

Nonetheless, the principal implications of psychic conversion for *systematic* theology are not hermeneutical in the strict sense of that term. Systematic theology is not appropriation of tradition but direct discourse grounded in part in such appropriation.[84] Psychic conversion adds a further resource to that direct discourse, and this in at least three ways.

First, it enables a fuller information of systematic discourse by the symbolic communication that is the medium or carrier of revelation,[85] or, if you will, a continuity of the formal and full meanings of both doctrinal and systematic theology with the elemental carriers of meaning in which God has revealed to the world the mystery of divine love. In many ways this is what von Balthasar is after in his insistence on the recovery of the transcendental *pulchrum* as a vehicle in which to do theology in direct discourse and in his emphasis on the manifestation of God in particular created aesthetic and dramatic forms. I am sympathetic with his intentions, for the most part, and for reasons that are directly theological. God's word is true, and God's purposes are good, but God's revelation of divine truth and goodness is in the elemental symbolic communication of dramatic and aesthetic disclosure. A theology that moves exclusively in the dimensions of intelligibility and truth, and an ethics that moves exclusively in the dimension of the good, can easily be closed to the underpinning operators that God employed to reveal the eternal mystery of God's kenotic self-transcendence in our regard. Those operators are aesthetic and dramatic. The meaning they express is elemental. It is a meaning that never will be exhausted in the categories of human thought, even as we do reach for and attain some imperfect and analogical understanding of the mystery. Theology, in the person of the theologian, must be open to, and in continuity with, those operators and the elemental meaning that they introduce into our lives.

And it must be able to express its understanding, its formal meaning, in a manner that transparently formulates something of the inexhaustible meaning of these elemental carriers. This is particularly true of any theology that, like Lonergan's, would find its grounding in the events that constitute the ongoing conversion of the one doing the theology.

Second, to the extent that one's appropriation of one's own symbolic system has itself been explanatory, relating symbolic deliverances to one another in genetic-dialectical fashion, one is equipped to employ symbols in one's systematics without relinquishing the systematic exigence. In fact, the most direct systematic-theological impact of such a move is the assertion that some of the categories to be employed in systematic theology can be symbolic without losing anything in systematic rigor. For the base of these categories and the source of their theological employment is not the common sense or undifferentiated consciousness that perhaps was responsible for the original employment of symbolic categories in the scriptures and other religious documents, but rather the interiorly differentiated consciousness that begins with bringing the operations of conscious intentionality as intentional to bear upon the operations of conscious intentionality as conscious, but that is now being extended to an appropriation of the psychic dimensions of consciousness in such a way as, in the limit, to give rise to an alternate and reoriented science of depth psychology. Thus categories may be employed in systematic theology that are symbolic and yet are derived with the same precision and differentiation that affect the categories derived from the base that Lonergan proposes in religious, moral, and intellectual conversion. At the moment I will have to leave these claims as more or less logical conclusions from methodological premises. They can be established more securely only *ambulando*, by doing systematics. I would, however, indicate that the claims are not unrelated to Lonergan's insistence that a scientific hermeneutics can provide explanatory understanding of nonexplanatory meanings.[86]

Third, psychic conversion is partly constitutive of (1) the social and cultural stance requisite for engaging in a systematics that would be a mutual self-mediation of Christian constitutive meaning with a cultural matrix, and (2) some of the central general theological categories that I will want to employ in such a systematics. I will leave further discussion of the second of these points entirely to the treatment in the next chapter of the dialectical structure of history. But let me comment briefly on the first of these points now.

I do not use the term 'social conversion' in *Theology and the Dialectics of History*, and I still shy away from it, mainly because to employ such terminology would imply that there is not already a fairly complete social and cultural stance involved in the other dimensions of conversion. However this may be, *Theology and the Dialectics of History* more than implicitly affirms a social-political dimension of conversion. In fact, it presents a transcendental argument in support of a preferential option for the poor, oppressed, and marginalized, and of their hermeneutic privilege in the interpretation of both the Christian tradition and contemporary situations. This argument follows upon reflection on the relations among the various levels of value that Lonergan organizes into a normative scale on the basis of the self-transcendence to which we are affectively carried in response to values at the different levels. And this reflection on the relations among the levels of value grants to cultural values a more prominent role than they seem to play in some liberation theologies.

This further foundational component will be stressed in the reflections that follow in the next chapter, and so I will not summarize or argue it here. What I wish to affirm at this point is the manner in which the openness of the structure of intentional consciousness *at both ends* further illuminates this social component of foundations. Attention to the 'lower' openness, if one is really serious about it, will serve to establish one in solidarity with those whose participation in the dialectic of history seems to mark them as the victims of the sin of the world; for negotiation of one's own psychic darkness will teach one that there are dimensions of the history of all of us that are not responsible for their own at times tragic disorder.[87] At the same time, a fidelity to the topmost operator, the operator that is constitutive of interpersonal relations and community will, to the extent that it is informed by the knowledge gained from the other levels of consciousness, ally one's sympathies with those most in need, those left unattended to in the normal course of events in a society where the social surd is a fact, 'an increasingly significant residue that (1) is immanent in the social facts, (2) is not intelligible, yet (3) cannot be abstracted from if one is to consider the facts as in fact they are.'[88] These emphases, which are the permanent legacy of liberation theology to the church, are also principal reasons for my insistence that a contemporary systematic theology will be, in its overall contours, a theology of history.

5 Expanding the Notion of Psychic Conversion

5.1 The Basic Thesis

I wish now to present a new application of the notion of psychic conversion.[89] It has to do with the reception of meanings and values in the movement that proceeds 'from above' in consciousness. I begin again with the issue of adjudicating the work of von Balthasar.

The theological significance of the notion of psychic conversion can be illustrated quite expeditiously by calling attention to the problems raised by a sympathetic reading of the major works of von Balthasar. A problem is raised by the title of the very first volume of von Balthasar's theological aesthetics, *Seeing the Form*, in German *Schau der Gestalt*.[90] For people educated by Lonergan, the title, of course, raises immediate suspicions of naive realism. The same suspicions are more pronounced when one considers the passages in the book where 'beholding' and 'perceiving' the form of revelation in Christ are also called *Wahrnehmen*, which literally means 'to take to be true.'[91] A difficulty arises if one finds that von Balthasar is basically correct in much of what he says, that his emphases are in many instances salutary. The problem is, How can his language avoid the charge of naive realism?

The clue to solving these problems lies in the reception 'from above' of meaningful data. The acknowledgment of this movement of reception 'from above' enables us to broaden or expand our account of what Lonergan calls empirical consciousness, the experience not only of the data of sense but also of the data of consciousness. Included among the data that occur to the attentive subject of a consciousness that is also invested with exigencies to be intelligent, reasonable, and responsible, and that is meant for love, are not only (and perhaps not even primarily) the spontaneous, immediate data of sense and consciousness. Nor are the materials limited to those data along with the symbolic and dramatic-aesthetic operators, including feelings, that I was attempting to pinpoint in earlier formulations of the notion of psychic conversion. Included as well are the materials that are intended in von Balthasar's 'seeing the form,' in Heidegger's preconceptual grasp of temporal, historical facticity, of what Heidegger, perhaps misleadingly, calls *Sein*, and in Wittgenstein's insistence on the public meaningfulness of ordinary language. The movement 'from above' introduces an empirical element into the other levels of consciousness, which function now not first of all as elevations of data of sense and consciousness to intelligibility, truth, and value, but as a form of mediated immediacy that receives empirically the intelligibility, truth, and value of communally sedimented meaning. This may mean in the long run that those of us who follow Lonergan might want to rename empirical consciousness in intentionality analysis, that rather than calling it 'experience' we might do better to call it something like 'reception.' Reception 'from below' has to do with the data of sense and consciousness that are the straightforward object of 'empirical consciousness' in the ordinary sense of the term. But reception 'from above' has to do with the meanings and values that are handed on to us in our communities. In each case there is an immediacy about the reception that qualifies it as 'empirical consciousness,' but in the second case empirical consciousness is also intelligent, judgmental, evaluative. In the movement from above downwards there is an empirical element, an element of immediacy, however mediated the immediacy may be, at the other levels of consciousness.

This notion provides an initial clue to articulating the dynamics that are operative in the movement within intentional consciousness 'from above downwards,' as we receive sedimented communal meanings and values as data. As Lonergan moved from cognitive interiority to existential interiority and then to religious interiority, and as I have added psychic interiority, so the point that I wish to make here is but an initial contribution to the elucidation of what we may call hermeneutic interiority, the movement from above downwards in the way of heritage and community. Psychic conversion, as having to do with empirical consciousness, is related to this hermeneutic interiority.

We will find, as we read Lonergan with these questions in mind, that he is already pointing in the direction that I am here indicating. The early Lonergan's notion of patterns of experience, where 'experience' refers to empirical consciousness and where empirical consciousness is already configured by input from communally transmitted meanings and values, is already open to this expansion of the meaning of 'empirical consciousness,' and it provides one link or bridge in Lonergan's work to the theological concerns of von Balthasar and to the philosophical concerns of both Heidegger and Wittgenstein. This is particularly clear in what Lonergan writes regarding the relative primacy of the dialectic of community over the dialectic of the subject. It is the community that sets the stage for the subject's dramatic pattern of experience. 'In this relationship the dialectic of community holds the dominant position, for it gives rise to the situations that stimulate neural demands, and it molds the orientation of intelligence that preconsciously exercises the censorship' over what will be allowed into consciousness.[92] That 'what will be allowed into consciousness' includes more than the elements in the sensitive stream that Lonergan enumerates: sensations, memories, images, emotions, conations. It includes the meanings and values handed on to one in one's education, socialization, acculturation. Again, there is a 'prior collaboration of imagination *and intelligence*' in which 'the materials that emerge in consciousness are already patterned, and the pattern is already charged emotionally and conatively.'[93] It may be asked whether this apprehensive reception from above, as it were, of an 'already patterned' set of materials can be related to Heidegger's *Verstehen*, and whether the emotionally and conatively charged character of the reception can be related to his *Befindlichkeit*, where *Verstehen* and *Befindlichkeit* are the two equi-primordial ways of being *Dasein*, the 'there' of *Sein*, where *Sein* has Heidegger's peculiar twist, something like 'the historically conditioned horizon of common meaning that affects the very reception of data.'[94]

Further grounds for this position are found in *Insight*'s discussion of 'the contextual aspect of judgment,' which exhibits something of the temporality that is to the fore in *Being and Time*, not the radical temporalizing, which remains problematic, but at least the dimensions of memory, presence, and anticipation. The contextual aspect of judgment is discussed in terms of 'the relation of the present to the past,' 'the relations within the present,' and 'the relations of the present to the future.' It is principally, though not exclusively, the relation of the present to the past that affects the point I am trying to make.

> [P]ast judgments remain with us. They form a habitual orientation, present and operative but only from behind the scenes. They govern the direction of attention, evaluate insights, guide formulations, and influence the acceptance or rejection of new judgments. Previous insights remain with us. They facilitate the occurrence of fresh insights, exert their influence on new formulations, provide presuppositions that underlie new judgments whether in the same or in connected or in merely analogous fields of inquiry. Hence, when a new judgment is made, there is within us a habitual context of insights and other judgments, and it stands ready to elucidate the judgment just made, to complement it, to balance it, to draw distinctions, to add qualifications, to provide defence, to offer evidence or proof, to attempt persuasion.[95]

I would like to adopt and adapt some of Heidegger's language at this point, and affirm that the habitual orientation formed by previous judgments and the habitual context of insights and other judgments help to constitute the intelligent and dispositional components of *Dasein* that function in the very reception of data in the movement from above. At the same time, I would suggest that Heidegger can benefit from Lonergan's contribution especially to the discussion of the relations within the present and of the relations of the present to the future. The relations of the present to the past have to do by and large with what Lonergan calls 'ordinary meaningfulness,' or with what Wittgenstein calls the public meaningfulness of language, while the relations within the present and the relations of the present to the future may release the processes that exhibit original meaningfulness. Heidegger and Wittgenstein, in quite different ways, illuminate the realm of ordinary meaningfulness, and Lonergan the realm of original meaningfulness, but all three exhibit a great deal of original meaningfulness no matter what it is that they are illuminating. Moreover, it may be that original meaningfulness may be the set of elements needed to transcend the radical temporalizing by which Heidegger places Being 'within' time rather than time 'within' Being.

The relations within the present, then, may be such as to show either mutual dependence and other connections or even conflicts among existing judgments. The connections stimulate logical efforts for 'organized coherence,' while conflicts 'release the dialectical process,' a process that gives rise to original meaningfulness. Again, the relations of the present to the future call attention to the dynamic structure of knowledge, something on which, it may safely be argued, Heidegger, at times associating or correlating Being with the transcendental imagination, does not lay sufficient stress. In brief, Lonergan says, 'All we know is somehow with us; it is present and operative within our knowing; but it lurks behind the scenes, and it reveals itself only in the exactitude with which each minor increment to our knowing is effected.'[96] But the same is true of all that we have received in the order of meaning and value. And I am asking whether all we know and all we have received reveals itself in the further reception of data, and whether those data include meanings and values. Is this not part of what is meant by the expression 'mediated immediacy'?

Another source of data from Lonergan in support of the position here being suggested is found in the following schematic representation, presented in the chapter on judgment:

I. Data. Perceptual Images.	Free Images.	Utterances.
II. Questions for Intelligence.	Insights.	Formulations.
III. Questions for Reflection.	Reflection.	Judgment.[97]

Lonergan says, 'The second level presupposes and complements the first. The third level presupposes and complements the second. The exception lies in free images and utterances, *which commonly are under the influence of the higher levels before they provide a basis for inquiry and reflection.*'[98] This quotation alone is probably all that is needed for me to make my point: there are presentations that occur empirically to the conscious subject that are already infused with intelligence and rationality and, we may add, with ethical overtones. These occur, I want to say, to a *Verstehen* that receives meaningful data before these data provide a basis for one's own inquiry and reflection, and so to this extent may be called 'empirical.' May it not be said that the basis for a potential and fruitful dialogue with both Heideggerian and Wittgensteinian strands in philosophy and with von Balthasar in theology is already contained in this brief selection?

The categories of 'mediated immediacy' and 'elemental meaning,' then, along with reflection on the movement from above in consciousness, suggest an expansion of our usual understanding of empirical consciousness, so that it is probably better designated in a generic way as 'reception.' From below upwards, as it were, it is primarily reception of data of sense and of consciousness, but from above downwards, it is reception of communally sedimented meanings and values involving all four levels of consciousness. The existential, reasonable, and intelligent levels of consciousness take on, in the movement from above, an empirical quality, receiving meanings and values from a communal heritage. The *Verstehen* and evaluation involved in this reception of meanings and values are distinct from the immanently generated insights, judgments, and decisions that give rise to the original meaningfulness that is one's own.

Now a problem presents itself immediately in what I am saying. For the category of 'elemental meaning' in Lonergan's writings does not refer exclusively to what I am suggesting we might call 'reception,' so that a one-to-one correspondence of reception and elemental meaning is not possible. The subject's own *immanently generated* insights are also instances of elemental meaning. What characterizes elemental meaning is that the distinction of subject and object has not yet arisen. Not only is it the case that the sense in act is the sensible in act, but also it is the case that the intellect in act, and very much in act in the 'Eureka!' of immanently generated insight, is the intelligible in act. 'Knowledge by identity' means there is a preconceptual unity of knower and known, whether in sensation or in the act of insight. But my question is whether we may also speak of an elemental identity of 'knower' and 'known' that, because it occurs in the reception of communally sedimented *meanings and values,* is not simply a matter of sense in act and sensible in act, but that, because it is also not a matter of immanently generated insight, of original meaningfulness, but rather of meaningful data in the sense of ordinary meaningfulness, is a form of empirical consciousness, or an empirical functioning of intelligent, judgmental, and evaluating consciousness.

In addition to the elemental meaning of acts of sensing and acts of insight as immanently generated knowledge, Lonergan speaks of the elemental 'meaning of the smile that acts simply as an intersubjective determinant, the meaning of the work of art prior to its interpretation by a critic, the meaning of the symbol performing its office of internal communication without help from the therapist.'[99] Can we not extend that category thus understood to many of the data that occur to us? As the dreams of the morning are the dreams of an intelligent subject, and so are already invested with meaning, may we not say that many of the data received by such a subject are already invested with a meaning that is a function of historical facticity, of personal and communal history? Is this meaning not elemental in the same sense as the smile or the work of art or the symbol, and yet in a sense that is different from the merely potential meaning of sensation? Further distinctions, of course, remain to be made, for at least the meaning of the smile is something that is not learned. It is natural and spontaneous. It does not have the same character of historical sedimentation that many of the other presentations to which I am referring exhibit. Still, this empirical givenness of structured meaning is undeniable and must be accounted for.

Moreover, this received meaning functions effectively and constitutively in the lives of those to whom it occurs. It does so even before they have subjected that meaning to critical examination, to a 'critique of beliefs,' if you will. Thus that meaning possesses an intelligibility that is more than the *merely* potential intelligibility of sense data but also less than formal and actual intelligibility in the strict sense of immanently generated meaning. And so I ask whether we must distinguish between the merely potential meaning of acts of sensing and the meaning of other received data that are invested with some kind of at least devalued formal and perhaps actual or full intelligibility. The effective and constitutive functions of meaning cannot be exercised by merely potential intelligibility, yet the mediated data of received intelligibility function effectively and constitutively in our lives. It is true that formal and actual intelligibility in the strict sense are a function of what Lonergan calls original meaningfulness, that is, of immanently generated knowledge and of the assent of faith in the fullest sense of that term. And the received intelligibility that I am suggesting is also the historical product of the original meaningfulness of the insights, judgments, and decisions of others who have preceded us, or of their biases, their failures to be intelligent, reasonable, and responsible, or of some combination of intelligence and bias. Still, we may speak of a formal and actual intelligibility that works in the very reception of the community's meanings and values. We need to speak perhaps of something like 'minor' and 'major' formal and actual intelligibility. What I am suggesting we might call 'minor formal intelligibility' and 'minor actual intelligibility' are connected with what Lonergan calls the 'ordinary meaningfulness' of publicly sedimented expression as this expression mediates the reception of data, and what I am suggesting we might call 'major formal intelligibility' and 'major actual intelligibility' are connected with what he calls 'original meaningfulness,' that is, to what proceeds (in the sense of *emanatio intelligibilis*) when the subject stands on his or her own two feet, raises his or her own questions for intelligence, reflection, and deliberation, answers these questions in acts of understanding and in judgments of fact and value, and formulates the answers in inner and outer words that contibute eventually, sooner or later, to the communal fund of ordinary meaningfulness.

Thus, the data that are received by the subject of ordinary waking consciousness (or for that matter, by the dreamer in the 'dreams of the morning') are already invested with a meaning that functions effectively and constitutively. These data are not mere data of sense or of consciousness arising in a state of unmediated immediacy. To speak of them as if they were is to engage in abstraction. They are rather already mediated by meaning to a subject whose consciousness receiving them is at once empirical consciousness and intelligent. They are data that are already invested with meaning, with an 'already given intelligibility,' with what I am suggesting we call 'minor formal and actual intelligibility.'

More strictly, *Verstehen* as understanding in this minor or devalued sense, ordinary meaningfulness, yields minor *formal* intelligibility. What accounts in this case for the judgmental component in the mediated immediacy of the subject – the judgmental component that is required for any intelligibility to approximate 'actual intelligibility' or 'full meaning' in Lonergan's sense of those terms – may be a function of one or more of at least three things: the 'always with us' quality of previous judgments, belief, or a suspicious suspension of belief. 'Belief' here can range all the way from comfortable embeddedness in a commonsense environment to religious belonging, and from these to something like the 'trust in being' that we either develop very early in life or go through life lacking, short of (I would add) the frequent miracles of grace. In the third of these in particular, we are talking more of *Befindlichkeit* than of *Verstehen*, more of 'state of mind' than of cognitive apprehension. In either case, however, the component of belief or unbelief is the function, proximately, of the personal history of the subject within the history of his or her community or network of communities (what Lonergan calls minor authenticity or unauthenticity) and, remotely and far more radically, of the communal history of that network itself (Lonergan's major authenticity or unauthenticity). Here, of course, I am using the terms 'major' and 'minor,' not in the sense of the suggestion of 'major and minor formal and actual intelligibility,' but in Lonergan's sense when he speaks of authentic and unauthentic existing.

> [E]xisting may be authentic or unauthentic, and this may occur in two different ways. There is the minor authenticity or unauthenticity of the subject with respect to the tradition that nourishes him. There is the major authenticity that justifies or condemns the tradition itself. In the first case there is passed a human judgment on subjects. In the second case history and, ultimately, divine providence pass judgment on traditions.[100]

Again, we may say that in the lives of each of us there is an intricate symbiosis of what, in one text alone (but a text that is extremely important), Lonergan refers to as ordinary meaningfulness and original meaningfulness. I have already anticipated that discussion several times, but allow me, please, a lengthy quotation at this point, with several interpolations of my own indicated by brackets.

> [T]he ordinary meaningfulness of ordinary language is essentially public and only derivatively private. For language is ordinary if it is in common use. It is in common use, not because some isolated individual happens to have decided what it is to mean, but because all the individuals of the relevant group understand what it means. Similarly, it is by performing expressed mental acts that children and foreigners come to learn a language. But they learn the language by learning how it ordinarily is used, so that their private knowledge of ordinary usage is derived from the common usage that essentially is public. [We may say the same, *mutatis mutandis*, of the ordinary meaningfulness of most other carriers of meaning, though some, like the smile, are 'natural and spontaneous.']
>
> ... [W]hat is true of the ordinary meaningfulness of ordinary language is not true of the original meaningfulness of any language, ordinary, literary, or technical. [By extension, we may say that it is also not true of the original meaningfulness of other carriers of meaning.] For all language develops and, at any time, any language [or any other set of public carriers of meaning] consists in the sedimentation of the developments that have occurred and have not become obsolete. Now developments consist in discovering new uses for existing words [or for other carriers of meaning], in inventing new words, and in diffusing the discoveries and inventions. All three are a matter of expressed mental acts. The discovery of a new usage is a mental act expressed by the new usage. The invention of a new word is a mental act expressed by the new word ...[101]

While Lonergan introduces the distinction of ordinary meaningfulness and original meaningfulness as a response to a Wittgensteinian objection to his position – and it is a legitimate response that in principle resolves many of the issues that Wittgensteinians might raise about Lonergan's work – it is also applicable *mutatis mutandis* to questions that might be presented from a Heideggerian perspective. What Heidegger is talking about when he insists on the preconceptual, 'given' intelligibility of the temporal and contextual contingencies of life is a subspecies of Lonergan's category of ordinary meaningfulness. And what Lonergan is talking about on almost every page of his writings, or at least what he is emphasizing and what represents his unique contribution to all of these discussions, is not the ordinary meaningfulness of historical facticity but the original meaningfulness that is responsible for 'healing and creating in history.' The two are not opposed, since in different ways one flows into the other. The original meaningfulness of one generation or even of one period in one's own life becomes the ordinary meaningfulness of a later generation or period, and problems with regard to ordinary meaningfulness give rise to the questions that issue in original meaningfulness. There is no reason for a philosophy or a theology to feel required to choose between them. The Scotist-inspired Heideggerian tendency and the Wittgensteinian tendency, whether Scotist-inspired or not, is to emphasize the ordinary meaningfulness of the public sedimentations as what is essential and to consider the original meaningfulness that issues from so-called mental acts as at best derivative. *That,* and not naive realism in the simple sense, would be the counterposition in these views. To appeal to Lonergan's dialectic of concept and performance, we might say that Wittgenstein and, perhaps to a greater degree, Heidegger display a great deal of original meaningfulness and ingenuity in their talk about ordinary meaningfulness. But Lonergan students should take care not so to stress the interior operations that give rise to original meaningfulness as to pass over in silence or even denial the fact that ordinarily, that is, in the ordinary meaningfulness of everyday life, we start from publicly sedimented expressions already invested with meaning.

5.2 *Related Considerations*

5.2.1 Understanding Data and Understanding Facts

The distinction of ordinary and original meaningfulness is related to the distinction of 'two orders or types of knowledge,' namely, understanding data and understanding facts. Again, while the latter distinction is introduced in a very specific context, in order to allow Lonergan to explain how systematics can be a matter of understanding what one already holds to be true, and so how systematics can be distinguished from doctrines, it is pertinent beyond that context. Lonergan writes:

> Now one can understand data and one can understand facts. The understanding of data is expressed in hypotheses, and the verification of hypotheses leads to probable assertions. The understanding of facts is a more complicated matter, for it supposes the existence of two types or orders of knowledge, where *the facts of the first type supply the data for the second type ...*
>
> Now the peculiarity of such understanding of facts is that two orders or types of knowledge call for two applications of the notion of truth. There is the truth of the facts in the first order or type.

> There is also the truth of the account or explanation reached in the second type or order. Moreover, while initially the second depends on the first, ultimately the two are interdependent, for the second can lead to a correction of the first.[102]

The distinction admits of many examples. While the proximate occasion for presenting the distinction in *Method in Theology* is the problem of finding a way to characterize the peculiarity of the functional specialty 'systematics' in relation to the functional specialty 'doctrines,' other examples of the two orders of knowledge are given first.

> [I]n critical history we distinguished two inquiries: a first inquiry aimed at finding out where one's witnesses got their information, how they checked it, how competently they used it; this was followed by a second inquiry that employed the evaluated information to construct an account of what was going forward in a given milieu at a given place and time. Similarly, in natural science one can start from the facts of commonsense knowledge and use them as the data for the construction of scientific theories; and inversely one can return from scientific theory through applied science, engineering, technology to bring about the transformation of the commonsense world.[103]

Again, with regard to the interdependence of the two orders,

> The critical historian's discovery of what was going forward can lead him to revise his evaluation of his witnesses. The scientific account of physical reality can involve a revision of commonsense views.[104]

Again, the eight, directly or indirectly interdependent functional specialties present a 'far more complicated' instance of the same twofold order of knowledge. For here all four levels of intentional consciousness are operative in each functional specialty, but each specialty intends the goal of one of the four levels

> So research is concerned to make the data available. Interpretation to determine their meaning. History to proceed from meaning to what was going forward. Dialectic to go to the roots of conflicting histories, interpretations, researches. Foundations to distinguish positions from counter-positions. Doctrines to use foundations as a criterion for deciding between the alternatives offered by dialectic. Systematics to seek an understanding of the realities affirmed in doctrines.[105]

Lonergan's concern in raising this distinction at this point is especially to draw attention to the relationship between doctrines and systematics. Doctrines presents facts to systematics, but these facts are for the systematician data to be understood. The task of systematics is not the understanding of data in the sense of the first order of knowledge, but only insofar as the facts established by doctrines are taken as the data that systematics attempts to understand. Functional specialization thus provides us with a highly differentiated instance of the manner in which the reception of meanings and values from above (here, from doctrines) is empirical even while being at the same time intelligent, judicious, and existential.

Of course, the truth of the doctrines, accepted as truth, functions constitutively in authentic Christian living before it is submitted to systematic understanding. The reception of belief precedes the understanding and critique of belief, and provides another, and perhaps the most common, example of the sort of thing I am talking about. Moreover, however much precisely as *doctrinal* truth beliefs are expressed in propositions, they can be carried also in art and symbols and intersubjectivity and the incarnate meaning of persons and their deeds, and precisely through such carriers function constitutively even when the propositions are not understood in any sophisticated fashion. As they so function, beliefs may be described in terms of Heidegger's *alētheia* or unconcealment. Here the facts of a first type of knowledge (here, belief) may supply data for the second type (understanding and critique). Then the truth of any new understanding of beliefs, including any new systematic understanding of the doctrines (such as Lonergan's four-point hypothesis linking the divine relations to created graces), can be likened to the truth of an original meaningfulness that proceeds proximately from one's reflective understanding that one's hypothesis is probably an acceptable set of analogues that gives us some imperfect glimpse of the meaning of the primal truth known judgmentally in doctrine and received as a given intelligibility and truth in belief. Doctrinal truth thus functions, or at least through genuine communications can be made to function, in the life of the community as a linguistic expression of a primal truth disclosed more elementally to believers. And in systematics it is submitted to further scrutiny by theologians attempting to understand it in a manner that approximates explanation. Thus, when Thomas Aquinas spoke of procession in God, he was employing what had become ordinary language in his faith tradition. But when he said that procession in God was *emanatio intelligibilis,* he was exhibiting the original meaningfulness of language, an original meaningfulness that was completely a function of his understanding of what divine procession had to be, an original meaningfulness that in this case subsequent theologians have rarely understood, and so one that has not really become ordinary meaningfulness even some seven centuries later, one moreover that is best understood if one submits to Lonergan's own maieutic of intelligent, reasonable, and responsible operations, that is, if one appropriates one's own acts of original meaningfulness.

5.2.2 Revelation and Reception

I wish to suggest another application. I begin with some citations from Lonergan. 'The word of God, the revelation God makes to man, is a matter of meaning … [T]hat revelation … would not be at all what [it is] without meaning.'[106] That meaning, moreover, is a reality. 'Our conscious living and the meaning that it carries are just as real as the realities of the spirit, and they do not belong to some shadowy world that really does not count. One mistakes the whole significance of meaning if one does not get that point correct: "intentional" is not opposed to "real."'[107] In this sense, then, Lonergan speaks in the same context of an ontology of meaning and an ethics of meaning.[108] And it is in this sense of the reality and morality of meaning that we can 'see the full impact and the full import of divine revelation. Revelation is God's entering into the world of human meaning.'[109] Again, the 'Word of God is God's entry into human reality as constituted by meaning.'[110] And the Word of God in this context may be 'taken as the word of the Bible, or the word of tradition, or the incarnate Word that is the incarnate meaning of the Son of God.'[111]

The ontological status of meaning is suggested again in the headings of the first two sections of the final chapter of *Method in Theology*, 'Meaning and Ontology' and 'Common Meaning and Ontology.' The first section will help me speak of revelation, and the second of reception.

'Meaning and Ontology' emphasizes that the four functions of meaning – cognitive, constitutive, communicative, and effective – have an ontological aspect. As cognitive, acts of meaning intend what is real. As constitutive, meaning 'constitutes part of the reality of the one that means': one's horizon, one's assimilative powers, one's knowledge, one's values, one's character. As communicative, meaning 'induces in the hearer some share in the cognitive, constitutive, or effective meaning of the speaker.' And as effective, meaning 'persuades or commands others or it directs [our] control over nature.'[112] Lonergan goes on:

> Such ontological aspects pertain to meaning, no matter what its content or its carrier. They are found then in all the diverse stages of meaning, in all the diverse cultural traditions, in any of the differentiations of consciousness, and in the presence and absence of intellectual, moral, and religious conversion. Again, they pertain to meaning, whether its carrier is intersubjectivity or art or symbol or

> exemplary or abominable conduct or everyday or literary or technical language.[113]

To these indications I suggest that we add Lonergan's earlier point regarding the relative dominance of the dialectic of community vis-à-vis the dialectic of the subject. And we might add the relative dominance of the dialectic of culture as well.[114] This relative dominance means that the horizon of the subject in his or her world, a horizon constituted by meaning, along with the world that is correlative to that horizon, are, prior to critical reflection on the part of the subject, largely a function of what Heidegger's language calls temporal and historical facticity, of 'being thrown' into existence in the world at this particular time and with these particular people, with their own horizons similarly determined for them by historical dialectics over which at the outset they have no control. All of this 'gives rise to the situations that stimulate neural demands, and it molds the orientation of intelligence that preconsciously exercises the censorship,'[115] so that the very reception of data that are also invested with meaning is itself constitutive of the subject's horizon. And it is precisely at this level, I think, that God's entrance into the world of human meaning takes place. Avery Dulles is on to this when, in his book *Models of Revelation*, he departs from 'model thinking' and takes his own stand, in a chapter in which he argues that divine revelation is best conceived along the lines of symbolic communication.[116] As we move to develop a theology of revelation in a systematic theology that finds its base in Lonergan – and revelation is not a theme to which Lonergan himself devoted a great deal of explicit theological attention – it is this level of elemental meaning, of the already given intelligibility of received data, that we have to ponder. God's entrance into the world of human meaning is God's effecting transformations in that already given intelligibility of 'world' that is correlative to our horizons – effecting transformations through the cognitive, constitutive, communicative, and effective functions of God's own meaning, of God's original meaningfulness, and ultimately of God's incarnate meaning, God's incarnate Logos, God's incarnate Word, the Son of the eternal Father, crucified, dead, and risen from the dead.

'Common Meaning and Ontology' is relevant to the dominant dialectics of community and culture. The 'formal constituent' of the community whose dialectic exerts a relative dominance over the dialectic of the subject is common meaning. Moreover, 'such common meaning is doubly constitutive. In each individual, it is constitutive of the individual as a member of the community. In the group of individuals it is constitutive of the community.'[117] Its genesis is 'an ongoing process of communication, of people coming to share the same cognitive, constitutive, and effective meanings.'[118]

There are more and less serious divisions resultant from divergent meanings. The serious divisions are those that arise from 'the presence and absence of intellectual, moral, and religious conversion.'[119] Radical dialectical opposition then affects 'community, action, situation. It affects community for, just as common meaning is constitutive of community, so dialectic divides community into radically opposed groups. It affects action for, just as conversion leads to intelligent, reasonable, responsible action, so dialectic adds division, conflict, oppression. It affects the situation, for situations are the cumulative product of previous actions and, when previous actions have been guided by the light and darkness of dialectic, the resulting situation [which, remember, stimulates neural demands] is not some intelligible whole but rather a set of misshapen, poorly proportioned, and incoherent fragments.'[120]

Now the 'state,' as it were, of the community, whether the community be religious or civil or some combination of both, affects the receptivity of both individuals and groups to the entrance of God's meaning into the world of human meaning through God's symbolic self-communication or revelation. In the wonderful sixth chapter of his *De Deo trino: Pars systematica*, Lonergan distinguished the habit of grace from the state of grace, and explicitly treated the state of grace as an intersubjective, indeed a social reality. '[T]he state or situation of grace refers to many different subjects together. Thus to constitute the state of grace there are required (1) the Father who loves, (2) the Son because of whom the Father loves, (3) the Holy Spirit in whom the Father loves and gives gifts, and (4) the just, who because of the Son are loved by the Father in the Holy Spirit, who consequently are endowed with sanctifying grace, whence flow the virtues and gifts, and who are thereby just and upright and open to receiving and eliciting acts that are directed toward eternal life.'[121] This 'divine-human interpersonal situation' (ibid.) is not simply a situation affecting four subjects: three of them divine and one human. Rather, the Latin term that is here translated 'the just,' namely, 'iusti,' is plural. It may be interpreted as signifying a community of subjects, so that when Lonergan writes that 'by reason of this state the divine persons and the just are in one another as those who are known are in those who know them and those who are loved are in those who love them,'[122] we may read him as referring to a communion of the divine subjects with a community of human subjects. In this sense, he may be said to have anticipated a contemporary discussion by explicitly treating 'the state of grace' as a social reality. Just as theologians some thirty years ago placed stress on sin as social and spoke of sinful social structures, so today we must work out the constitution of grace-filled social structures.

The dominance of the dialectic of community over the dialectic of the subject means that the relations of the present of the subject to the past are relations not only to the subject's own past but also to the past of his or her community or network of communities. And these relations decisively affect the orientation or habitual context within which the reception of data occurs. These relations decisively affect what for any given subject in whatever milieu constitutes ordinary meaningfulness. That ordinary meaningfulness may be more or less sinful, more or less under the influence of grace. Revelation as God's entrance into the human world of meaning shifts the probabilities in favour of graced ordinary meaningfulness. And that shift in probabilities affects the reception, or better, the receptive potential, of subjects in community to the divine meaning intended by God when God enters our world of meaning.

Much more could be said about the theology of reception in its ecclesial significance, but this is not the place for that. Let me just indicate that I believe that the ecclesial notion of reception, as in 'reception of church teaching,' must be understood in this context of the meaning of revelation and of human reception of God's entrance into our world of meaning.

5.2.3 Revisiting the Notion of Psychic Conversion

The occasion of my original insight regarding psychic conversion was research on a paper on the Heideggerian roots of Rudolf Bultmann's hermeneutical theory. I was reading *Kant and the Problem of Metaphysics* and taking extensive notes on this very important work of Heidegger's, when the notion of psychic conversion emerged. In most of the explanations of what I mean by psychic conversion I have focused on a release into an openness on the part of intentional consciousness to the *Befindlichkeit* dimension of *Dasein.* I have addressed dramatic bias and scotosis, and acknowledged the need to extend this discussion to the organic. Scotosis is the sort of thing that Max Scheler refers to in the following words:

> Beyond all conscious lying and falsifying, there is a deeper 'organic mendacity.' Here the falsification is not formed in consciousness but at the same stage of the mental process as the impressions and value feelings themselves on the road of experience into consciousness. There is 'organic mendacity' whenever a man's mind admits only those impressions and feelings which serve his 'interest' or his instinctive attitude. Already in the process of mental reproduction and recollection, the contents of his experience are modified in this direction. He who is 'mendacious' has no need to lie! In his case, the automatic process of forming recollections, impressions, and feelings is involuntarily slanted, so that conscious falsification becomes unnecessary.[123]

And so I have stressed how important it is that intentional consciousness take cognizance of the underlying 'tidal movement that begins before consciousness, unfolds through sensitivity, intelligence, rational reflection, responsible deliberation, only to find its rest beyond all of these,' in 'being in love.'[124] As beginning before consciousness that tidal movement reveals itself in our dreams. As unfolding through sensitivity, intelligence, rational reflection, and responsible deliberation, it is experienced in our feelings, both intentional and nonintentional – and I have suggested that non-intentional feelings may be more important than might be obvious from reading Lonergan, especially if Ignatian 'consolation without a cause,' as consolation with a content but without an apprehended object, must be understood as having an original nonintentional moment, at least in the sense that it is not a response to such an object.[125] And as finding rest beyond the levels of intentional consciousness, the tidal movement is the operator of community. But what I overlooked in my presentation, or simply assumed that Lonergan was providing, was, in Heidegger's terms, the *Verstehen* component of *Dasein*. I believe now that Heidegger's *Verstehen* is not Lonergan's insight as a release to the tension of inquiry, whether that insight be direct, inverse, or reflective, but rather an intelligent component that is at work in the very reception of meaningful data 'from above.' If that is the case, and if what I called psychic conversion is indeed a habitual *conversio ad phantasma*, a habitual being-at-home with, not being alienated from, the stream of an empirical consciousness that receives data mediated by meaning, then psychic conversion is a retrieval or re-establishing of a link between the inquiring and critical spirit and the mediated immediacy of the movement from above in consciousness. At the first Lonergan Workshop, in 1974, I spoke of a 'psychic rift' for which I was attempting to find some healing. And by that expression, 'psychic rift,' I meant not only dramatic bias, from 'below,' but also something very much like what Heidegger perhaps is naming when he speaks of the forgetfulness of Being, at least if he means the forgetfulness of an already given, temporally and historically conditioned facticity that is mediated by meaning, from above.

6 The Question of Truth

Still, any effort such as the present one to mediate these concerns cannot avoid the question of truth. Heidegger and Lonergan may be taken as figures representative of the tendencies that I seek to mediate. But these two thinkers present very different notions of truth. And the same could be said in comparing von Balthasar's *Wahrnehmen* and Lonergan's notion of truth as issuing from an immanently generated grasp of the virtually unconditioned. Two papers of Lonergan's point the way beyond an impasse, I think, namely, the first two of the Donald Mathers Lectures delivered at Queen's University, Kingston, Ontario, in 1976, 'Religious Experience' and 'Religious Knowledge.' The overall objective of the three lectures that Lonergan delivered in this series is to work out 'a single but complex viewpoint' that would regard religious studies and theology as 'distinct and complementary' disciplines. That is not my concern here. But the first two of the lectures contain material that I find directly pertinent to the present issues.

'Experience,' in the paper 'Religious Experience,' does not mean the whole of knowledge (one possible meaning for the term 'experience,' as when we speak of a person of experience) but 'an element within a larger compound, an infrastructure that easily is unnoticed until it is rounded off in combination with a manifold of further elements.'[126] In science, a distinction is made between a scientific hypothesis and the data to which it appeals, but even the data as appealed to are not yet the infrastructure that corresponds to 'experience.' For as appealed to, the data are named, and the naming supposes the scientific suprastructure with its technical language, as well as the earlier ordinary language that one employed before learning the science and that one continues to employ in one's everyday living.

> Only when one goes behind ordinary language and commonsense knowing does one come to the infrastructure in its pure form. It is pure experience, the experience underpinning and distinct from every suprastructure. As outer experience it is sensation as distinct from perception. As inner experience it is consciousness as distinct not only from self-knowledge but also from any introspective process that goes from the data of consciousness and moves towards the acquisition of self-knowledge.[127]

Still, Lonergan tells us in *Insight* 'how abstract it is to speak of a sensation,' since all acts of sensing, all activities of what here is called 'outer experience,' 'occur in some dynamic context that somehow unifies a manifold of sensed contents and of acts of sensing.'[128] Moreover, the data of consciousness, of 'inner experience,' are the very operations not only of sensing and perceiving, but also of inquiring, understanding, conceiving, reflecting, grasping the unconditioned, affirming, deliberating, evaluating, deciding, and of the feelings that accompany these and that change as different operations are performed. They are these operations and states, not as named but as experienced. These operations and states, precisely as experienced, and whether they are named or not, are precisely the operations and states that effect 'the world mediated and constituted by meaning.'

Thus it is, in the language of the paper 'Religious Experience,' that 'we become normal human beings only by mastering vast systems of symbols and adapting our muscles, our nerves, our cerebral cortex, to respond to them accurately and precisely.'[129] In this sense 'the cultivation of religious experience is its entry into harmony with the rest of one's symbolic system, and as symbolic systems vary with the culture and the civilization, so too does the cultivation of religious experience.'[130] Already we are removed, then, from the 'pure experience' that is nothing but infrastructure. Already we are the subjects of symbolic systems that mediate the world by meaning.

But within this framework there arises the question of the validity or objectivity or truth of the various symbolic systems. The paper 'Religious Knowledge' addresses this issue precisely with respect to religious convictions. '[H]ow can one tell whether one's appropriation of religion is genuine or unauthentic and, more radically, how can one tell one is not appropriating a religious tradition that has become unauthentic[?]'[131] The question can be generalized, to extend to the other components of one's historically and culturally inherited symbol system. There may be no more significant question in the whole of human life than this: how can I tell whether the convictions that I have been taught to live by are a function of a tradition or set of traditions that have become unauthentic? Or to use language that we found useful earlier, how can I judge whether the ordinary meaningfulness that constitutes my present horizon, historically and culturally conditioned as it is, is a function of an unauthentic or an authentic tradition? And the answer can be discovered only by the release of the original meaningfulness by which we submit our beliefs and convictions to an immanent critique, in order to ascertain their genuineness. The answer is found in the self-transcendence that is the criterion of authenticity or genuineness, a self-transcendence that, in the stage of cultural development that is advanced by a Lonergan, can be submitted to self-appropriation. Once again, Heidegger is speaking mainly about the ordinary meaningfulness that constitutes present horizons, and Lonergan about the original meaningfulness that submits ordinary meaningfulness to critique and, probably, to transformation: to 'healing and creating.' The operations that constitute original meaningfulness, then, alone are able to pass judgment on the truth of the ordinary meaningfulness of present horizons. The immanently generated affirmation that emanates from the grasp of the virtually unconditioned is alone capable of ascertaining the truth of the unconcealedness of the mediated immediacy with which the process toward original meaningfulness begins. Heidegger's unconcealedness alone will not do, nor will von Balthasar's *Wahrnehmen.* Both must be confirmed by some sort of process that leads either to immanently generated knowledge or to the reflective understanding that grasps as virtually unconditioned the value of deciding to believe. If they cannot be so confirmed, they must be subjected to the process of transformation that is best succinctly summed up in the wonderful expression 'healing and creating in history.' The 'minor formal or actual intelligibility' of mediated immediacy must either be confirmed or corrected by the 'major formal or actual intelligibility' attained by the operations that Lonergan has clarified. It is not the case, in the last analysis, that the truth of judgment is merely a derivative of a primal unconcealedness. It is rather the case that the truth of the primal unconcealedness of mediated immediacy is a function of the major authenticity of the cultural and religious traditions that have bequeathed us this heritage. If that is lacking, then our responsibility is to correct the major unauthenticity of the received tradition; and the only way we can do that is by exercising the original meaningfulness that, under God's gift of grace, is the sole source and guarantee of such healing and creating in history.

Still, this does not mean that Heidegger is entirely mistaken in his notion of truth as unconcealedness, nor that his appeal to overcome the forgetfulness of what he calls Being is itself on entirely the wrong track. What he is all about, if I have been interpreting him correctly, or at least if I may put the best possible interpretation on his words, is intimately related to the healing and creating in history that Lonergan is promoting: healing the forgetfulness of an already given, temporally and historically conditioned facticity that is mediated by meaning, as a starting point for the exercise of the operations by which original meaningfulness creates. What his notion of truth as unconcealment is about is what Lonergan's first transcendental precept, Be attentive, is urging. Insights are only as good as the images in which they grasp intelligibility. Forgetfulness of the images reduces and in the limit eliminates the probability that we will have the insights we need, not only to get on with our individual lives, but also to fulfil our historical responsibilities. Insight into image is infallible, but if the images are distorted, so too will be the insights. And until the forgetfulness of the data is overcome, the marshalling of the evidence for a reasonable judgment will be lacking essential components. This is what psychic conversion is all about. Whether it is defined from below, as it were, as the transformation of the censorship over neural demands from a repressive to a constructive functioning, or explained from above in language that appeals to a healing of the forgetfulness of historical facticity, it is a transformation that effects a renewed link between the creative, inquiring human spirit and the materials, the elemental meaning, the mediated immediacy that at any given time constitute the starting point of the creative process.

10

System and History

We come at last to the relation between the systematic ideal and the reality of historical consciousness or historical mindedness. I would distinguish at least four meanings of the expression 'system and history.'[1] The first two, 'Developing Synthesis' and 'System as Witness,' are methodological: How can the systematic ideal be reconciled with historical relativity? The third, 'History as Mediated Object of Systematic Theology,' completes the heuristic anticipation presently possible for the unified field structure of systematic theology. Discussion of this third meaning takes up most of the present chapter. The fourth meaning, 'Theology as Praxis,' treats the historical responsibilities of systematics.

1 Developing Synthesis

The fact that human understanding, however systematic, always occurs within contexts, that all concepts have dates because the acts of understanding that ground them are historically conditioned in multiple ways, is responsible for the first two of these meanings of the expression 'system and history.' These two meanings coincide with the first two anticipations mentioned above, in chapter 8.

The first meaning can be expressed both positively and negatively. Positively, my proposals anticipate the possibility of *an ongoing genetic sequence of systematic theologies.* But perhaps this positive meaning is best clarified if we indicate what I am *not* about.

Lonergan writes, 'When the classicist notion of culture prevails, theology is conceived as a permanent achievement, and then one discourses on its nature. When culture is conceived empirically, theology is known to be an ongoing process, and then one writes on its method.'[2] It is not my intention to adopt a classicist concern with theology's nature, but rather to ask about the operations to be performed, the objectives to be pursued, and the procedures to be followed by a collaborative community that, at least in principle, will extend into an indefinite future. There must be acknowledged an indefinite series of efforts to construct systematic theologies. And there must be rejected the possibility of some single definitive *Summa* of theological understanding. While we acknowledge that some systematic achievements are in fact permanent contributions that can only be built upon, not gone back on, and while we grant that some of these achievements were in fact arrived at in the medieval *Summae*, we also insist that higher viewpoints are always possible. Higher viewpoints are 'higher' not just because they are more inclusive but also and mainly because they call for a shift in the basic terms and relations of the entire discipline and consequently for a rearrangement of everything else, even of the permanent achievements.[3] The systematic theology for which the present work is a methodological grounding will be part of an ongoing sequence of theologies. Any genuine achievement that it may attain is always likely to assume a different position and status in a later theology that grasps more than we do or that comprehends more deeply what we may grasp less adequately.

Sometimes higher viewpoints are occasioned by cultural developments that are relatively independent of theology, while at other times they are the fruit of deepened insight into the mysteries of faith themselves, in their distinctive supernatural reality. It is probably the case that the latter advance, more often than not, is the contribution of those theologians who also are saints, since deepened insight into the mystery of God is a function of mystical gifts of understanding and wisdom. The former type of advance, that due to cultural developments, while it demands great faith, emanates principally from the understanding of intelligent men and women attempting to comprehend what they believe and to do so on the level of their own times.

Such culturally occasioned advance is particularly influential when the higher viewpoints occur in the realm of the categories that theology shares with other contemporary disciplines. Lonergan calls such categories 'general.' If we are familiar with the theology of Thomas Aquinas, we know something about what general categories are and how they function. For the introduction of Aristotle's metaphysics and psychology into the systematic theology of Aquinas supplied that theology with its general categories. And it was because of its general categories that this theology was able to mediate 'between a religion and the significance and role of a religion' in Thomas's cultural matrix.[4] A theology that does not pay sufficient attention to the genesis and development of its general categories fails to perform such mediation. At best, as for example in the theology of Karl Barth, such a theology exercises a self-mediation from the events of revelation to the contemporary faith of the church. A major and crucial methodological problem lies precisely here: how to achieve or reach a theological synthesis that really does issue from a mutual self-mediation with culture, but that does so without falling into the conceptualist and reductionist trap of some versions of the method of correlation. I suggested above a way of avoiding such a trap, by regarding the relation of the general categories to the special categories along the lines of the relation of obediential potency that obtains between nature and grace.

From a more positive standpoint, the first meaning of 'system and history' reflects the fact that the present work, too, anticipates a series of systematic theologies in a manner that is somewhat new. The newness lies, not in a lack of continuity with great achievements of the theological past, but in the fact that the series will quite knowingly and deliberately take its stand *on a ground that is generative of all such achievements.* The ground has only recently begun to be cleared. Lonergan would have been the first to acknowledge that his work was but a beginning. As yet no series of systematic theologies has been explicitly and deliberately built upon this work. But the nature of the ground is such that in principle such a series could extend indefinitely, even as the clearing of the ground goes forward beyond the articulations with which Lonergan began this work. We can envision today, I dare say for the first time in the history of Catholic theology, the possibility of an ongoing genetic sequence of systematic statements grounded in an ongoing clarification of the basic terms and relations. The expression 'system and history' refers in part to the formal-methodological constituents of such a sequence. It indicates that, because of advances in the clarification of theology's method and foundations, we now can envision a developing synthesis, a synthesis, moreover, that in any of its stages will never be complete in any one person's mind, a synthesis that will reside rather in the collaborative community itself. We can envision a synthesis that can grow over the centuries, exhibiting perhaps something analogous to the ongoing history of the more successful empirical sciences.

2 System as Witness

If the first meaning of 'system and history' anticipates a future history of systems, the second meaning has to do with recovering the past.

As we have seen, Lonergan comments, in the first chapter of an early version of his systematics of the Trinity, that 'today's scholars resemble twelfth-century compilers more than they do thirteenth-century theologians.'[5] He does not mean this statement as a criticism, but as a factual comment on the historical situation in which he found himself in 1957, when these words were published. Far from making a merely negative assessment of the positive research of the recent past, even from a systematic standpoint, he regards this research as anticipating a new step in the comprehension of the history of Christian constitutive meaning. For he goes on to say, 'Besides systematic exegesis, there exists a historical exegesis that *no longer omits the accidentals but includes them in a synthetic manner.* Besides systematic theology, there exists *a more concrete and comprehensive theology that considers and seeks to understand the economy of salvation in its historical development.* This new step in comprehension has been in preparation for a long time, thanks to so much biblical, conciliar, patristic, medieval, liturgical, ascetical, and other research; *but its synthetic character has not yet clearly appeared.*'[6]

Now to speak of this more concrete and more comprehensive theology as having a synthetic character is to add a new series of meanings for the term 'systematic theology.' The more concrete and comprehensive theology that Lonergan envisions may be 'praeter theologiam systematicam' as systematic theology has traditionally been conceived, and even as Lonergan himself continued to conceive it. But if it is genuinely synthetic, then it is systematic in some new and yet to be developed fashion. Yet for such a concrete and comprehensive theology to be developed in a manner that is synthetic and systematic, some principle has to be discovered and articulated that will function for theology much as the calculus functioned for physics. That is to say, theology needs a principle, something that is first in some order, that will make possible an understanding of religious and theological *history* that is not only narrative and descriptive but also synthetic, systematic, and explanatory. The difference between narrative, descriptive history and synthetic, systematic, explanatory history is analogous to the difference between the notion of 'going faster' and the notion of acceleration as the second derivative of a continuous function of distance and time. But what kind of principle can do that for theology? It is narrative, descriptive history that Lonergan is concerned with in *Method in Theology*'s chapters on history (even when he is concerned with 'critical history') and, I might add, that Paul Ricoeur is also concerned with (in views that are basically complementary to Lonergan's) in *Time and Narrative.*[7]

It is possible (though by no means certain) that Lonergan is commenting favourably in the passages in *Divinarum personarum* on the *ressourcement* emphases of *la nouvelle théologie* (which was still under suspicion in some Vatican circles in 1957). But if this is the case, he is also subtly suggesting that *ressourcement* is not enough. What will issue from this new movement in theology, indeed from positive research in general, is in fact some new kind of synthesis, which was not the objective of the *ressourcement* movement. In addition to the ongoing doctrinal movement that is continually establishing and within dogmatic limits changing the community's constitutive meaning, and in addition to the more familiar systematic movement that would understand the realities named in doctrines, there will emerge a new mode of understanding, a new movement towards what is perhaps even a new theological goal. I am calling this third movement explanatory history. Explanatory history is history in all its concreteness, yet history governed by a set of heuristic notions that would enable theologians to relate *to one another* in genetic and dialectical fashion various stages in the evolution of the meanings constitutive of the Christian church. The key notion of explanatory history is not 'what was going forward.' This remains the heuristic notion of the narrative, descriptive history that will always be a particular 'functional specialty' in theology's indirect discourse, in the phase that is concerned with the words and deeds of others. But the key heuristic notions of explanatory history, the notions that enable the discernment of relations among the stages themselves, will be something else. They will be supplied by a development in the notion of *dialectic.* Lonergan suggests as much in his opening treatment of dialectic in *Insight.*[8] Key elements will be the notions of differentiation and conversion: differentiations of the basic notions of the intelligible, the true and the real, and the good, and conversion in the intellectual, moral, religious, and psychic or affective domains. The base that enables one to employ these notions will be interiority analysis. Such analysis equips one with heuristic notions that constitute an always *potential* totality of viewpoints that can be employed to understand the relations among various sets of historical data. Explanatory history may be correlated with a type of diachronic structuralism,[9] an explanatory grasp of the relations among *stages,* where the relations are both genetic and dialectical.

Again, the theology that emerges from such a new movement will not be systematic theology in the traditional sense of that term. It will be *praeter theologiam systematicam.* It will be something new. It will include systematic theologies. In the ideal order it would include all of them. But it will include them precisely as dimensions of the past history of the community, of doctrine, of theology, and in fact of the religions and religious thought of humankind. Its comprehension of history will not be simply narrative and descriptive. It will be in principle synthetic and explanatory, however piecemeal its explanatory grasp of relations may be. Its synthesis will emerge as it traces genetic and dialectical relations among various moments in history. If there is to be a new systematic theology in the strict sense of that term, namely, an understanding of the realities intended in the community's constitutive meaning, it will include, however much in a subordinate position, a theology of theologies, just as Lonergan's *Insight* includes and grounds a philosophy of philosophies. This is the point to the second meaning of 'system and history.'

The emphasis that we are stressing here resembles the methodical and scientific hermeneutics of philosophical statements that Lonergan proposed in chapter 17 of *Insight.* I suspect that this material is among the least understood of Lonergan's writings. And unless I am mistaken, its reflections are among those on which he came to lay less stress as his work proceeded.[10] I have reviewed it in greater detail and tried to resurrect it in the context of a proposal regarding the ontology of meaning.[11] But I am here indicating its relation to systematic theology. While it is indeed different from systematics as traditionally conceived, it will be a dimension of systematics as that discipline or 'functional specialty' is emerging. It may be worked out in dialectic, but in itself it does not belong to that phase of theology where theology mediates from the past into the present. It is a dimension of what is mediated into the present in direct discourse in this 'new stage of meaning' grounded in interiority analysis. It is a theology of religious expressions and of theological understanding, an explanatory grasp of the genetic and dialectical relations that obtain (1) among religious moments, (2) between religious moments and their theological articulations, and (3) among the theological articulations. And it is this, not in the abstract but in the concrete, in the details that historical research itself provides for this new, synthetic understanding.[12]

3 History as Mediated Object of Systematic Theology

The third meaning of 'system and history' has to do with further and more substantive dimensions of the objective of systematics. We touched briefly on this meaning above, when discussing the unified field structure for systematics, but now we must fill out the heuristic anticipation of that very structure by adding in very brief compass the basic terms and relations of the theory of history that would form one dimension of that structure.

3.1 Data from the Lonergan Archives

This third meaning of 'system and history' is affirmed quite clearly in some papers that can be studied in the Lonergan Archives in Toronto, papers that were penned by Lonergan at and shortly after the time of his breakthrough, in February of 1965, to the notion of functional specialties. In these papers Lonergan states that the 'mediated object' of systematics is history, *Geschichte.* If it is true that limiting the mediated object of systematics to the theology of theologies of which we just spoke is to submit to an idealism of a Hegelian variety, then a broader notion of history is required

– broader than the history of theological ideas – if we are to be true to Lonergan's meaning and to systematics itself.

The notion of functional specialization is what enabled Lonergan to write *Method in Theology*. Theology is conceived according to operational specializations and structured as a multiform process from data to results. The notion is already quite familiar, and so I will say only as much about it here as is needed to present the third meaning of 'system and history.'

First, then, there are two phases to theology. There is a mediating theology, that is, a phase of theology that mediates from the past into the present, a phase of indirect discourse in which researchers, exegetes, and historians report on what others have said and done. This is theology as hearing, as *lectio divina*. And there is mediated theology, a phase in which theologians stand on their own two feet and say, not what others have said but what they wish to say on their own account and of their own responsibility. Mediated theology is direct theological discourse in the present and with an eye to the future. It is a phase, not of hearing but of saying, not of *lectio divina* but of questions and answers, and of questions and answers not about what others have said and done but about the realities affirmed in the faith of the church. As in the structure of the medieval *quaestio*, various views on any issue have been considered ('Videtur quod non' and 'Sed contra'), and now one speaks what one holds to be correct and attempts to provide an understanding of what one judges to be true ('Respondeo dicendum'). At one point in the archival papers that date from the breakthrough to functional specialization, Lonergan calls the first phase 'theology as openness' and the second 'theology as action.'

Second, each phase is structured into four distinct but related sets of theological operations. The operations are determined by the goals appropriate to four similarly distinct but related levels of intentional consciousness, but all four levels of intentional consciousness conspire to meet the respective objectives of any one level. Thus in the first phase: (1) the data are made available though *research*, and the availability of data is the goal appropriate to empirical consciousness; (2) the data are understood in *interpretation*, which corresponds to intelligent consciousness; (3) what was going forward especially in the doctrinal development of the tradition is narrated in *history*, which is headed to the facts known in true judgments; (4) conflicts are resolved by reducing them to their roots through the procedures of *dialectic*, where encounter with the values and beliefs of others moves one to decision. The second, mediated phase proceeds from (5) an objectification of the additional grounds for one's positions in *foundations*, again correlated with decision, through a statement (6) of what one holds to be true (judgment) in *doctrines*, to (7) an understanding of one's doctrines in *systematics*, and finally (8) to the mediation of Christian constitutive meaning in contemporary pastoral, interdisciplinary, and interreligious situations in *communications*, where the data are established that, among other things, will be made available in future research, when what for us is the present age becomes for our successors something to be studied in the first, mediating phase of a future theology.

The conception is brilliant. In principle and in Lonergan's intention it includes everything that goes on in theology, every operation that theologians perform. It offers a potential totality of theological operations, and provides the framework for the coalescence of the operations into distinct but related specializations or, in Lonergan's phrase, functional specialties. While more is to be done by way of clarifying all of the functional specialties, the achievement of differentiating them in the first place is of extraordinary intellectual importance.

Now, on a handwritten piece of paper[13] that perhaps represents the earliest extant record of Lonergan's breakthrough to this notion of the structure of the entire discipline of theology, the four specialties of the 'hearing' phase of theology are called research, interpretation, history, and conversion; 'history' is further specified by the use of the German word *Historie*; and the four specialties of the 'saying' phase are called foundations, doctrine, explanation, and communication.[14] Furthermore, in an important step that for some reason did not find its way into *Method in Theology*, there is specified a 'mediating object' for each of the specialties of the first phase and a 'mediated object' for each of the specialties of the second phase. The 'mediating subject' is introduced at the end of the first phase as catalyst of the transition from hearing to saying, from mediating objects to mediated objects.

The first phase, again, mediates from the past into the present, and so the respective objects of each of the functional specialties in this phase will contribute to the mediating function of the whole phase, and so can be called 'mediating objects.' Thus, the mediating object of research is the given (that is, data). The mediating object of interpretation is meaning. The mediating object of history (*Historie*) is truth, in the sense of 'what really happened.' And the mediating object of 'conversion' is encounter.

In addition to these mediating *objects*, however, there is a mediating *subject*. What grounds the self-mediation of the subject, the grounding later called 'foundational reality,' lies outside the domain of theology itself but is required if one is to move into the second phase, and its objectification is required if that move is to be methodical. For the mediating objects of the first phase are not sufficient of themselves to enable one to speak the mediated objects of direct discourse in one's present situation.[15] There is required an additional and invariant foundation, objectified in the functional specialty 'foundations' but occurring, happening, not in theology but in life. Such is the mediating subject.

Moreover, each functional specialty of the second phase has a mediated object, an object that is mediated through the offices of the mediating objects of the first phase as processed by the mediating subject who is the theologian. The respective objects of the second phase are mediated into the present by the subject's processing of the data, meanings, facts, and encounters intended in, disclosed by, research, interpretation, history, and dialectic. At this early point in Lonergan's conception of the specialties, the mediated object of 'foundations' is said to be God; the mediated object of 'doctrine' is said to be redemption; the mediated object of 'explanation' is said to be history, but history now not as *Historie* but as *Geschichte*; and the mediated object of 'communication' is said to be 'world.'

As the book *Method in Theology* emerged, there occurred several shifts from this initial conception. While the terms 'mediating object' and 'mediated object' do not occur in *Method in Theology*, in fact the object mediated in foundations is, it seems, not God but the mediating subject, that is, the differentiated and converted horizon within which the constitutive meaning of the church can be affirmed in doctrines, understood by the systematic theologian, and communicated in many ways to different audiences. The same horizon is what makes possible the derivation of the special and general categories, which is another task or function of the specialty 'foundations.' Again, the mediated object of doctrines is not specified in *Method in Theology* as redemption. From the book *Method in Theology* itself, we might assign a more generic mediated object to this functional specialty: the affirmed meanings constitutive of this particular faith community as these meanings are appropriated in specifically theological discourse. (The 'as' phrase here is important: 'doctrines' as a functional specialty includes more than statements found in creeds and in church doctrines; it includes as well those theological doctrines that a given doctrinal theologian holds to be true.) It may be that Lonergan would still have intended these meanings to take the general form of a doctrine on redemption, but he does not state this in the book. Again, in *Method in Theology*, the de facto mediated object of communications is, perhaps, not 'world,' but the reign of God within the world.

But what of systematics? This is our concern. Again the point that Lonergan makes in the notes we are discussing is not pursued in *Method in Theology*. And again it is something to which I wish to return here. The mediated object of the functional specialty 'explanation' or systematics is history, *Geschichte*, the history that is written about as contrasted with the history that is written. A contemporary understanding of the truth of Christian faith affirmed in ecclesial and theological doctrines would take the form of a theological theory (explanation) of history. This, I believe, is what Lonergan is saying in the notes under consideration, and this is what I am affirming here.

Further data along these lines are supplied by other items in the same folder in the Lonergan Archives. It is not my purpose here to give anything even remotely resembling a thorough exposition of Lonergan's papers in preparation of *Method in Theology*. Let me mention only a set of handwritten pages.[16] Here Lonergan calls the seventh functional specialty 'theories' (pages 1 and 2), 'theories pure [that is, explanatory]' (page 6), and 'theory' (page 8). Page 8 of this item calls the first phase 'Theology as Openness' and the second phase 'Theology as Action.' 'Theory' is explicitly related to 'systematic' theology, just as 'foundations' is to 'fundamental,' 'doctrine' to 'dogmatic,' and 'communication' to 'pastoral.' It is as if Lonergan is providing new words for traditional theological disciplines; but the new words indicate as well that the meaning or function of the traditional disciplines is being transformed. In these pages he seems not to want to use the words 'fundamental theology,' 'dogmatic theology' or 'dogmatics,' 'systematic theology' or 'systematics,' and 'pastoral theology.' Use of these terms will distort his meaning, for he is talking about something new. In this 'something new,' 'foundations' will play something of the role that used to be played by 'fundamental theology,' but it will not be the old fundamental theology at all. 'Doctrine' will play something of the role that used to be played by 'dogmatic theology,' but it will not be the old dogmatic theology at all. 'Theory' or 'explanation' will play something of the role that used to be played by 'systematic theology,' but it will not be the old systematic theology at all. And 'communication' will play something of the role that used to be played by 'pastoral theology,' but it will not be the old pastoral theology at all.

What constitutes the difference between the old disciplines and the new specialties? For one thing, the old disciplines that were called fundamental theology, dogmatic theology, systematic theology, and pastoral theology were a function of what Lonergan calls 'subject specialization,' whereas the new specialties are a matter of functional or operational specialization. That is to say, the old disciplines were a function of dividing up the results of particular investigations, and so the *objects*, whereas the new specialties are a function of classifying the recurrent *operations of subjects*, operations that are responsible for the process from data to results. The key to method as conceived by Lonergan by the time he arrived at functional specialization is the move from objects, material and formal, to operations as constituting the basis of specialization. Clearly, object and operation are correlated. This is shown by the fact that Lonergan's notes on operational specialization also mention mediating and mediated objects. But just as clearly, the key role is now assigned to operations.[17] Thus Lonergan says toward the very beginning of a 1962 institute on method:

> The consideration of method ... is not directly the consideration of objects. According to St Thomas in *Summa Theologiae*, 1, q. l, a. 7, *Theologia tractat de Deo et de aliis quae ad Deum ordinantur.* That is the object of theology. Consideration of method is not directly concerned with the object, not with God, with scripture, with the councils, with the Fathers, with the liturgy, or with the Scholastics, but with me and my operations. It is concerned with the theologian and what the theologian does. It does not imply a total neglect of the object – that is impossible. If you eliminate the object you eliminate the operation, and if you eliminate the operation the subject reverts to the state of sleep, and there are no operations at all. But it is not directly concerned with the objects, and insofar as it considers objects it considers them through the operations. Similarly, it considers the subject not purely as subject without any operations, but as operating. Accordingly, while it is necessary to begin from objects, still objects are considered simply as means to pin down the operations that are involved. It considers objects not for their own sakes, but as discriminants of operations.[18]

This much of a difference is apparent from *Method in Theology* itself, where the differential establishing the specialties is strictly methodological. But there appears in the material we are now considering another and strictly theological differential: the concern for history in the very theological content of specialties of the second phase. 'Doctrine' is to be a doctrine on history, emphasizing redemption. 'Explanation' is to be a theological theory of history. 'Communication' is directed to historical action in the constitution of the reality that is here called 'world.' This was new, radically new, for Catholic theology at the time of the breakthrough.

Let us examine just a bit more of the data. The twelfth page of the item that we are considering is headed 'operational specializations.' History as a functional specialty in the first phase, as *Historie*, has to do with a 'sequence of ideas and doctrines.' It employs 'comparative, organistic, genetic, [and] dialectical methods.' Such history 'moves towards [a] synthesis of interpretations.' Its dialectical component 'sets [the] fundamental alternatives of judgment.'[19] *'Conversion' as a functional specialty is 'my encounter with history, religious, moral, intellectual.'* 'Foundations' treats 'conversion made thematic, categories, recurrent questions.' 'Doctrines' (now plural) rests on a 'functional relation': 'understanding [the] history of [a] doctrine' is functionally related to 'understanding [the] doctrine [itself].' These understandings 'plus conversion and deployment in foundations' lead to 'synthesis in a doctrine about history, role of Church as continuing redemption.' 'Theories' is related to 'interpretation' because of the relation between *intelligere verba* (understanding the words: interpretation) and *intelligere rem* (understanding the reality: theories, explanation, systematics). It offers 'solutions to doctrinal problems,' 'developed conceptualization for doctrines, of foundational categories.' All of that is quite in keeping with the traditional conception of systematics. But here Lonergan adds that this functional specialty results in a 'synthesis in a theory of history.' And 'communications' (now plural) is 'historical action, handing on tradition effectively in accord with cultural differences, changes, with individual and group needs and exigencies.'[20]

The entire process of the complete discipline of theology consists in a movement, then, from 'theology as openness' (the first, hearing, mediating phase) to 'theology as action' (the second, saying, mediated phase). Again, it consists in a movement from 'mediating to mediated object,' from 'moving to terminal object,' from 'hearing to saying, *lectio* to *quaestio*, learning to teaching,' from 'Christ and Church to God and all in relation to God,' from 'historical, positive, apologetic resources to fundamental, dogmatic, systematic, pastoral,' from *oratio obliqua* to *oratio recta*, from a phase in which there is 'no confusion [between] Paul and me, Aquinas and me' to a phase in which there is a 'clear distinction,' from a phase in which I study what is 'there ... to be learnt' to a phase in which 'my responsible addition [is] vital.'[21]

The thirteenth page speaks of 'history' (*Historie*) as concerned with 'development in sapientia intelligentia scientia – heading to judgment.' 'Conversion' is 'existential interpersonal decision.' 'Foundations' is 'decision made thematic,' distinguishing 'positions and counterpositions.'[22] 'Doctrines' expresses 'judgment as mine within Church – *a doctrine on history*.' 'Theories' expresses 'understanding of doctrines – *a theory of history*.' And 'communications' is '*historical action* – data as produced.'[23]

My concern in presenting these materials at this point is to indicate that, when Lonergan arrived at the notion of theology's structure and method according to the interrelation of distinct functional specialties, he also clearly stated (1) that the sixth functional specialty, 'doctrine' or 'doctrines,' was to come together in a 'doctrine about history' and the 'role of [the] Church as continuing redemption'; and (2) that the seventh functional specialty, which is not in these pages called systematics but 'explanation' or 'theories,' and which is the attempt to understand doctrines, was to find 'synthesis in a theory of history.' The transposition of what one has learned in the 'hearing' phase of theology into the categories in which one is to 'speak' the truth and explain and communicate it in one's own cultural matrix occurs as one develops ways of speaking about the process of history itself and about the constitutive meaning of Christian living in relation to the historical process. Anticipating the language that Lonergan would use ('systematics'), we may say that a contemporary systematic theology is to be a systematics of history. Clearly, that was Lonergan's option, and it is one that I will attempt to follow. The particular manner in which I will try to develop such a systematics is, of course, my own responsibility, and whatever defects it may have cannot be blamed on Lonergan. Nonetheless, if someone wishes to correct my attempts in an effort to be more faithful to Lonergan, at least it is clear that one should not go back on the basic option that the seventh functional specialty, which later came to be called 'systematics,' is to be a theory of history. Clearly that was Lonergan's option as well.

What, then, is this 'history' that is to be the mediated object of systematics?

3.2 Lonergan on the Dialectic of History

Lonergan's interest in the analysis of history dates from at least the late 1930s, when he wrote a series of papers on the philosophy of history which were discovered only posthumously.[24] In reflecting many years later on the insights that guided his reflections on this subject, he wrote:

> It was about 1937–38 that I became interested in a theoretical analysis of history. I worked out an analysis on the model of a threefold approximation. Newton's planetary theory had a first approximation in the first law of motion: bodies move in a straight line with constant velocity unless some force intervenes. There was a second approximation when the addition of the law of gravity between the sun and the planet yielded an elliptical orbit for the planet. A third approximation was reached when the influence of the gravity of the planets on one another is taken into account to reveal the perturbed ellipses in which the planets actually move. The point to this model is, of course, that in the intellectual construction of reality it is not any of the earlier stages of the construction but only the final product that actually exists. Planets do not move in straight lines nor in properly elliptical orbits; but these conceptions are needed to arrive at the perturbed ellipses in which they actually do move.
>
> In my rather theological analysis of human history, my first approximation was the assumption that men always do what is intelligent and reasonable, and its implication was an ever increasing progress. The second approximation was the radical inverse insight that men can be biased, and so unintelligent and unreasonable in

> their choices and decisions. The third approximation was the redemptive process resulting from God's gift of his grace to individuals and from the manifestation of his love in Christ Jesus.[25]

Lonergan goes on in the same context to highlight chapter 20 of *Insight* as the place where 'the whole idea' is presented, while chapters 6 and 7 present 'the sundry forms of bias' and chapter 18 'the notion of moral impotence.'

This is not the place for a detailed study of the development of Lonergan's notion of the dialectic of history. Much work is needed still on this topic.[26] Several articles have appeared debating the status of the general notion of dialectic in Lonergan's thought and especially in *Insight*.[27] I have expressed my own opinion on the issue, especially in chapter 3 of *Theology and the Dialectics of History*. But I admit that in that chapter I am presenting my own notion of dialectic and claiming that this notion is a development on what remain coincidental comments in *Insight*, a development that is based in accepting psychic conversion as foundational.

I do not intend in the present chapter to repeat here the exegesis of *Insight* already expressed in *Theology and the Dialectics of History*. Rather I will simply relate my own views to what is probably Lonergan's most nuanced version of his own position on the dialectic of history, however brief it may be: that which appears in the 1977 paper 'Natural Right and Historical Mindedness.' In this paper the analysis of history is recast in terms of *meaning*, and especially in terms of what in many other places Lonergan calls the meaning constitutive of human communities.

History now is viewed as rooted in a total and dialectical source of meaning. The same progress-decline-redemption structure that is found in Lonergan's earlier analyses still obtains. Thus the same three steps remain in effect (though the third has to be pieced together from comments spread throughout the paper), but they are now spoken of primarily in terms of the dialectic of the development of meaning.

The dialectic of history is introduced here in the context of a more far-reaching question: is there a possibility of establishing, as a reality in history, what we have come to call collective responsibility? Lonergan proposes to address this issue by attempting to bring into conjunction his own development of the Greek philosophical notion of natural right and the modern notion of historicity. The issue thus becomes one of determining whether, once historicity is acknowledged, there can still be said to be norms in history, and if so, how these norms can be appealed to, not simply in the individual, whom they affect directly and proximately, but also in the community.

Lonergan begins with historicity. 'Historicity is what man makes of man,'[28] and the actual changes that mark the progress and decline in that process are at their core changes of meaning. Are there to be determined any norms in such a process? Is there any permanent and binding force that underpins the variety of human manners and customs and the meaning that is constitutive of these? That distinctly contemporary question is the issue at stake in the paper.

Natural right was the 'component or factor' that the Greeks affirmed, 'underneath the manifold of human lifestyles,' to contain the 'universality and permanence of nature itself.'[29] Is there any possibility of rehabilitating such a notion? Well, if a rehabilitation of such a notion is to help us actually to determine any norms in 'man's making of man' and in the changes of meaning that such historicity entails, then the notion of natural right will have to be interpreted, not in terms of 'universal propositions, self-evident truths, naturally known certitudes,' but in terms of nature itself as it concretely operates.[30]

Lonergan works, then, from Aristotle's definition of nature as 'an immanent principle of movement and of rest' to find such a principle in the human spirit raising and answering questions. 'As raising questions, it is an immanent principle of movement. As answering questions and doing so satisfactorily, it is an immanent principle of rest.'[31] From there, of course, it is an easy step to proceed to the familiar analysis of the three types of questions that we raise – questions for intelligence, questions for reflection, and questions for deliberation – and to show how in each of these the human spirit manifests itself as an immanent principle of movement and of rest. The three types of questions are not three natures, since they form a series in which 'what the several principles attain are only aspects of something richer and fuller,' and 'the several principles themselves [are] but aspects of a deeper and more comprehensive principle.'[32]

What is that deeper and more comprehensive principle? We have seen it already. It is itself a nature, at once a principle of movement and of rest, and it is described here as 'a tidal movement that begins before consciousness, unfolds through sensitivity, intelligence, rational reflection, responsible deliberation, only to find its rest beyond all of these,' in 'being-in-love.'[33] This tidal movement, this deeper and more comprehensive principle, is now the *normative source of meaning in human history*, the normative source of the meaning that is constitutive of the world in which we live. Collective responsibility (the central topic of the paper) is treated in terms of the effects of such an immanent source of meaning as these effects are embodied in the social and cultural realities that are, respectively, the infrastructure and superstructure of the human community.[34] And this social and cultural context brings Lonergan to his new formulation of the dialectic of history. The entire 'ongoing process of self-transcendence' that he has described as natural right, the tidal movement that is the deeper and more comprehensive principle, in itself reveals only individual responsibility. But 'inasmuch as the immanent source becomes revealed in its effects, in the functioning order of society, in cultural vitality and achievement, in the unfolding of human history, ... the manifold of isolated responsibilities coalesce[s] into a single object that can gain collective attention.'[35] That single object is the meaning constitutive of a given social order, and any treatment of it must be not only hermeneutical but also dialectical.

The first step in the dialectic is again the affirmation of the principle of progress, but here that principle, that 'tidal movement' of ongoing self-transcendence, is also a *normative source* of constitutive meaning. While this normative source reveals directly individual responsibility – what in the shorthand language of the 'transcendental precepts' Lonergan would specify as 'Be attentive, Be intelligent, Be reasonable, Be responsible' – the manifold of such individual responsibilities coalesces into the unfolding of history. This manifold thus sublates individual intelligence and reasonableness and becomes the hypothetical source of 'ever increasing progress,' which now exists in the *community* that is faithful to the exigencies of ongoing self-transcendence.

Second, however, the normative source of meaning is not the total source of meaning. The norms constitutive of normative responsibility can be violated not only by isolated individuals but also by the manifold of individual responsibilities that has coalesced into the functioning order of a society. And so 'from the total source of meaning we may have to anticipate not only social order but also disorder, not only cultural vitality and achievement but also lassitude and deterioration, not an ongoing and uninterrupted sequence of developments but rather a dialectic of opposed tendencies.'[36] The total source of meaning in history is dialectical. The dialectic of history thus becomes essentially a conflict immanent in the society's carriers and embodiments of constitutive meaning.

The elements of that dialectic are set forth under six headings. Because history is now conceived as rooted in a total, dialectical, and communal source of *meaning*, at the core of these elements there lies the issue of the development of meaning.

(1) The first point is that human meaning, whether technical, social, or cultural, develops and expands in human collaboration.

(2) Second, these expansions occur on a succession of plateaus. What here are called plateaus correspond to what in *Method in Theology* are called stages of meaning.[37] The first plateau entails the development of practical intelligence, intelligence in the realm of doing, and the style of the development is 'the spontaneous accumulation of insights into the ways of nature and the affairs of men.'[38] Whatever awareness there may be of

reality being more than nature and humanity 'has little more than symbolic expression in the compact style of undifferentiated consciousness.'[39] The second plateau involves a cumulative development and specialization of *language*. It 'has to do mainly with speech,'[40] and it leads to an eventual differentiation of consciousness in philosophy, mathematics, and science. And the third plateau, which we are only beginning to inhabit in our time, and precariously so, is marked by a movement to concern with 'developments generally,' where the 'central concern is with human understanding where developments originate, with the methods in natural science and in critical history which chart the course of discovery, and more fundamentally with the generalized empirical method that underpins both scientific and historical method to supply philosophy with a basic cognitional theory, an epistemology, and by way of a corollary with a metaphysics of proportionate being.'[41]

The differences of plateau give rise to different conceptions of the dialectic operative within history.

> The notion of fate or destiny or again of divine providence pertains to the first plateau. It receives a more detailed formulation on the second plateau when an Augustine contrasts the city of God with the earthly city, or when a Hegel or a Marx set forth their idealistic or materialistic systems on what history has been or is to be. A reversal towards the style of the first plateau may be suspected in Spengler's biological analogy, while a preparation for the style of the third plateau may be discerned in Toynbee's *A Study of History*. For that study can be viewed, not as an exercise in empirical method, but as the prolegomena to such an exercise, as a formulation of ideal types that would stand to broad historical investigations as mathematics stands to physics.[42]

What, then, would be 'an exercise in empirical method' with regard to history? How is the dialectic of history conceived on the third plateau? The remaining four points formulate the answer to this question. In anticipation of what will emerge from these points, Lonergan comments that the notion of a dialectic of history that emerges on this plateau 'has its origins in the tensions of adult human consciousness, its unfolding in the actual course of events, its significance in the radical analysis it provides, its practical utility in the invitation it will present to collective consciousness to understand and repudiate the waywardness of its past and to enlighten its future with the intelligence, the reasonableness, the responsibility, the love demanded by natural right.'[43]

(3) Third, then, on the third plateau there emerge specific ideals of

enlightenment and emancipation, ideals that are different from those trumpeted in the eighteenth century in the context of the second plateau.[44] The enlightenment specific to the third plateau 'aims to be such self-awareness, such self-understanding, such self-knowledge, as to grasp the similarities and the differences of common sense, science, and history, to grasp the foundations of these three in interiority which also founds natural right and, beyond all knowledge of knowledge, to give also knowledge of affectivity in its threefold manifestation of love in the family, loyalty in the community, and faith in God.'[45] And emancipation in the same context is 'such self-transcendence as includes an intellectual, a moral, and an affective conversion. As intellectual, this conversion draws a sharp distinction between the world of immediacy and the world mediated by meaning, between the criteria appropriate to operations in the former and, on the other hand, the criteria appropriate to operations in the latter. Next, as moral, it acknowledges a distinction between satisfactions and values, and it is committed to values even where they conflict with satisfactions. Finally, as affective, it is commitment to love in the home, loyalty in the community, faith in the destiny of man.'[46]

(4) Fourth, such ideals enable us to engage as well in a 'critique of our historicity, of what our past has made us,' a critique that is 'concerned with the operative meanings constitutive of our social arrangements and cultural intercourse.'[47] The critique will be a matter not only of 'the research that assembles the data, the interpretation that grasps their significance, the history that narrates what has been going forward'[48] but also of the dialectical principles that expect a diversity of results rooted in opposed horizons: 'If some have been through the threefold conversion, others will have experienced only two, others only one, and some none at all. Hence we must be prepared for the fact that our researchers, our interpreters, our historians may exhibit an eightfold diversity of results, where the diversity does not arise from the data but rather from the horizon, the mindset, the blik, of those conducting the investigation.'[49] Moreover, the basic division of materials in the investigation will now be a division of *meanings* provided by the three plateaus themselves: 'the proper locus of the distinction between the plateaus is not time but meaning.'[50] Thus, 'there will be meanings such as prove operative in men of action; further meanings that involve a familiarity with logical techniques; and a still further plateau of meanings that attain their proper significance and status within a methodical approach that has acknowledged its underpinnings in an intentionality analysis.'[51] Finally, the basic categories of analysis in this critique of what our past has made us and of the constitutive meanings that have emerged from that history will distinguish (1) developments, (2) the handing on of developments, (3) completeness and incompleteness in developments, and

(4) completeness and incompleteness in the handing on of developments. Lonergan's analysis here is rich. It reflects a specification of his late insistence on movements from below (here, developments) and from above (here, handing on of developments) in consciousness.

> Development may be described, if a spatial metaphor is permitted, as 'from below upwards': it begins from experience, is enriched by full understanding, is accepted by sound judgment, is directed not to satisfactions but to values, and the priority of values is comprehensive, not just of some but of all, to reveal affective conversion as well as moral and intellectual. But development is incomplete when it does not go the whole way upwards: it accepts some values but its evaluations are partial; or it is not concerned with values at all but only with satisfactions; or its understanding may be adequate but its factual judgments faulty; or finally its understanding may be more a compromise than a sound contribution.
>
> Again, the handing on of development may be complete or incomplete. But it works from above downwards: it begins in the affectivity of the infant, the child, the son, the pupil, the follower. On affectivity rests the apprehension of values. On the apprehension of values rests belief. On belief follows the growth in understanding of one who has found a genuine teacher and has been initiated into the study of the masters of the past. Then to confirm one's growth in understanding comes experience made mature and perceptive by one's developed understanding. With experiential confirmation the inverse process may set in. One now is on one's own. One can appropriate all that one has learnt by proceeding as does the original thinker who moved from experience to understanding, to sound judgment, to generous evaluation, to commitment in love, loyalty, faith.
>
> It remains that the process of handing on can be incomplete. There occur socialization, acculturation, education, but education fails to come to life. Or the teacher may at least be a believer. He can transmit enthusiasm. He can teach the accepted formulations. He can persuade. But he never really understood and he is not capable of giving others the understanding that he himself lacks. Then it will be only by accident that his pupils come to appropriate what is sound in their tradition, and it is only by such accidents, or divine graces, that a tradition that has decayed can be renewed.[52]

(5) Fifth, there are ambiguities of completeness. First-plateau minds that find meaning only in action can live in a second-plateau context. Or first-

plateau and second-plateau minds can dwell in third-plateau contexts. Or third-plateau contexts can be marked by methodological blocks; thus – and these are Lonergan's examples, not mine – in the contemporary academy we find the confinement of philosophy to ordinary language, or the restriction of knowledge to the exact sciences, or the insistence that human studies must be value-free, or the limited openness to values that proscribes transcendence to God – or, we might add, the postmodern emphasis on otherness that also does not acknowledge the ongoing process of self-transcendence to the other as a normative source of meaning.

(6) Sixth, dialectic is not the final word. '[I]t can be more helpful, especially when oppositions are less radical, for the investigators to move beyond dialectic to dialogue, to transpose issues from a conflict of statements to an encounter of persons. For every person is an embodiment of natural right. Every person can reveal to any other his natural propensity to seek understanding, to judge reasonably, to evaluate fairly, to be open to friendship. While the dialectic of history coldly relates our conflicts, dialogue adds the principle that prompts us to cure them, the natural right that is the inmost core of our being.'[53]

Arguably, this late statement represents Lonergan's most nuanced position on the dialectic of history, and it is to this statement that I would here address the further considerations that I began to express in detail in *Theology and the Dialectics of History.*

3.3 The Psyche and the Normative Source of Meaning

These further considerations advance the notion of the normative source of meaning in history, and they do so in two ways. First, psychic conversion brings certain nuances to that notion by developing the notion of dialectic. This is the topic of the present subsection. Second, as we will see in the next subsection, this expanded notion of dialectic is part of a broader attempt to develop Lonergan's statements in *Method in Theology* and elsewhere regarding a normative scale of values. Developed positions on dialectic and the scale of values, then, expand Lonergan's notion of the normative source of meaning in history, by drawing out implications that I believe are already coincidentally present in his work. As we will see, these developments are instances of what Lonergan himself recommends as 'complicating the basic structure' of conscious intentionality.

We begin with the affirmation that there is a particular dimension of the total and dialectical source of constitutive meaning in history that is distinct from intentional operations, from the levels of intentional consciousness that these operations constitute, and from the biases that affect these levels of intentional consciousness. This dimension underpins, accompanies, and reaches beyond the operations of intelligence, reasonableness, and moral responsibility. Like these operations themselves, it finds objectification in the working order of a society. And like these operations, it too is affected by a bias, the bias that in *Insight* Lonergan begins to objectify in his pages about dramatic bias.[54] This bias too finds objectification in the working order of a society, as do the individual, group, and general biases that affect our intentional operations. Like the latter three biases, dramatic bias introduces a dialectical element into that working order, into its structures, into its institutions, and most of all into the intersubjectivity that constitutes the primordial infrastructure of the social order, and the personal relationships that constitute the flowering of that same order. To the extent that this dimension is relatively free from such bias, it aids the coalescence of individual responsibilities into an authentic working order in a society, and so the effective achievement of genuine collective responsibility. But to the extent that it is under the influence of bias, it militates against such coalescence and consequent collective responsibility.

The dimension to which I am referring is the *aesthetic and dramatic* dimension of human living and its underlying neural base. What I have called psychic conversion aids both its appropriation and the healing of its dramatic bias. If the dialectic of history is grounded in a *total and dialectical* source of constitutive meaning, if the dialectical element is introduced because of the various forms of bias, if the *normative* source of meaning in history is authenticity free from or healed of bias, then, since dramatic bias and psychic conversion affect that source just as the other biases and the other conversions do, consideration of dramatic bias and psychic conversion will profoundly affect our understanding of the dialectic of history itself. Such are the grounds of the argument.

First, however, it will help us to grasp better these grounds themselves if we recall Lonergan's statement that the normative source of meaning in history is 'a tidal movement that begins before consciousness, unfolds through sensitivity, intelligence, rational reflection, responsible deliberation, only to find its rest beyond all of these,' in love. Bias can affect not only intelligence, rational reflection, and responsible deliberation, but also sensitivity, its underlying neural manifold, feelings, receptivity, and the context of interpersonal relations and community into which the entire tidal movement heads. If intentionality analysis leads to the appropriation of intelligence, rational reflection, and responsible deliberation, of their operators, and of the subtle devices that militate against their authentic exercise, a parallel analysis or, perhaps, a parallel set of practices might be expected to facilitate the appropriation of the other elements and operators and biased devices as they function in this total and dialectical source of meaning in history.[55]

Next, then, talk of other *operators* leads us to reflect on Lonergan's expressions in two other papers. First, as we have seen, in 'Mission and the Spirit,' what in 'Natural Right and Historical Mindedness' is a 'tidal movement' is called 'the passionateness of being,' and that passionateness of being is said to have 'a dimension of its own' that underpins, accompanies, and reaches beyond 'the subject as experientially, intelligently, rationally, morally conscious,' that is, the subject governed by the operators of questions for intelligence, reflection, and deliberation.[56] What underpins intentional consciousness is 'the *quasi-operator* that presides over the transition from the neural to the psychic'; what accompanies intentional consciousness is 'the mass and momentum of our lives, the color and tone and power of feeling'; and what reaches beyond or overarches intentional consciousness is 'the topmost *quasi-operator* that by intersubjectivity prepares, by solidarity entices, by falling in love establishes us as members of community.'[57]

Second, we have also already mentioned the posthumously published 'Philosophy and the Religious Phenomenon,' which does not use 'operator' language in regard to the topmost level, but does employ the term 'symbolic operator' for the factor that in 'Mission and the Spirit' is called a lower quasi-operator. 'The intellectual operator that promotes our operations from the level of experience to the level of understanding may well be preceded by *a symbolic operator* that coordinates neural potentialities and needs with higher goals through its control over the emergence of images and affects.'[58] Regarding the topmost level, Lonergan says, '[B]eyond the moral operator that promotes us from judgments of fact to judgments of value with their retinue of decisions and actions, there is a further realm of interpersonal relations and total commitment in which human beings tend to find the immanent goal of their being and with it their fullest joy and deepest peace.'[59] I would propose that we might speak of an operator here, too, just as 'Mission and the Spirit' appealed to a topmost quasi-operator. And I would appeal to the following quotation from *Method in Theology* to help us specify just what this operator is: 'It is as though a room were filled with music though one can have no sure knowledge of its source. There is in the world, as it were, a charged field of love and meaning; here and there it reaches a notable intensity; but it is ever unobtrusive, hidden, inviting each of us to join. And join we must if we are to perceive it, for our perceiving is through our own loving.'[60] The topmost operator is *gratia operans.*

Thus, Lonergan says, the structure of intentional consciousness 'may prove open at both ends.'[61]

From these various sources, I draw the notion of *an aesthetic and dramatic operator.* It functions in three ways, and these are specified in 'Mission and the Spirit' as characterizing the 'dimension of its own' that is proper to the passionateness of being. First, as underpinning the operations of intentional consciousness, it is what in 'Philosophy and the Religious Phenomenon' is called a symbolic operator. Or, more generically, we might speak of it as the operator that produces the phantasms that, among other things, are required for insight. Psychic conversion would, then, effect a habitual attitude of *conversio ad phantasmata*, a return to this 'natural orientation' of the human spirit in this world, just as intellectual and moral conversion are the rehabilitation of the natural orientations of intelligence, reason, and existential responsibility. Second, as accompanying intentional operations, it affects the mass and momentum of feeling that makes even our exercise of these operations a dramatic sequence of events. Third, as overarching these operations, it is the power of love that meets us as we are, that brings rest to our intentional striving and psychic restlessness, and that releases in us the capacity for total commitment, whether in the intimacy that constitutes genuine families, the loyalty that enjoins responsibility for the well-being of our fellow men and women, or the unrestricted being in love that, under whatever form it may be found, precisely because it is unrestricted, the Christian is enabled to name being in love with God.

This threefold aesthetic and dramatic operator – symbolic, sensitive, and agapic – joins the intentional operators of intelligent, rational, and moral consciousness to form the *normative* source of meaning in history. What constitutes the normative source of meaning in history is not the open structure of intentional consciousness alone but that structure *in* the total context within which it exists, a context that includes the factors introduced by the aesthetic and dramatic operator. We must, therefore, grant to the aesthetic and dramatic operator a significance for history that parallels the significance accorded by Lonergan to the operators of intellectual and moral development 'from below,' that is, to questions for intelligence, questions for reflection, and questions for deliberation.

The 'dimension of its own' that is proper to the passionateness of being, along with the lower, intermediate, and higher workings of the aesthetic and dramatic operator that is distinct from the operators of intelligent, rational, and moral consciousness, are what is released into the possibility of some appropriation by what I have called psychic conversion.

Again – to appeal to the categories that I employed in *Theology and the Dialectics of History* – if the normative order of intentionality, as it functions in the dramatic pattern of everyday living, can be called the search for direction in the movement of life, then the element that underpins, accompanies, and reaches beyond this order, the passionateness of being as it becomes conscious in the dimension that is its own, is the very movement of life itself. Psychic conversion is the release of dimensions of this movement into a capacity for appropriation.

My writings to this point on this and related subjects have emphasized what in 'Mission and the Spirit' Lonergan calls the underpinning quasi operator, and in 'Philosophy and the Religious Phenomenon' the symbolic operator. And it is true that, *from below*, this operator is the root of everything else in the 'dimension of its own' proper to the passionateness of being; that is, it is the root of the feelings that accompany intentional consciousness and of the intersubjectivity and sense of solidarity that prepare the subject for interpersonal relations and total commitment. Let me repeat what Lonergan says of it in 'Mission and the Spirit':

> It ushers into consciousness not only the demands of unconscious vitality but also the exigences of vertical finality. It obtrudes deficiency needs. In the self-actualizing subject it shapes the images that release insight; it recalls evidence that is being overlooked; it may embarrass wakefulness, as it disturbs sleep, with the spectre, the shame of misdeeds. As it channels into consciousness the feedback of our aberrations and our unfulfilled strivings, so for the Jungians it manifests its archetypes through symbols to preside over the genesis of the ego and to guide the individuation process from the ego to the self.[62]

My earlier writings emphasized that symbolic or psychic operator as what is released into potential appropriation through what I am calling psychic conversion. But what I am after in speaking of psychic conversion includes as well the other two dimensions of what now I am calling an aesthetic and dramatic operator, and they were never totally excluded from my intentions or neglected in what I tried to say regarding this foundational dimension.[63] My earlier emphases were influenced by the factors of personal history that led me into this domain through an existential wrestling with Jung and the world view that emerges from his writings. And because this 'symbolic operator' is the root from below of all that happens in this 'dimension of its own' on the part of the passionateness of being, these earlier emphases cannot be passed by as we extend our consideration to the other two elements of this operator: its role as accompanying the operations of intentional consciousness in feeling, and its role as overarching the entire structure of intentional consciousness in moving us beyond intersubjectivity and solidarity into personal and existential relation with the other. In fact, even with the extension of the notion of psychic conversion to these other areas of the aesthetic and dramatic operator, I would still hold to the definition that I have already given of psychic conversion. Psychic conversion is the transformation of the censorship exercised by dramatically patterned intentionality and imagination over the neural infrastructure of the aesthetic dimension, a transformation from a repressive to a constructive functioning. For that censorship operates *all along the line,* and not just in the initial transition from the neural to the psychic that can be opened up for appropriation by dream analysis and interpretation. In fact, even genuine dream analysis and interpretation opens intentional consciousness not only to its preconscious base but also to the feelings that accompany and either facilitate or else impede the operations of intentional consciousness, and to the charged field of love and meaning that operates the opening of the psychic and intentional subject into community and interpersonal relations. Furthermore, let me point once again to the hermeneutical extension of the same notion that I presented above in chapter 9.

On the basis of this distinction in relation between intentionality and psyche, between the search for direction and the movement of life, between intentional consciousness and the dimensions to which it lies open on either end and even in its own immanent structure, I propose, then, to offer an addition to what Lonergan says about the dialectical structure of history. Intentionality and psyche *together* are the total and dialectical source of meaning in history, and this correspondence of the operators of the two areas of conscious human development[64] will have implications for the notion of dialectic itself.

Let me state these implications in the briefest possible terms, and let me do so in three steps that parallel Lonergan's threefold approximation to the concreteness of the historical dialectic.

First, then, there is a tension between intentional consciousness and this 'dimension of its own' proper to the passionateness of being, and the only authentic negotiation of this tension is to bring it fully into consciousness and let it function as a creative source of one's further development by preserving a correspondence between the respective operators of psyche and intentional consciousness in its spiritual dimensions of intelligence, reason, and moral deliberation.[65] In my own terminology, intentionality and psyche, the search and the movement, constitute a *dialectic of contraries* that is to be affirmed, strengthened, and assumed as the foundation of one's conscious dramatic living. That *integral dialectic of the subject,* and not just the operators of intellectual, rational, and moral development, constitutes, I believe, the normative source of meaning in history, fidelity to which would imply 'ever increasing progress.'

Second, skewing that dialectic in favour of either psyche or intentionality, either the movement or the search, is the source or root of personal and social decline. Thus, in addition to the dialectic of contraries, there is a dialectic of contradictories, an either/or. But the either/or is not between psyche and intentionality, the movement and the search, but between the integral dialectic of psyche and intentionality and their distorted dialectic, where distortion would be a function of granting undue predominance to either of these two co-constitutive factors. The dialectic of contradictories introduces the second component in the total dialectical process: *either* the solidary and creative tension of psyche and intentionality, of movement and search, as normative source of meaning, *or* the dissolution of this tension through neglect of *either* pole.

Third, the redemptive process resulting from the gift of grace and manifested in Christ Jesus is required for the integrity of the dialectic of psyche and intentionality, and is to be understood in part, with the use of general categories, in terms of that integrity.

Thus would I restate Lonergan's three approximations to the concreteness of the historical dialectic.

While I must accept responsibility for the position here stated (and argued at length in *Theology and the Dialectics of History*), two passages from chapter 7 of *Insight* provide coincidental anticipations of the distinction between (1) an integral dialectic of contraries both as normative and as source of progress in history, and (2) a dialectic of contradictories that affects the integrity of the dialectic of contraries itself.

> [D]ialectic rests on *the concrete unity of opposed principles*; the dominance of either principle results in a distortion, and the distortion both weakens the dominance and strengthens the opposed principle to restore an equilibrium.[66]

> ... [G]eneralized method has to be able to deal, at least comprehensively, not only with the data within a single consciousness but also with the relations between different conscious subjects, between conscious subjects and their milieu or environment, and between consciousness and its neural basis. From this viewpoint, dialectic stands to generalized method as the differential equation to classical physics, or the operator equation to the more recent physics. For dialectic is a pure form with general implications; it is applicable to any concrete unfolding of linked but opposed principles that are modified cumulatively by the unfolding; it can envisage at once the conscious and the nonconscious either in a single subject or in an aggregate and succession of subjects; *it is adjustable to any course of events, from an ideal line of pure progress resulting from the harmonious working of the opposed principles, to any degree of conflict, aberration, breakdown, and disintegration*; it constitutes a principle of integration for specialized studies that concentrate on this or that aspect of human living, and it can integrate not only theoretical work but also factual

> reports; finally, by its distinction between insight and bias, progress and decline, it contains in a general form the combination of the empirical and the critical attitudes essential to human science.[67]

These two coincidental anticipations need to be integrated and systematized in a higher viewpoint on the whole issue of dialectic, and that integration and systematization is what I am suggesting by bringing psychic conversion to bear on the elucidation of the historical dialectic.

3.4 Dialectic and the Scale of Values

3.4.1 Three Instances of the Dialectic of Psyche and Intentionality

This dialectical heuristic formal structure has three concrete realizations. They are interrelated, but they are also distinct. Each of them has roots in both the psyche and intentional consciousness, and so in the total source of meaning in history.

Two of the concrete realizations of dialectic are amply discussed by Lonergan in the chapters on common sense in *Insight.* The foundational realization is *the dialectic of the subject,*[68] where, as Lonergan makes clear, the respective poles are the censorship exercised by dramatically patterned intentional consciousness and imagination, on the one hand, and the neural demands that would reach a conscious integration in image and affect, on the other hand. As we have already said, this censorship operates all along the line in the tidal movement that begins before consciousness, extends through intentional consciousness, and finds its rest in love. Psychic conversion is the transformation of that censorship from a repressive to a constructive functioning, thus releasing the aesthetic and dramatic operator into the freedom from repression that is required if it is to perform its function. But Lonergan also speaks about a *dialectic of community,*[69] where the respective poles are the practical intelligence responsible for technological innovations, economic systems, and the political and legal stratum, on the one hand, and the intersubjectivity that prepares the way for the function of the topmost operator, on the other hand. In my formulation, when these principles are working together harmoniously, they constitute an integral dialectic of community.

To these two instances of the pure form of dialectic I have added a *dialectic of culturally constitutive patterns of meaning,*[70] drawing on Eric Voegelin to distinguish anthropological and cosmological constitutive meaning.[71] For Voegelin these sets of meaning are patterned symbolizations of the experience of life as a movement with a direction that can be found or missed or, once having been found, lost. I believe they are ideal types or models that are extremely handy to have around when it comes to describing or explaining the meaning constitutive of concrete real situations.

Cosmological constitutive meaning finds the paradigm of order in cosmic rhythms, which are drawn upon to inform first the life of the community, and then, through the order of the community, the order of individual life. In societies governed by cosmological constitutive meaning, the movement of constitution runs from the cosmic measure of integrity to the integrity of the community, and from the integrity of the community to order in the life of the individual.

Anthropological constitutive meaning is based on the insight that the measure of integrity is world-transcendent, and that it orders first the life of the individual, and through well-ordered individuals, the life of the community; in Plato's terms, as interpreted by Voegelin, the soul is the measure of society, but God is the measure of the soul.[72] An insight with at least some of these anthropological characteristics is to be found, it seems, in all of the breakthroughs that for Karl Jaspers constitute an epochal or axial juncture in human history,[73] a juncture that would correspond to the movement from Lonergan's first to his second plateau.

Voegelin mentions as well soteriological symbolization. Soteriological constitutive meaning is, in my understanding, the condition of the integral dialectic of anthropological and cosmological constitutive meanings. More precisely, that integral dialectic does not yet exist in any recurrent fashion, and it is our responsibility to evoke it as constitutive of a world-cultural humanity. As theology and the preaching of the gospel evoke that world-cultural mentality, they will call excessively cosmological societies to the anthropological freedom to take responsibility for their own history; and they will call excessively anthropological societies to acknowledge their connection with 'nature' understood as distinct in its schemes of recurrence from those introduced into history by inquiry, insight, reflection, judgment, deliberation, and decision.

3.4.2 The Scale of Values

These three dialectical processes are related to one another, and their interrelations can be understood by first placing them at respective levels in the scale of values that Lonergan suggests in *Method in Theology*, and then determining the relations among the levels of value. Thus the integral dialectic of the subject constitutes personal value, the integral dialectic of culture constitutes cultural values, and the integral dialectic of community constitutes social values. Here is what Lonergan says of the scale of values:

> Not only do feelings respond to values. They do so in accord with some scale of preference. So we may distinguish vital, social, cultural, personal, and religious values in an ascending order. Vital values, such as health and strength, grace and vigor, normally are preferred to avoiding the work, privations, pains involved in acquiring, maintaining, restoring them. Social values, such as the good of order which conditions the vital values of the whole community, have to be preferred to the vital values of individual members of the community. Cultural values do not exist without the underpinning of vital and social values, but none the less they rank higher ... Over and above mere living and operating, man has to find a meaning and value in his living and operating. It is the function of culture to discover, express, validate, criticize, correct, develop, improve such meaning and value. Personal value is the person in his self-transcendence, as loving and being loved, as originator of values in himself and in his milieu, as an inspiration and invitation to others to do likewise. Religious values, finally, are at the heart of the meaning and value of man's living and man's world.[74]

3.4.3 The Analogy of Dialectic

We can approach the question of the interrelation of the three dialectical processes, and so of personal, cultural, and social values, by speaking first of an *analogy of dialectic*, that is, an analogous relation that obtains among the three dialectical processes, and then of the constitution of society. Regarding the analogy of dialectic, six points are relevant.

First, each of the dialectical processes (the dialectic of the subject, the dialectic of culture, and the dialectic of community) embodies a tension of limitation and transcendence. It is not, of course, the case that the principle of limitation is always to be located in the sensitive or psychic component of the dialectic – in neural demands and their conscious integration in images and affects (the subject), in cosmological constitutive meaning (culture), and in spontaneous intersubjectivity (community) – and the principle of transcendence in the intentional order – in the dramatic pattern of self-constitution (the subject), in the anthropological shaping of cultural meanings and values (culture), or in practical ideas (community). The tension of limitation and transcendence is a tension of the *integrators and operators* of development, where development is moving beyond, and so transcendence in the sense in which the term is being employed here. The initiative of such development, whether in the subject, culture, or the community, can originate anywhere. Thus the principal operator of a specific personal development can be symbolic; it can occur, for example, in a dream. In that case there is a task of adapting one's dramatic self-understanding to the initiative for development that has arisen proximately in the psychic dimension, rather than of adapting one's sensitivity to new ideas. So in each instance there is a need to specify the respective sources of integration and of operation of further development. The matter is complex. In the example just given, it is true that no development will take place unless questions for interpretation, reflection, and deliberation follow upon the dream that initiated the movement forward, and so the question as operator comes into correspondence with the psychic operator, and intentionality assumes the role of guiding transcendence. But it first had to bring *itself* into correspondence with the psychic operator, not the other way round. And the integration of the initiated development is essentially in the intentional order, in a new set of concepts expressing a modified self-understanding. The point, then, is that the limitation-transcendence dialectic is not to be mechanically or conceptualistically fitted to correspond to the interactions of psyche and intentionality; it is not the case that the psychic component is always limiting and the intentional always moving beyond.

Second, as we have seen, each of these dialectical processes is in its integrity a dialectic not of contradictories but of contraries. The processes of social, personal, and cultural change represent the more or less integral or distorted unfolding emergent from both of the constitutive principles in the respective dialectic. The opposition between these principles is to be reconciled by their functional interdependence, whereas a dialectic of contradictories can be overcome only by the choice of one principle to the exclusion of the other: the true rather than the false, the good rather than the evil.

Third, then, each dialectical process is integral to the extent that the relevant processes of change are a function of the harmonious interaction of the two internally constitutive principles, and distorted to the extent that the changes are a function of one of the internally constitutive principles at the expense, or to the exclusion, of the other.

Fourth, in each case the integrity of the dialectic is a function, not of one or the other of its internally constitutive principles, but of a third principle of higher synthesis. Thus the integrity of the dialectic of the subject is a function of grace: proximately of the conjugate forms of charity, hope, and faith, and of sensitive participation in them, and remotely of the communication of the very life of God that is a created change that affects, indeed effects, a topmost level of consciousness, a completion, a resting from intentional striving and psychic restlessness. Again, the integral dialectic of cosmological and anthropological constitutive meaning is a function of soteriological constitutive meaning, of the outer word of God's revelation spoken to and appropriated by cultures transformed by its message. Yet again, the integrity of the dialectic of community is a function of the integrity of the dialectic of culture itself.

Fifth, around the respective principles of higher synthesis there functions a dialectic of contradictories, and it decides the fate of the dialectics of contraries. Thus, (1) the rejection of the life of grace ipso facto distorts the dialectic of neural demands and dramatically patterned self-constitution, whereas the acceptance of grace incrementally heals the division in the subject; (2) a culture's effective rejection of the message of salvation, no matter how much it may use and abuse Christian language, distorts the dialectic of cosmological and anthropological constitutive meaning, whereas its acceptance of that message heals the one-sidedness of culture; (3) the neglect of culture as form of community distorts the dialectic of intersubjective spontaneities with social structures and systems, whereas attention to cultural integrity at the same time establishes or encourages a flourishing community.

Sixth, inversely, the integrity of the dialectics of contraries provides criteria by which one can ascertain the authenticity of the principle of any supposed higher synthesis. Thus (1) a supposed 'grace' that would ultimately divide rather than integrate the dialectic of neural demands and dramatic self-constitution is not grace but illusion; (2) a declaration of the word of God that promotes either a cosmological fatalism or an anthropological neglect of cosmic rhythms and purposes is fraudulent; and (3) a set of cultural meanings and values that promotes the neglect of intersubjective groups within the society or the biased disregard of timely and fruitful practical ideas is an inauthentic mindset or mentality. Clearly, then, the issue of good and evil centres around the principles of higher synthesis of each dialectic; it is not an issue between the respective poles of each dialectical process, such that emphasis of one is good and of the other evil; rather, it is an issue of their integral dialectical tension (good) or of the breakdown of that tension (evil).

3.4.4 The Constitution of Society

We can move closer to specifying the relations among the levels of value by considering the constitution of society. The elements of society are (1) intersubjective spontaneity, (2) technological institutions, (3) the economic system, (4) the political order, and (5) culture. Moreover, culture is distinguished into the two dimensions of the everyday set of meanings and values informing a given way of life, and the reflexive level arising from scientific, scholarly, philosophic, and theological understanding of the everyday. The crucial question has to do with how these five elements are related to one another.

My position can be stated in six points.

First, the spontaneous intersubjectivity that is one of the constitutive principles of the dialectic of community is also, on its own, one of the five elements constitutive of society.

Second, practical intelligence, the other constitutive principle of the dialectic of community, is the source of three of the other constitutive elements of society: technology, the economic order, and the political and legal stratum of society.

Third, these three elements must be kept in a taut dialectical tension with spontaneous intersubjectivity, since, again, 'the dominance of either principle results in a distortion, and the distortion both weakens the dominance and strengthens the opposed principle to restore an equilibrium.'[75]

Fourth, the integrity or distortion of this dialectic of community is a function proximately of the everyday level of culture, and remotely of the reflexive level of culture.

Fifth, from a normative viewpoint, spontaneous intersubjectivity, technology, economic relations, politics, and the everyday level of culture constitute the infrastructure of a society, and the reflexive level of culture constitutes the superstructure, where, again, culture at both levels is the condition of the possibility of an integral dialectic of community.

Sixth, there is needed at the superstructural level of culture a dimension of consciousness that would inform an intellectual collaboration to assume responsibility for the dialectic of community by attending to the integrity of cultural values themselves at both superstructural and infrastructural levels. This dimension of consciousness Lonergan calls cosmopolis,[76] and I have elaborated it further into what I call world-cultural consciousness.[77]

Since Marxism seemed until recently to pose the most serious challenge on the contemporary scene to the affirmation that the integrity of culture is the condition of possibility of the integral dialectic of community, I judged when writing *Theology and the Dialectics of History* that a clarification by contrast of my own position with the Marxist analysis of society may prove helpful. Such a clarification would reveal at least four differences between my position and that of Marx.

First, on my position the *basic* social dialectic is between primordial human intersubjectivity and the practical intelligence responsible for what Marx calls forces and relations of production as well as for the political process, whereas for Marx the basic social dialectic is between the forces and relations of production themselves. Such a dialectic, if it exists – and there is good reason to doubt its permanent status – would be a dialectic *within* practicality, but for me there is a more basic dialectic *between* the whole of practicality and human intersubjectivity.

Second, regarding the dialectic of forces and relations of production, Marx did not foresee the current macroeconomic structure of capitalism, which in many ways is very different from the capitalism that he criticized. In his own day the crucial point of critique was that ownership units must be at least as large, complex, and differentiated as the potentials of productive planning in the forces of production, or the ownership unit will fetter the unit of technological production, thus setting the stage for the latter to burst the bonds of the former through revolution. But today the scale of ownership units *overreaches* that of technological units, and what is required is the scaling *down* of economic units to the proportions demanded by the dialectic of community. This raises the question of culture as the condition of possibility of the scaling down, and in fact by this question the entire set of basic terms and relations in the Marxist theory of society (to say nothing of capitalist market expansion) is seriously challenged.

Third, the paradigm of praxis is for me an artistic paradigm, where the artistry in question is the dramatic artistry of the delicate dialectic of limitation and transcendence.[78] Because of his identification of praxis with production, Marx always displaces this tension in the direction of transcendence, even when, as in his descriptions of praxis in the communist utopia, he *does* employ an artistic analogy.

Fourth, technology, economic relations, *and* the legal and political stratum, in dialectical relation with intersubjective communicative action, where the dialectic is constituted as a function of the everyday level of culture, constitute the base or infrastructure of a healthy society, and its superstructure lies in the reflexive scientific, scholarly, philosophic, and theological dimensions of culture, one of whose functions is to keep in the infrastructure what belongs in the infrastructure, including the realm of politics. Cultural integrity is thus responsible for the infrastructural dialectic, and one of the ways in which it meets that responsibility is by keeping the legal and political *in* the dialectic rather than allowing them to usurp the prerogatives of culture *above* the dialectic, as they must do according to Marx, and as they most often in fact do in capitalist societies.

An option on the relation of cultural and social values is taken at least implicitly in every contemporary theology that attempts to be direct discourse. The tendency or danger of liberation theologies in this regard is to overlook the fact that it is *culture* that is responsible for social integrity. And the tendency or danger of theologies that are afraid of liberation emphases is to forget or repress the fact that one of the responsibilities of culture is precisely *social integrity*. Whatever option a theology makes on this issue ultimately determines whether the theology in question will represent a major surrender of intelligence or whether it will embody, not only the empirical, but also the critical, dialectical, and normative capacities of intelligence. Will the theology be a function of what Lonergan calls cosmopolis, that is, of a dimension of consciousness that informs a collaborative responsibility for culture as the condition of the possibility of recurrent social values, or will it be instead a contribution to a series of ever less comprehensive syntheses constituting decline? A theologian today must take an explicit stand on the relation of cultural values to the social order.

This part of my option on history deals, then, with a question about the structure of the situation which a theology is addressing and of the situation which a theology is evoking. Implicit assumptions in regard to this question, and especially about the relation of culture to politics, the economy, and technology, are present in any contemporary theology *in oratione recta*, and these issues have to be made explicit from the outset.

3.4.5 Relations among the Levels of Value

From the reflections of the last two subsections we may proceed to determine the relations that obtain among the levels of value. There are relations both 'from above' and 'from below.' From above, the more inclusive levels are the condition of the possibility of successfully functioning schemes of recurrence at the more basic levels. From below, besides the obvious reverse conditioning, questions emerging at more basic levels evoke operations that will lead to consolidations at higher, more inclusive levels.

First, then, the effective recurrence of schemes at the more basic levels is a function of the recurrence of schemes at higher levels. Thus (1) the effective and recurrent distribution of vital values to the whole community is a function of the social order, which in its integrity is constituted by the dialectic of spontaneous intersubjectivity and the practical intelligence that institutes technological, economic, and political structures. (2) The effective integrity of the dialectic of the social order is a function of the cultural values that inform the everyday life of the community. These in turn, especially in an age of increasingly differentiated consciousness, depend on the superstructural level of scientific, scholarly, philosophic, and theological meaning. (3) Both dimensions of cultural value are a function of the integrity of persons in community. And (4) personal integrity is a function of grace. Thus we have our first set of relations: schemes at the higher levels of value condition schemes at the more basic levels.

But the problems that emerge on the more basic levels condition the emergence of the questions that, if pursued freely, will result in changes at the more inclusive levels so as to meet the problems emergent at the more basic levels. Moreover, the scale or proportion of the problems that exist at the more basic levels determines the extent of the changes that must take place at the higher levels. In other words, the proportions of the relevant higher synthesis required to meet the problem of more basic schemes of recurrence are set by the difficulties of the more basic levels themselves.

Now, if we follow through on the further implications of this analysis, we will see that in our current situation, which is the situation that a contemporary systematic theology must address, the problem of the effective and equitable distribution of vital goods is global, and so its solution must thus call for new technological, economic, and political structures on a global scale, and for new visions of intersubjective and interpersonal flowering. And the socio-economic relations and political realities, as well as the new interpersonal ethics, that could constitute a globally interdependent commonwealth will call for the generation of cultural values that are somehow crosscultural. Thus the culture that is adequate to the proportions of a globally interdependent technological, economic, and political order in dialectical relationship with a crosscultural intersubjectivity is at best emergent in our present situation; and the obstacles to its truly effective emergence and survival are monumental in scope and power. A theology that would mediate in direct discourse between a cultural matrix and the significance and role of a religion within that matrix will be mediating what Christians believe as true and value as good, not with a relatively stable set of cultural meanings and values, but with an emergent set required to meet the exigencies of the present social order. More precisely, its mediation with prevailing cultural values will be for the sake of catalysing the emergence of a new set of cultural values, a set that itself is crossculturally generated. Systematic theology today will be contributing to the emergence of a new cultural matrix, in a fashion that can truly be called axial or epochal. It will be forging some of the very materials of constitutive meaning required for the emergence of a legitimate alternative to the present situation.

Elements of such constitutive meaning appear, I believe, in the notion or model of the integral dialectic of culture. The integral dialectic of culture, again, is constituted by the tense interplay of cosmological and anthropological constitutive meaning, under the higher synthesis provided by soteriological constitutive meaning. Cosmological constitutive meaning, when exclusive of anthropological insight and truth, binds the schemes of recurrence of social and individual development too stringently to the schemes of recurrence of nonhuman nature; cosmological consciousness is thus prone to succumbing massively to a fatalism that seems inscribed in cosmic rhythms, especially when these rhythms are known only descriptively; and cosmological cultures become very easily the victims of other cultures whose exclusively instrumental use of intelligence and reason has effected a release from cosmic fatalism, perhaps, but only at the expense of destroying our ecological participation in nature. On the other hand, anthropological constitutive meaning exclusive of cosmological insight and truth is insensitive to its biological base in the body's and the psyche's rhythmic participations in nonhuman nature, and so to an entire dimension of the passionateness of being or tidal movement that is the normative source of meaning in history. Especially when it loses its original revelatory experience of being drawn beyond the cosmos for its standard of integrity, anthropological constitutive meaning becomes exclusively instrumental. And if it also lacks the cosmological pole of limitation, it will become imperialistic, in Joseph Schumpeter's sense of imperialism as the objectless disposition on the part of a state or other macrosystem to unlimited forcible expansion.[79] The end result, as Hannah Arendt has shown historically[80] and as Lonergan has argued philosophically,[81] is the totalitarian state or, today, the macroeconomic structure that controls even the state.

3.5 *Complicating the Structure*

The nuances on dialectic that I have offered and the interrelation of the three dialectical processes, while they are intended as advancing Lonergan's own discussion of a theory of history, nonetheless remain continuous with his formulations of his own insights, and in this and the next subsection (3.6) they will be integrated into his more inclusive analysis. The base of our additions lies in psychic conversion and the enlarged notions (1) of dialectic and (2) of the normative source of meaning that psychic conversion renders possible. And our reflection on the scale of values expands or differentiates further Lonergan's notion of value itself as a component in the structure of the human good.[82] I wish now to show how both the nuances and the expansion proposed here may be understood as instances of what Lonergan once referred to as 'complicating the structure.'

3.5.1 The Basic Issue

The issue of 'complicating the structure' arose in the lectures that Lonergan delivered on method at Boston College in the summer of 1968. At one point he asked the question, How does one get from transcendental method to general categories? And his answer was as follows: 'I indicate five ways of going about it. One starts from the basic structure, the transcendental notions, the operations, the structure of the operations, and from the correlative objects. One can: (1) complicate the structure, (2) turn to concrete instances of it, (3) fill it out, (4) differentiate it, (5) set it in motion.'[83] It is primarily the first of these 'ways of going about it' that I wish to address here, though we will see that others are also brought into play.

Lonergan gave four examples of complicating the basic structure. The first is 'the commonsense development of intelligence studied in chapters 6 and 7 of *Insight*.' A second way distinguishes at least four differentiations of heuristic structures: 'the classical, statistical, genetic, dialectical heuristic structures worked out in *Insight*: classical, in classical science; statistical, when you start taking concrete events into account; genetic, in biology; dialectical, dealing with the concrete, the dynamic, and the contradictory.' A third way is by developing the integral heuristic structure that is a metaphysics. 'It complicates the fundamental business of experiencing, understanding, judging, and deciding by having several instances of this in certain relations.' And finally, the notion of functional specialties represents a fourth complication of the basic structure. 'We have the four things (experiencing, understanding, judging, and deciding) occurring in two phases; and the effort concentrates on the end of the first level, the second level, the third level, and the fourth level. This happens twice, and so you get eight. It's a complication of the basic structure.' To these four I would add Lonergan's later development of a way of speaking about a movement 'from above downwards' in the structure as another instance of complicating the structure, one that in fact is heralded by functional specialization's movement from foundations through doctrines and systematics to communications in the second phase of the theological enterprise.

The example of functional specialization embodies a form of 'complicating the structure' that is evident in other instances as well. The key to functional specialization's complication of the structure lies in the technique of bringing the operations of all four levels of conscious intentionality to bear upon achieving the ends peculiar to each of the four levels, and this in two phases, one in indirect discourse, relating the words and deeds of others, and the other in direct discourse, taking responsibility for one's own words and deeds.

3.5.2 The Scale of Values as a Complication of the Structure

In effect I introduced in the last chapter a further complication of the movement from above downwards, in speaking of the reception of communally transmitted meanings and values. And now I wish to suggest that the elaboration of the scale of values that I attempted in *Theology and the Dialectics of History* and that I have summarized here represents a further instance of complicating the structure. And both of these arise from bringing the operations of all four levels to bear upon achieving the objectives of distinct levels. In the first instance, the four levels of intentional consciousness are brought to bear upon the 'empirical' reception of meaningful data. In the second instance, we must first distinguish the pursuit of the scale of values from the philosophic account of the scale. In the pursuit, all four levels of intentional consciousness are brought to bear on achieving the objectives of each of the levels of consciousness. And in the reflective elaboration of that scale, this multiple complication itself is accounted for. In either case the integral pursuit of the scale of values is a complication of the basic structure, and this is what accounts for the transcendental and transcultural validity of the scale itself. Moreover, our analysis is in effect an exercise in at least two more of Lonergan's 1968 canons or precepts, namely, turning to concrete instances of the complicated structure and setting the complicated structure in motion. At this point we are right into the issue that Lonergan himself was addressing in 1968, namely, deriving the general categories for a doctrinal and systematic theology. Moreover, as we will see, we have here at least the beginnings of a set of categories for a doctrine and theology of social grace, and a contribution to Lonergan's efforts, especially in 'Natural Right and Historical Mindedness,' to articulate a basis for collective responsibility.

Lonergan never tells us how he derived the ascending scale of values: vital, social, cultural, personal, religious. But it has always seemed obvious to me that the scale is based on the increasing degrees of self-transcendence to which one is carried or to which a community is carried in response to values at the different levels. And it has also seemd right to assume that the levels of value are isomorphic with the levels of consciousness, so that vital values correspond to experience, social values to understanding, cultural values to reflection and judgment, personal values to deliberation and decision, and religious values to God's gift of love. We are dealing here with a complication of that basic structure of consciousness.

Insofar as we are speaking of the deliberate pursuit of values, we are speaking always of fourth-level activity. But in our pursuit of values at the different levels of the scale, all four levels of intentional consciousness, within the horizon effected by the gift of God's love, are brought to bear upon the realization of the objectives of one level, in a manner that is analogous to the manner in which the four levels operate in each of the functional specialties to bring about the objectives of different levels in any given specialty. Thus, while vital values entail more than experience, still they have some correspondence to particular goods, which in Lonergan's scheme of the human good are correlated with the level of experience. Again, while the social value of the good of order entails more than understanding, still for Lonergan it is always a function of understanding. Again, while cultural values entail more than reflection and judgment, still they have some correspondence to judgment. Finally, while personal values entail more than decision, they have some correspondence to the existential moment in which one discovers for oneself that it is up to oneself to decide for oneself just what one is going to make of oneself. The scale of values is a function of the structural invariants of intentional consciousness, and is indeed isomorphic with them, even as the pursuit and realization of any one of the levels of value (at least of vital, social, cultural, and personal value) entails bringing the intentional operations of all four levels to bear upon attaining the objective of one level. The scale of values, in fact, entails what Lonergan calls a fresh apprehension of the structural invariants themselves, and so its elaboration is itself a development in the realm of cultural values.[84] And if I am correct in insisting on these relationships, if the scale of values is derived from the basic structure of the invariant features of intentional consciousness, then it does indeed provide a legitimate complex of general categories for a systematic theology that would be a theology of history.

This position on the scale of values remains static, however, until we turn to two more suggestions from Lonergan's 1968 presentation: 'identify concrete instances of the complicated structure' and 'set the complicated structure in motion.' Since I devoted a great deal of attention to those tasks in *Theology and the Dialectics of History*, it will be sufficient here to summarize what appears there and to bring it up to date by harmonizing it with the new methodological perspectives that have emerged in this book and by relating it to the issues of social grace and collective responsibility.

We return, then, to Lonergan's statement in 'Natural Right and Historical Mindedness' that the normative source of meaning in history is 'a tidal movement that begins before consciousness, unfolds through sensitivity, intelligence, rational reflection, responsible deliberation, only to find its rest beyond all of these,' in love.[85] I will now argue (1) that this statement shows that what I have called psychic conversion is itself a further complication of the basic structure; (2) that this statement supports the distinction of a dialectic of contradictories and a dialectic of contraries as a further complication of the structure; (3) that this statement can be employed also to complicate and fill out the structure of the scale of values (which is already a complication of the structure); and (4) that when this latter task is done, the way is open both for a fuller account of the collective responsibility that was Lonergan's principal concern in 'Natural Right and Historical Mindedness' and for a new moment in the theology of grace, namely, a theological grounding of the notion of social grace or grace-filled social structures. Our comments on the first two of these will simply review material that we have already seen.

3.5.3 Psychic Conversion as a Complication of the Structure

First, then, this statement from 'Natural Right and Historical Mindedness' demands a further complication of the account of the structure of the subject's authenticity. In the context in which the statement appears in 'Natural Right and Historical Mindedness,' the statement stipulates or at least implies that we must grant that what I have called the symbolic operator at the base of the structure, as well as the feelings that permeate the structure itself and the topmost operator of interpersonal relations and total commitment, provide a needed complement to the operators of intellectual and moral development specified in Lonergan's intentionality analysis. This is confirmed by the fact that the statement that I have quoted appears in 'Natural Right and Historical Mindedness' as an answer to a question: because what is attained by the several principles that are operators of conscious intentionality (questions for intelligence, questions for reflection, and questions for deliberation) 'are only aspects of something richer and fuller, must not the several principles themselves be but aspects of a deeper and more comprehensive principle?'[86] Lonergan's answer to that question is another question: 'And is not that deeper and more comprehensive principle itself a nature, at once a principle of movement and of rest, a tidal movement that beings before consciousness, etc.' The whole movement, which is 'an ongoing process of self-transcendence,'[87] is explicitly identified as 'the normative source of meaning' in history.[88]

This normative source 'reveals no more than individual responsibility,' and so Lonergan has not yet answered the central question that he posed in the paper, namely, the question regarding the structure of collective responsibility. 'Only inasmuch as the immanent source becomes revealed in its effects, in the functioning order of society, in cultural vitality and achievement, in the unfolding of human history, does the manifold of isolated responsibilities coalesce into a single object that can gain collective attention.'[89] But we will come back to that topic later. The scale of values will be the key to discerning how that immanent source becomes revealed in society, culture, and history.

As we have seen, the subjective context of the operators of conscious intentionality is mentioned also in the slightly earlier paper 'Mission and the Spirit,' where Lonergan's term corresponding to what in 'Natural Right and Historical Mindedness' is called 'a tidal movement' is referred to rather as 'the passionateness of being.' To repeat what I have already quoted several times, the passionateness of being 'has a dimension of its own' that enables it to underpin, accompany, and reach beyond 'the subject as experientially, intelligently, rationally, morally conscious.' As underpinning this intentional subject, it is what at this point he calls 'the quasi-operator that presides over the transition from the neural to the psychic'; as accompanying intentional operations it is 'the mass and momentum of our lives, the color and tone and power of feeling'; and as reaching beyond or overarching conscious intentionality it is 'the topmost quasi-operator that by intersubjectivity prepares, by solidarity entices, by falling in love establishes us as members of community.'[90]

My own proposal is that this dimension, distinct from but related to intelligent, rational, and moral operations, is released into the possibility of some appropriation by specifying a set of aesthetic-dramatic operators that mediate between the two dimensions, as these operators promote something that underpins, accompanies, and reaches beyond intentional operations. The set of aesthetic-dramatic operators consists of (1) the symbolic operators that effect the transition from the neural to the psychic, (2) the affective operators that consist in the feelings that permeate all intentional operations, and (3) the intersubjective operators that found community. Again as we have seen, in the posthumously published (indeed posthumously discovered) paper 'Philosophy and the Religious Phenomenon,' Lonergan extends his analysis of consciousness to include six levels of consciousness, four of which are the levels of intentional consciousness with which we are familiar.[91]

3.5.4 Dialectic as a Complication of the Structure

Next, it is on the basis of this distinction-in-relation between intentionality and psyche that I posited a certain dialectical nature to the normative source of meaning in history. It was from my study of Jungian psychology that I first learned how essential it is to distinguish two kinds of opposed principles of change. Jung and his disciples tend to treat all opposition as capable of reconciliation in some kind of higher synthesis. This works fine for such principles of change as consciousness and the unconscious, spirit and psyche, or the masculine and feminine dimensions of the psyche itself, but it wreaks havoc and disaster when the opposed principles are self-transcendence and the refusal of self-transcendence, authenticity and inauthenticity. For then one is engaged in the fruitless and indeed very dangerous quest to reach a position beyond good and evil. But there would be a reverse sort of havoc were Lonergan students to treat the opposition between neural demands and the censorship, for example, or between intersubjectivity and practical intelligence, as if one of these principles of change were somehow a source of evil or falsehood and only the other principle a source of the good and the true. We have to acknowledge something like what, for better or for worse, I have called dialectics of contraries, such as the dialectic of the subject in chapter 6 of *Insight* and the dialectic of community in chapter 7, and dialectics of contradictories, such as the dialectic of 'thing' and 'body' introduced in chapter 8 of the same book and the dialectic of authenticity and inauthenticity that features so prominently in Lonergan's later work. Dialectics of contraries are grounded in a tension between intentional consciousness and the passionateness of being that *has a dimension of its own.* The only satisfactory negotiation of this tension is to bring it fully into consciousness and let oneself be established in it as the creative source of one's further development and one's efforts at world constitution. Lonergan's presentation of genuineness in chapter 15 of *Insight* supports this analysis. Neither limitation nor transcendence is to be neglected; the tendency to such neglect, in either direction, is, theologically viewed, concupiscence, and capitulation to the tendency is basic sin. Intentionality and psyche constitute a *dialectic of contraries* that is to be affirmed, strengthened, and assumed as the foundation of one's conscious dramatic living. That dialectic constitutes the normative source of the subject's authenticity. Fidelity to the dialectic would imply progress. Skewing that dialectic in favour of either psyche or intentionality, either the movement or the search for direction in the movement, is the source or root by default of personal decline.

There is, however, a *dialectic of contradictories*: *either* the solidary and creative tension of psyche and intentionality as normative source of authenticity, *or* its dissolution by neglect of *either* pole. That either/or is the basis of the either/or of what is authentic or inauthentic. Lonergan's usual, though I would maintain not his sole, use of the term 'dialectic' has to do with the concrete, the dynamic, and the *contradictory*, and so with the dialectic of contradictories. But in *Insight* there is a single but complex notion of dialectic that can be reduced to some manageable clarity only by grasping the distinction between consciousness and knowledge. There is a duality to both consciousness and knowledge, but the duality is to be negotiated in a different manner in each case. The duality of consciousness is precisely the duality of intentionality and 'tidal movement' or 'passionateness of being' or sensitive psyche or vertically finalistic undertow (or whatever one chooses to call it), where the latter has 'a dimension of its own.' But there are also two kinds of knowing that exist without differentiation and in an ambivalent confusion until they are distinguished explicitly and only one of them is acknowledged to be full human knowing. Thus the duality of knowing is to be negotiated, Lonergan says, by 'breaking' it and affirming oneself a knower in the sense of a concrete unity, identity, whole that performs cognitive operations on the three levels of experience, understanding, and judgment. But breaking the duality of knowing entails affirming, maintaining, and strengthening the unity *in duality* of consciousness, a concrete unity of opposed principles, both of which are 'I' and neither of which is merely 'It.' The duality of sensitive and intellectual consciousness is constitutive of full human knowing. To break the duality of consciousness in favour of either sense or intellect to the exclusion of the other would be to invite, indeed to guarantee, conflict, aberration, breakdown, and disintegration in the unfolding of the linked but opposed cognitive principles of sensitive and intellectual consciousness, whereas to preserve that dialectic results in the cognitive progress consequent upon the harmonious working of these principles. The basic position on knowing affirms the unity in duality of consciousness, while the basic counterpositions break that unity in duality. Moreover, preserving that unity in duality is a realization of the tension of limitation and transcendence that constitutes genuineness. That tension is not mere homeostatic balance but conscious finality, in which psychic spontaneity heads toward the transforming enrichments effected by successive sublations in virtue of further questions, or, as Lonergan puts it, in which 'the operator is relentless in transforming the integrator.'[92] Thus the experience of movement and rest changes as one moves from level to level. And the feeling of the creative tension is the affective indication of integrity in the process of inquiry whereby one arrives at the intelligible, the true, and the good.

The two quite distinct kinds of realization of this single but complex notion are unified by the fact that there is a dialectic when there is a concrete unfolding of linked but opposed principles of change, where the principles themselves are modified cumulatively by the unfolding. But they are distinct because a dialectic of contraries calls for a choice of *both* generative principles in their functional interdependence, while a dialectic of contradictories demands that we choose *one* principle of the process and reject the other. But this either/or bears upon the harmonious working of the internally constitutive principles of the dialectic of contraries: either the creative tension of the two (authenticity) or the displacement of this tension in one direction of the other (inauthenticity).

The distinction that I am drawing is not unrelated, I believe, to a use of the term 'dialectic' that appears in some of Lonergan's early writings on dialectic and history, where he distinguished a natural dialectic, a dialectic of sin, and a supernatural dialectic. The dialectics of contraries that, as we will see in a moment, I am locating at the personal, cultural, and social levels of the scale of values would be complications of the structure of what Lonergan called a natural dialectic, where there is 'a series of ascending general principles each followed by expansion, antithesis, and a soluble problem.'[93] The term 'natural dialectic' thus corresponds to the term 'progress' in the familiar theory of history as progress-decline-redemption, just as 'dialectic of sin' corresponds to 'decline' and 'supernatural dialectic' to 'redemption.' If the normative source of meaning in history is now the 'tidal movement that begins before consciousness, unfolds through sensitivity, intelligence, rational reflection, responsible decision, only to find its rest beyond all of these' in love, then that tidal movement takes the place that previously was assigned to the 'natural dialectic' of 'progress.' And if this is the case, then that 'natural dialectic,' now identified with the 'deeper and more comprehensive principle,' the 'something richer and fuller' than intentional consciousness alone,[94] is dialectical precisely in the sense that I am appealing to in speaking of a dialectic of contraries.

Dialectic is a relatively a priori component in the heuristic structure of human science, when this science studies data that lie beyond those that are to be found within a single consciousness, whether in the relations between consciousness and the unconscious, or in the relations among different conscious subjects, or in the relations between conscious subjects and their historical milieu. 'Dialectic' functions in the study of these data much as the differential equation functions in classical physics: as the physicist anticipates that the correlation that will provide an explanatory account of the relations among sense data will be the solution of a differential equation, so the human scientist anticipates that the relations between consciousness and the unconscious, between different conscious subjects, and between conscious subjects and their milieu will be some realization of dialectic.

Note that with the notion of dialectic applied in this way we are inching toward some greater specification of the structure and constitution of collective responsibility, that is, toward something that would be more than simply the affirmation, regarded by Lonergan as unsatisfactory, that 'as [people] individually are responsible for the lives they lead, so collectively they must be responsible for the resultant situation.'[95] We will come closer still when we flesh out this discussion with a consideration of the scale of values.

3.5.5 Complicating the Scale of Values

Third, then, the same statement from 'Natural Right and Historical Mindedness' concerning the normative source of meaning in history can be applied to complicating and filling out the structure of the scale of values.

In *Theology and the Dialectics of History* I argued that the dialectical structure of the normative source of meaning has at least three realizations, and that these are intimately interrelated, while remaining distinct. There is a *dialectic of the subject,* where the respective poles are the censorship exercised by dramatically patterned intentional consciousness and imagination, on the one hand, and the neural demands that would reach a conscious integration in image and affect, on the other hand. There is a *dialectic of community,* where the respective poles are the practical intelligence responsible for technological innovations, economic systems, and the political and legal stratum of society, on the one hand, and the intersubjectivity that prepares the way for the function of the topmost operator, on the other hand. And there is a *dialectic of culturally constitutive patterns of meaning.*

Cosmological constitutive meaning finds the paradigm of order in cosmic rhythms, which are drawn upon to inform first the life of the community, and then the order of individual life. Anthropological constitutive meaning is based on the insight that the measure of integrity is world-transcendent, and that it orders first the life of the individual, and, through well-ordered individuals, the life of the community. The dialectics of the subject and of community are found in Lonergan (chapters 6 and 7 of *Insight*, respectively). The dialectic of culture is my own contribution, drawing on suggestions that I found in Eric Voegelin's work but taking these suggestions in directions that are different from those of Voegelin, who does not envision anything like a dialectic of contraries between these cultural meaning systems.

All of this is preparatory to the task of setting our increasingly more complicated structure in motion. That is done by specifying how the three dialectical processes of subject, culture, and social community are related to one another. The interrelations of the three dialectical processes can be understood by relating them to respective levels in the scale of values: the dialectic of the subject to the level of personal value, the dialectic of culture to the level of cultural values, and the dialectic of community to the level of social values. The interrelations of these three levels will then be by identity the interrelations of the three dialectical processes. These interrelations are determined by setting the complicated structure in motion. And this will give us an approximation to the notion of collective responsibility and to a theology of social grace.

3.5.6 Collective Responsibility and Social Grace

Fourth, with the complication of the scale of values that is introduced by pairing it with an analogy of dialectic at the levels of social, cultural, and personal value, the way is open both for a fuller account of the collective responsibility that was Lonergan's principal concern in 'Natural Right and Historical Mindedness' and for a new moment in the theology of grace, namely, a theological grounding of the notion of social grace or grace-filled social structures. It has barely been acknowledged that the principal impetus for a theology of social grace is provided by Lonergan himself in the final chapter of the systematic part of his *De Deo trino*, where 'the state of grace' is distinguished from 'the habit of grace,' and is identified as a social and intersubjective situation, where the subjects involved in the situation are the three divine subjects and a very widely inclusive community of human subjects, namely, all those who have said 'Yes,' either explicitly or implicitly, to God's offer of God's own love.

First, then, collective responsibility. Lonergan begins 'Natural Right and

Historical Mindedness' by commenting on the difficulty of the notion of collective responsibility and even more on the difficulty of ever achieving its reality. Still, he says, 'if collective responsibility is not yet an established fact, it may be a possibility. Further, it may be a possibility that we can realize. Finally, it may be a possibility that it is desirable to realize.'[96] His efforts to clarify the notion take the form of the conjunction of the notion of natural right and human historicity. If the complications of the basic structure that I have suggested here have any validity at all, they would represent contributions to the articulation of these two conjoined realities. And if that is the case, then perhaps we are closer to realizing an adequate account of collective responsibility.

I begin the chapter on the scale of values in *Theology and the Dialectics of History* by drawing on chapter 7 of *Insight* to posit a fivefold constitution of society: (1) intersubjective spontaneity, (2) technological institutions, (3) the economic system, (4) the political order, and (5) culture. Then, again with Lonergan, I distinguish culture into the two dimensions of the everyday set of meanings and values informing a given way of life, and the reflexive level arising from scientific, scholarly, philosophic, and theological understanding. The question then becomes, How are these elements related to one another? And I argue that the answer lies in developing Lonergan's notion of the scale of values, which I am here suggesting is a complication of the basic structure of the normative source of meaning in history.

The social, cultural, and personal levels of value, then, are immanently constituted as dialectics of contraries or 'natural dialectics': the dialectics, respectively, of community, culture, and the subject. Each is a dialectical finalistic tension of limitation and transcendence or going beyond. The foundation and prime analogate lies in the twofold dialectic of the subject. The dialectic of the subject is twofold in that there is a basic dialectic of consciousness in its entirety, psyche and intentionality, with the unconscious, and a derived dialectic within consciousness between the psychic and the spiritual dimensions of consciousness.

The following schema setting up the scale of values is somewhat different from that offered in the book (pp. 95–97), but it contains all of the essential elements of that schema and is simply another way of formulating it.

First, the spontaneous intersubjectivity that is one of the constitutive principles of the dialectic of community is also one of the five elements constitutive of society.

Second, practical intelligence, the other constitutive principle of the dialectic of community, is the source of three of the other constitutive elements of society: technology, the economic order, and the political and legal stratum of society.

Third, these three elements must be kept in a taut dialectical tension with spontaneous intersubjectivity: '[T]he essential logic of the distorted dialectic is a reversal. For *dialectic rests on the concrete unity of opposed principles*; the dominance of either principle results in a distortion, and the distortion both weakens the dominance and strengthens the opposed principle to restore an equilibrium.'[97]

Fourth, the integrity or distortion of this dialectic of community is a function proximately of the everyday level of culture, and remotely of the reflexive level of culture; and general bias is connected to a refusal to acknowledge the significance of the reflexive level for the well-being of the social order.

Fifth, spontaneous intersubjectivity, technology, economic relations, politics, and the everyday level of culture constitute the infrastructure of a healthy society, and the reflexive level of culture constitutes society's superstructure; and culture at both levels is the condition of the possibility of an integral dialectic of community.

Sixth, there is needed at the superstructural level an orientation that would take responsibility for the dialectic of community by attending to the integrity of cultural values at both the superstructural and the infrastructural levels. This orientation or mentality is what Lonergan calls cosmopolis.

Seventh, the foregoing can be expanded into a reflection on the relations that obtain among all the levels of value. The relations among the levels are isomorphic with those among the levels of consciousness. Moreover, from below, more basic levels are required for the emergence of higher levels, but they also set problems that only proportionate developments at the higher levels can solve; whereas from above, these proportionate developments are the condition of possibility of the appropriate schemes of recurrent events at the more basic levels. Thus while people cannot devote their energies to creating and maintaining a social order if they are starving, and so while the emergence and development of effective schemes of recurrence in the good of order rests on previous schemes of vital values, conversely the effective and recurrent distribution of vital goods to the whole community is a function of the social order, which in its integrity is constituted by the dialectic of spontaneous intersubjectivity and the practical intelligence that institutes technological, economic, and political structures. Next, while culture rises on the base of social institutions, the effective integrity of the dialectic of the social order is a direct function of the cultural values that inform the everyday life of the community, and these in turn depend on the superstructural level of scientific, scholarly, philosophic, and theological meaning. Third, while personal integrity emerges in the context of cultural traditions, still both dimensions of cultural value are a direct function of the integrity of persons in community. Fourth, while the religious development of the person builds on and perfects natural development, personal integrity is a direct function of God's grace, and natural development is incapable of sustained development without that grace.

The same scale is related also to dialectics of contradictories. '[J]ust as sensitivity can suffer a breakdown under the cumulative misinterpretation of experience, so the social schemes required for distributing vital goods can be responsible instead for the maldistribution of these goods. And as a reinterpretation of experience is required for the healing of the psyche, so new technological, economic, and political schemes are required for the redistribution of vital goods. Again, as a reinterpretation of experience requires a shift in one's meanings and values, so the new social schemes need new cultural values to inform and motivate their emergence and sustenance. Again, as the new meanings and values required for a reinterpretation of experience are a function of religious, moral, intellectual, and psychic conversion, so the new cultural values informing new social structures are a function of the conversion of persons as their originating values. Finally, as conversion is the work of grace in personal life, so too the originating values of authentic culture are God's instruments for the renewal of the face of the earth.'[98]

The heuristic structure of these relations of progress and decline includes the following: (1) the breakdown of the effective recurrence of events at the more basic levels provides problems that can be resolved only by emergent transformations at the more complex levels; and (2) the proportions of the problems at the more basic levels determine the range and efficacy that the more complex developments must achieve if they are truly to meet the problems. The dynamics are spelled out in the following paragraph from *Theology and the Dialectics of History*.

> From above, then, religious values condition the possibility of personal integrity; personal integrity conditions the possibility of authentic cultural values; at the reflexive level of culture, such integrity will promote an authentic superstructural collaboration that assumes responsibility for the integrity not only of scientific and scholarly disciplines, but even of everyday culture; cultural integrity at both levels conditions the possibility of a just social order; and a just social order conditions the possibility of the equitable distribution of vital goods. Conversely, problems in the effective and recurrent distribution of vital goods can be met only by a reversal of distortions in the social order; the proportions of the needed reversal are set by the scope and range of the real or potential maldistribution; the social change demands a transformation at the everyday level of culture

> proportionate to the dimensions of the social problem; this transformation frequently depends on reflexive theoretical and scientific developments at the superstructural level; new cultural values at both levels call for proportionate changes at the level of personal integrity; and these depend for their emergence, sustenance, and consistency on the religious development of the person.[99]

The integrity of the superstructure thus conditions the integrity of the infrastructure. The breakdown of infrastructural integrity calls for proportionate developments at the superstructural level of culture. While personal integrity and authentic religion in one sense stand beyond both infrastrucure and superstructure, they are essential to the integral functioning not only of a just society but also of the entire scale of values. A systematic theology that would integrate this view of history with the four-point theological hypothesis regarding created participations in the divine relations would articulate religious values precisely in terms of these participations.

There is an expansion of this basic structure in several directions, and the expansion is both a further complication of the structure and a further setting in motion. One implication is that, if the scale or proportion of the problems that exist at the more basic levels determines the extent of the changes that must take place at the more complex levels, then today, when the problem of the effective and equitable distribution of vital goods is global, so its solution must entail new technological, economic, and political structures that, while always local, form global networks, as well as commensurate intersubjective spontaneities and interpersonal relations. These socio-economic, political, and interpersonal relations in turn will depend on the generation of cultural values that in some sense are crosscultural (the dialectic of culture). The theoretical developments required to institute alternative technologies, economies, polities, and communities are a function of the superstructure of culture, where the refinement of the dialectic of culture can be elaborated and where particular communities can communicate and collaborate in the institution of social schemes that promote a just social order. Again, this dialectic of culture will depend on the appropriation of crosscultural psychic and intentional constituents of personal authenticity. And finally, such authenticity is itself dependent on the universal gift of God's grace, that is, on what Christians would call the universal mission of the Holy Spirit and what the systematic theology being proposed here would call created participations in the divine relations of active and passive spiration.

If this analysis is correct, then the kind of self-appropriation of the crosscultural constituents of personal integrity that Lonergan's work joined with psychic conversion makes possible is a culturally necessary form of self-transcendence at the present time. There is required on the part of a creative minority of subjects – and cultural leadership is always taken by a creative minority – the achievement of interiorly differentiated consciousness. There is also required something like a post-interiority mentality at the level of common sense, an attention to and recognition of the factors facilitating authentic progress on a transcultural basis. Moreover, the work of God's grace in our contemporary situation includes this movement to interiorly differentiated consciousness as an agent of a world-cultural network of alternative communities. We must look to the dialogue of world religions as a principal arena for the crosscultural generation of world-cultural values. And religion, to be authentic, must be concerned not only with personal transformation but also with cultural and social change, again in accord with the structure of the scale of values.

A key insistence of *Theology and the Dialectics of History*, and one that I believe is very much in keeping with Lonergan's own convictions, has to do with the significance of the cultural superstructure. The breakdown of everyday cultural values can often be reversed only by prolonged and difficult artistic, theoretical, scientific, philosophic, and theological work. The cultural values of a healthy society are constituted by the operative assumptions resulting from the pursuit of the transcendental objectives of the human spirit: of the beautiful in story and song, ritual and dance, art and literature; of the intelligible in science, scholarship, and common sense; of the true in philosophy and theology; and of the good in all questions regarding normativity. Such operative assumptions alone permit the subordination of practicality in the origination and development of capital and technology, the economy and the state, to the construction of the human world, of human relations, and of human subjects as works of art. These pursuits cultivate an interiority that maintains practicality in a creative tension with intersubjective spontaneity.

We can specify further relations within the structure (and so still one more complication of the structure) by focusing on the elements that constitute the infrastructure. What are the relations among technology, the economy, and politics when these practical elements are a function of integral praxis constituting the human world as a work of art? The answer lies in what Lonergan calls the political specialization of common sense. Legal and political institutions are an element, not of the superstructure, as Marx would maintain, but of the infrastructure, where they are to mediate between culture in its everyday dimension and the economic and technological institutions of a society, with a view to seeing that the latter are placed in dialectical relation with intersubjective interaction. While the specialization of intelligence or mentality that Lonergan calls cosmopolis mediates from the superstructural to the infrastructural level of culture, the mediation from the infrastructural level of culture to the economy, to capital formation, and to the intersubjective community is the responsibility of the political specialization of common sense. When the integral scale of values is neglected, the legal and political institutions slip out of the infrastructure and become the lowest rung of a mendacious superstructural edifice erected to preserve a distorted economic order in which intersubjective interaction in its autonomous capacity is overlooked and instead is twisted through group bias into becoming an ally of a practicality distorted by general bias. Politics should be the institution whereby the whole community can be persuaded by rational argument and symbolic example to exist and change in the tension of the opposites of vital spontaneity and practical ideation. What it becomes under the dominance of group bias allied with general bias is an instrument of the distortion of the dialectic of community through a displacement of that tension, a mendacious but quite public determinant of the meanings and values that inform the way of life of segments of the community rather than a mediator to economic institutions of meanings and values that flow from the pursuit of the transcendental objectives of the human spirit. Culture itself then becomes an instrument of distorted practicality, and the superstructure becomes a surd when the political invades its domain. As culture retreats, morality and religion follow suit: personal values are ignored or amputated, and religious values are either explicitly denied or twisted into supports for a distorted culture and society. The entire structure is upset by the derailment of the political, a derailment rooted in the loss of the tension of practicality and intersubjectivity that it is the responsibility of culture to inform and of politics to implement.

In Lonergan's terms practical intelligence *evokes* technology and capital formation, technology *evokes* the economy, and the economy *evokes* the polity. 'Evokes' suggests relations 'from below,' relations of differentiation and creativity. '[T]echnology arises and develops because of the recurrent intervention of practical intelligence to devise means to meet more readily the recurrent desires of the community for the particular goods that satisfy their vital needs. The recurrent interventions call forth a division of labor and an economic system ... for the sake of meeting the problems set by the distribution of the consumer goods emergent from the technological institutions ... The economy ... evokes the polity, for the sake of effective agreement on the integral unfolding of the dialectic of community ... [P]olitics meets the problems occasioned by the tension of the economic and technological orders with the intersubjective spontaneity of the groups who compose the society ... by giving each pole of the tension its due place in determining the unfolding history of the community. But when it displaces its function, politics becomes the instrument, not of the common good, but of one or other of the groups constituted by the economic order.'[100]

So much for the contribution that my efforts here might make to Lonergan's attempt to frame a notion of collective responsibility adequate for our time. I wish only to add a final note regarding the ulterior theological significance of this notion. If it is the case that the scale of values is a complication of the basic structure that fills out the notion of collective responsibility that Lonergan grounded in that structure, then it must also be maintained that the relation of vital, social, cultural, and personal values taken together to religious value must be isomorphic with the relation of experience, understanding, judgment, and decision taken together to grace: a relation of obediential potency. Our next task in the theology of grace, I suggest, is to relate this point to the constitution of a society that is ordered in accord with the scale of values. If I am correct on this point, then it may very well be that the considerations of the present chapter are circling around the starting point for the next development that must take place in the theology of grace, namely, developing a doctrine of social grace corresponding to the recent development of the theological doctrine of social sin. All I can do at this point is suggest the possibility of such a development and the lines along which fruitful exploration might be possible.

3.6 Systematic Theology as a Theory of History

I will now proceed in a very generic fashion to relate the developments here expressed to the six points in which Lonergan sets forth the dialectic of history in 'Natural Right and Historical Mindedness.'

The *first* of these points, again, is that technical, social, and cultural meaning develops and expands in human collaboration, and the *second* that these expansions occur on a succession of plateaus corresponding to *Method in Theology*'s three stages of meaning: the development of practical intelligence; the specialization of language and differentiation of consciousness in philosophy, mathematics, and science; and the turn to the operations whence all developments originate. The *third* point is that the third plateau has quite specific ideals of enlightenment and emancipation, defined respectively in terms of the advancing differentiation of consciousness and the cumulative processes constituting the ongoing conversion of the subject. The *fourth* point is that these ideals, to the extent that they are achieved, provide grounds for a genetic and dialectical retrieval of what our past has made us. The *fifth* point has to do with the ambiguities that survive when people do not advance to the context rendered possible once a given stage or plateau has been reached, or, in the third stage, when the basic clarifications of interiority differentiation have not yet taken hold. And the *sixth* point is the invitation to conversation amidst these ambiguities, where people reveal, before they appropriate, their native drive to understanding, reasonable judgment, fair evaluation, friendship, and love.

Amplifying Lonergan's *first* and *second* points, then, we can say that psychic conversion, in the explicit sense intended here, is a distinctly third-plateau series of events, complementing the intellectual conversion to which Lonergan's work beckons us. Amplifying his *third* point, we can say that on the third plateau itself psychic conversion contributes to the interiorly differentiated consciousness that, if and when shared in conversation and dialogue, can, ever so slowly, advance the enlightenment and emancipation demanded for a new maieutic of meaning. Amplifying his *fourth* point, we can say that psychic conversion can join intellectual conversion to become an aid to the further clarification of the first two plateaus on which human collaboration develops and expands meaning; more specifically, psychic conversion enables a retrieval of the elemental and symbolic manifestations of meaning in their genetic and dialectical relations to one another; thus in the articulation of the three dialectical processes, it reveals the source of the psychic, intersubjective, and cosmological poles of these processes, and in so doing joins intellectual conversion to form the twofold foundation of a dialectical self-appropriation needed for the further advance and expansion of meaning and for the self-conscious community fidelity to the integrity of the scale of values. All of this, of course, occurs within a horizon that is not only interiorly but also religiously differentiated, for the reception of God's gift of love is the radical source of historical integrity. Finally, amplifying Lonergan's *fifth* and *sixth* points, we can say that the ambiguities of the third plateau receive a further complication when people accept intellectual conversion but reject psychic conversion; these ambiguities reveal that further dialogue and conversation are required.

It is, then, in terms of history conceived (1) in terms of Lonergan's formulations of dialectic but also (2) with the addition of my own specifications, that I would attempt to elaborate a systematic understanding of transposed church doctrines, transposed theological doctrines, and the new theological doctrines that emerge from applying the functional specialties to contemporary situations. A systematic theology grounded in interiorly and religiously differentiated consciousness is to be a theology of history, where history is understood in these nuanced dialectical terms. We have now filled out what earlier we called the unified field structure of systematic theology by adding the basic categories of a theory of history to the four-point hypothesis that sublates the medieval theorem of the supernatural into the relation of four created supernatural realities to the four divine relations.

This option means concretely that the realities named in systematic theology by special categories – from the Trinity at the beginning to the theological understanding of the concrete structure of the church at the end – are to be understood in terms of or in relation to the dialectical process of history, its flourishing and breakdown, and the authentic and distorted relations among the diverse elements that constitute the process. The immanent intelligibility of historical process consists in the more or less integral or distorted functioning of, and relations among, the three dialectics of the subject, culture, and community, as these are open to religious values 'at the top' and to vital values 'from below.' My understanding of these dialectical processes is grounded in the notion of psychic conversion. The integrity of each dialectic is understood in terms of the tension or poised equilibrium of limitation and transcendence, integrator and operator, that in chapter 15 of *Insight* is presented as constituting the form or pattern of all authentic development.[101] I understand the normative relations among the three dialectics in accord with my analysis of the scale of values. The theological option that this analysis entails is to the effect that the principal special-categorial realities that will be treated in systematic theology will be understood in relation to these three dialectics, their flourishing and breakdown, and the authentic and distorted relations among them. The upshot of such an option is that systematic theology is a theology of history, where history will be understood as a function of the more or less integral or distorted dialectics of the subject, culture, and community, and where the relations among these dialectics are understood in terms of an analysis of the relations that should obtain among all of the levels of the scale of values. The latter analysis is itself a complication of the basic structure of the normative source of meaning in history.

4 Theology as Praxis

The fourth meaning of 'system and history' is suggested by Lonergan's expression 'theology as action.' There is a praxis component or, better, a praxis orientation to systematic theology. There is a relation to 'historical action,' to the 'data as produced,' that is the concern of communications. This component will be more pronounced in future systematic theologies than has been the case in the past. In particular, there is an insistence emergent from theologies of liberation on the preferential option for the poor in church ministry and in our retrieval of the gospel and the gospel's effective history in the tradition. It is an insistence that has already become part of the Catholic Church's official teaching, even though it has yet to be integrated with the most significant theological achievements of the Catholic tradition, past and present. Contemporary and future systematic theologies must be concerned with this integration, with the orientation of systematic theology not only toward the theological understanding of history but also toward the making of history through 'theology as action.'

The pitfalls of such an emphasis cannot be underestimated, but they must not lead the theologian to abandon the emphasis itself. Lonergan, perhaps unwittingly, provides the key to avoiding the pitfalls when he says, 'A theology mediates between a cultural matrix and the significance and role of a religion within that matrix,'[102] for the principal praxis issues for theology have to do with *culture* and *mediation.*

What is direct discourse in theology? Whether in doctrines or systematics or communications, direct discourse will be informed by and continuous with those achievements of the tradition that one judges genuine and that one wishes to carry forward. 'Foundations' as a distinct functional specialty names only part of the real foundations, for a major part is diagnosed by work in research, interpretation, history, and dialectic.[103] Anyone engaging in direct theological discourse must be always engaged as well in a continual *ressourcement.* But direct discourse is more than just continuing the effective history of the classic texts of the tradition, however permanent one may judge the significance of some contributions to be, and however much direct discourse will always partly be a matter of transposing that significance into contemporary contexts. To limit direct discourse to such a continuation of the tradition's effective history is to limit its mediating function to a self-mediation of Christian constitutive meaning, a mediation from revelation and tradition to the contemporary faith of the church. And that is only part of theology's mediating function. For contemporary contexts themselves are further theological sources. They give rise not only to questions that can at times be answered by transposing insights from the tradition, but also to the very insights that will develop the tradition and so become part of what we will hand on to those who come after us.

This means, as we have said, that Lonergan's statement about theology's task of mediation is best understood as referring at least in part to a *mutual self-mediation* of the historically constituted community of faith and its contemporary cultural contexts. The mutual self-mediation in question here results from an encounter and dialogue of persons with different horizons.

Horizons[104] can be related in complementary, genetic, or dialectical manners. Sometimes mutual self-mediation is explicitly dialectical, the reflection of mutual repudiation and negation. This can be for at least two reasons. First, the community of faith will always find itself in interchange with futile ways of life from which it must pray for its own liberation; and to the extent that it allows the prayer to be answered it can also always invite others to share in its freedom. Second, however, the church itself in its concrete practice will always stand under the judgment both from within and from without of women and men of intellectual, moral, religious, and affective integrity. Elements in the culture itself can occasion a conversion on the part of the church from biased and sinful elements in the horizon operative in ecclesial praxis. However much authenticity is in the last analysis a function of divine grace, it stands above and beyond church affiliations.

But mutual self-mediation can also reveal both a complementarity in horizons and genetic relations that go both ways. So the church will at times offer an advance on a line of development in a culture; and a culture will at times invite the community of faith to grow beyond immature, fearful, culturally relative, or undifferentiated stances.[105]

We have already emphasized that there is a doctrinal component in the methodological insistence that the mediation that theology performs is a mutual self-mediation between 'a cultural matrix and the significance and role of a religion within that matrix.' That doctrinal component has to do with the universality of the mission of the Holy Spirit. Christians ought not expect that the 'significance and role' of authentic Christianity within a cultural matrix is the only carrier of divine grace or human authenticity within that matrix. As authentic Christianity meets or interacts with a given cultural matrix, part of the drama that is going forward lies in the fact that the work of God embodied in a genuine Christian community and proclaimed in its explicit message is meeting up with the work of God already present in elements of the cultural matrix: present sometimes quite explicitly, at other times awaiting a more proper and more adequate expression and formulation, and at still other times operative even without any recognizable contribution from the church and its tradition. Failure on the part of the church to recognize the varieties of grace in history, the fact of the gift of the Holy Spirit beyond the boundaries of church affiliation, has resulted in some of the most conspicuous mistakes in the mission of the church throughout the course of Christian history. These mistakes continue into our own day.

In this book, then, I have built on the foundational effort that I published in 1990 as *Theology and the Dialectics of History*. There I attempted to set a context, objectify a horizon, and derive some of the principal categories, for a contemporary systematic theology, and so to meet at least some of the demands posed by Lonergan for work in the functional specialty 'foundations.' I relied on Lonergan's notions of intellectual, moral, and religious conversion, while adding my own explicit call for psychic conversion. I tried to highlight as well the social dimension of the conversion process that, among other things, honours liberation theology's option for the poor. But I emphasized a particular standpoint on the relation of cultural to social values that easily can be overlooked in liberation theologies. With earlier statements on psychic conversion Lonergan had indicated substantial agreement. The social emphases are based in part on Lonergan's explicit statements on culture and society and in part on reflection on the relations among the various levels of value in the scale of values that he proposes in *Method in Theology*. So I would claim, despite the novel additions, a fundamental continuity with Lonergan's intentions, a continuity that, in the case at least of psychic conversion, he explicitly affirmed.

This work in foundations was from the beginning oriented to systematic theology, and beyond systematics to communications. The functional specialty 'foundations' grounds direct theological discourse, discourse *in oratione recta,* discourse that does not so much report on history as make history: theological discourse on the level of one's own time, theology as itself a form of praxis, the praxis of constitutive meaning. And so 'foundations' has a set of ulterior purposes. A first is to enable one to select, transpose, and perhaps even propose for the first time the theological doctrines that one judges to be true. A second is to ground the construction of a systematic understanding of these doctrines. And a third is to aid church ministry in working out for concrete contexts the ultimate transpositions and implications of the judgments of fact and the judgments of value that one holds to be constitutive of the Christian community's existence and praxis.

Direct theological discourse on the level of one's own time, but in continuity with the genuine achievements of the tradition, thus imposes several strenuous demands on the theologian. One needs to have understood the tradition's contributions in their own contexts, through the appropriate exegetical and historical methods or in reliance on others familiar with these methods. One needs to have objectified a horizon for appreciating the permanent significance of many of these contributions and for transposing and developing them in ways that will be intelligible to one's contemporaries. One needs to derive requisite categories from that objectified horizon and to rely on that horizon for the appropriation of categories from the tradition. And one needs constantly to be alert to contemporary situations as a source not only of theological questions but also of insights not previously entertained in the tradition, or of better expressions of what perhaps is only inchoate in the tradition, expressions in which what may have been left in the realm of elemental or potential meaning can now be elevated to formal, actual, and constitutive meaning, and so, being spoken, can also be incorporated into the ongoing tradition of the community. My insistence on the permanent validity of two emphases of the theology of liberation – the preferential option for the poor and their privileged position in the interpretation of contemporary situations and ultimately of the tradition itself – provides one example of what I am talking about here. So does John Courtney Murray's doctrine on religious liberty. So, I hope, does the contribution that Lonergan's work in economics will make to the church's moral theology. Readers will no doubt supply their own contemporary examples of areas of church teaching and practice where similar endeavours are required and eventually will succeed. And theology's historical action lies partly here, in its function of mutual self-mediation between the religious tradition and the contemporary cultural matrix.

This fourth meaning of 'system and history' can be illuminated also from the standpoint of the analysis of the scale of values. To repeat what I said above (p. 178), in our current situation, in the situation that a contemporary systematic theology must address, the problem of the effective and equitable distribution of vital goods is global, and so its solution must call for new technological, economic, and political structures on a global scale, and for new visions of intersubjective and interpersonal flowering. Moreover, the socioeconomic relations and political realities, as well as the new interpersonal ethics, that could constitute a globally interdependent commonwealth, will call for the generation of cultural values that are themselves crosscultural. The culture that is adequate to the proportions of a globally interdependent technological, economic, and political order in dialectical relationship with a crosscultural intersubjectivity is at best emergent in our present situation, and the obstacles to its truly effective emergence and survival (some of them, unfortunately, working from within the church) are monumental in scope and power. A theology that would mediate in direct discourse between a cultural matrix and the significance and role of a religion within that matrix will be mediating what Christians believe as true and value as good, not with a relatively stable set of cultural meanings and values, but with an emergent set required to meet the exigencies of the present social order. More precisely, its mediation with prevailing cultural values will be for the sake of catalysing the emergence of a new set of cultural values, a set that itself is crossculturally generated. Systematic theology today will be contributing to the emergence of a new cultural matrix, in a fashion that can perhaps be considered axial or epochal. It will be forging some of the very materials of constitutive meaning required for the emergence of a legitimate alternative to the present situation.

We cannot shrink before the large challenge confronting systematic theology, however difficult it may be to meet it. It is already past time – one might even say three centuries past time[106] – to begin constructing a systematic theology in contexts set by modern and, now, postmodern developments.[107] The cultural context in which Scholasticism could provide an effective medium of communication between a situation and the significance of Christian faith in that situation is now long dead. Any intellectual integration analogous to that provided by the best of Scholasticism, but on the level of our times, must be largely heuristic and operational because grounded in a method that recognizes that theology is an ongoing development.[108] Yet the fact of *fides quaerens intellectum* has not been cancelled in the process. Lonergan offers part at least of the heuristic and operational ground for a new, open intellectual integration, and the work of constructing a contemporary systematic theology in fundamental accord with the method that he has left us, and with the inspiration behind it, has to begin.

Central to that work will be the responsibility of maintaining a continuity with the methodological insistence of the best of Scholasticism, and especially of Aquinas, on the interrelation in theology of general and special categories, and especially of the realities named by each set of categories. Lonergan's insistence on both sets of categories, presented in his chapter on foundations, and alluded to subsequently as he speaks of work in theological direct discourse, is entirely in continuity with Aquinas. It is true, of course, that the ground of each set of categories is now able to be differentiated, whereas Aquinas left that ground for the most part implicit. And it is true as well that especially the general categories, but the special categories as well, will now include far more than Aquinas, in his own intellectual context, could envision. All of science was for Aquinas and for several centuries after him entirely in continuity with, and a development upon, basic philosophical and especially metaphysical categories. Only in the early modern period did science become methodologically and materially independent of philosophy, and so only then did it begin to develop its own categories.[109] Of course, philosophical and metaphysical categories, including many of those which Aquinas inherited from Aristotle, will remain as general categories in a contemporary systematics constructed in line with Lonergan's inspiration; there will even be metaphysical equivalences drawn with scientific categories.[110] But Lonergan's book *Insight*, which is the principal guide to the derivation of the general categories, presents a general heuristic anticipation for the derivation and employment of properly scientific categories as well. Such derivation is ongoing, as my own book *Theology and the Dialectics of History* demonstrates, and as its chapter 19, on the ontology of meaning, tries to explain; and this is one of the principal reasons that systematic theology itself will continue to develop its understanding of the faith, its *intelligentia fidei*.

Finally, mutual self-mediation of a set of religious constitutive meanings with contemporary cultural matrices is not the only mediation that theology, even systematic theology, performs. If we are putting an emphasis on it, this is because, while the opening sentence of *Method in Theology* demands such an emphasis, the emphasis appears in the body of *Method in*

Theology only in the last chapter. The rest of the book highlights, not a mutual self-mediation of religion and culture, but primarily a self-mediation immanent to the Christian tradition itself. This self-mediation is an important task of theology, but it is not enough. Theology's mediating function includes more than a mediation between the data on revelation and tradition, on the one hand, and the contemporary faith of the church, on the other hand. Our insistence on expanding the notion of systematics beyond what appears in *Method in Theology* is directly dependent on the judgment that theology's mediation is more than a self-mediation of constitutive meaning from revelation to faith. It is also a mutual self-mediation with culture, in which the constitutive meaning itself of the faith community is constantly open to development, change, and refinement. The dogmas that it is the principal function of systematics to understand provide permanent parameters of such development, change, and refinement; but understanding them is not the only function of systematics, and it is crucially important to emphasize the other functions, if indeed systematics is responsible for more than a self-mediation from the primary sources and the rest of the tradition to the contemporary faith of the church.

5 Concluding Summary

If the complications of the basic structure that I have attempted here are correct, then the initial general categories are in place for work in the functional specialty 'systematics,' where the task is one of providing a theological synthesis in a theory of history. Those initial categories are constituted by an analogy of dialectic (subject, culture, and community) set in motion by the interrelations among the levels of value. Systematics, of course, is an ongoing process, and we can and should expect no more than a genetic sequence of systematic syntheses, where part of the development will come from advances in the theory of history itself. But at least one piece is sufficiently in place to enable us to begin, namely, the basic terms and relations of a theory of history. That much was provided in my earlier book, *Theology and the Dialectics of History.* The present work has attempted further definition regarding methodological questions in systematics, and has offered a more precise way of specifying the relation between the general categories of a theory of history and the special categories peculiar to theology. In that relation there lies a unified field structure for systematics. The theorem of the supernatural has been sublated into a four-point hypothesis that speaks of created participations in the Trinitarian relations, while the general categories are now derived from Lonergan's *Grund- und Gesamtwissenschaft* of cognitional theory, epistemology, metaphysics, and existential ethics. The four-point hypothesis is the central core of the realm of religious values, and the dimensions of personal, cultural, social, and vital values in their interrelation with one another stand in a relationship of obediential potency to the created participations in the Trinitarian relations that are articulated in the four-point hypothesis.

I conclude by repeating and amplifying a bit what was first introduced at the end of chapter 7. The recurrent intelligent emanation of the word of authentic value judgments and of acts of love in human consciousness (personal value) is due to the grace of the mission of the Holy Spirit (religious value) and is also the source of the making of history, of historical progress through schemes of recurrence in the realms of cultural, social, and vital values. But the mission of the Holy Spirit *is* the eternal procession of the Holy Spirit linked to a created, contingent external term that is the consequent condition of the procession being also a mission, or of the proceeding Holy Spirit also being sent. Thus the intelligent emanation in God of the Holy Spirit, the eternal procession in God of the Holy Spirit from the Father and the Son, joined to the created, contingent, consequent external terms that are sanctifying grace and the habit of charity, as well as to the operative movements that are known as *auxilium divinum* or actual grace – the eternal intelligent emanation of the Spirit in God from the Father and the Son as also their Gift in history – is the ultimate condition of possibility of any consistent or recurrent intelligent emanation of authentic judgments of value and schemes of recurrence rooted in acts of love in human beings. This collaboration of intelligent processions, divine and human, is the condition of the possibility of the consequent authentic performance of the normative source of meaning in history. And if such personal value conditions the possibility of functioning schemes of recurrence in the realms of cultural, and then social, and then vital values, if that normative source, functioning communally, is the origin of progress in history, then the mission of the Holy Spirit, which is identical with the eternal procession of the Spirit linked to the created, contingent, consequent term of charity, and so the Spirit as Gift of Father and Son, is the very source of progress in history. Conversely, wherever genuine progress (measured by fidelity to the scale of values) takes place, the Spirit of the Father and the Son is present and active. The combination of the four-point hypothesis with the theory of history thus enables us to relate Trinitarian theology, even the theology of the immanent Trinity, directly to the processes not only of individual sanctification but also of human historical unfolding. Not only is the discernment of the mission of the Holy Spirit in all its concrete details the most important ingredient in humankind's taking responsibility for the guidance of history, as we said above, but conversely, the appropriation of the integral scale of values, again as much as possible in all its concrete details, would represent the contribution of systematics to the church and to various local Christian communities in their communal discernment of the mission of the Holy Spirit. As the theology of a very recent generation disengaged in a new way the notion of social sin, so the theology of this generation, if it begins with the four-point hypothesis in the context of a theory of history, will elaborate the notion of social grace, or, to use Lonergan's own expression in the final chapter of the systematic part of his *De Deo trino,* the notion of the state of grace, not as an individual habit but as a social situation, as an intercommunion of the three divine subjects, one of them being the incarnate Word of God, with all of those who have said yes to the offer of a created participation in divine life and as the consequent intercommunion of these human subjects with one another in the incarnate Word.

Notes

Preface

1 Robert M. Doran, *Theology and the Dialectics of History* (Toronto: University of Toronto Press, 1990, 2001).

Chapter 1

1 See Robert M. Doran, 'The First Chapter of *De Deo Trino, Pars Systematica*: The Issues,' *Method: Journal of Lonergan Studies* 18:1 (2000) 27–48; '*Intelligentia Fidei* in *De Deo Trino, Pars Systematica*,' *Method: Journal of Lonergan Studies* 19:1 (2001) 35–83; and 'The Truth of Theological Understanding in *Divinarum Personarum* and *De Deo Trino, Pars Systematica*,' *Method: Journal of Lonergan Studies* 20:1 (2002) 33–75. I hope to follow up these articles with further studies along the same lines.
2 Ivo Coelho, *Hermeneutics and Method: A Study of the 'Universal Viewpoint' in Bernard Lonergan* (Toronto: University of Toronto Press, 2001). Attention must also be called to Matthew Ogilvie's fine study of Lonergan's notion of systematics, *Faith Seeking Understanding: The Functional Specialty 'Systematics' in Bernard Lonergan's* Method in Theology (Milwaukee: Marquette University Press, 2001).
3 Bernard Lonergan, *Method in Theology* (latest printing, Toronto: University of Toronto Press, 2000).
4 Many of these papers can be found in *A Third Collection*, ed. Frederick E. Crowe (Mahwah, NJ: Paulist Press, 1985). Others appear in volume 17 of Collected Works of Bernard Lonergan, *Philosophical and Theological Papers 1965–1980*, ed. Robert C. Croken and Robert M. Doran (Toronto: University of Toronto Press, 2004).

5 Bernard Lonergan, *De Deo trino, Pars systematica* (Rome: Gregorian University Press, 1964). The work is currently being translated and will be issued with Latin and English facing pages as volume 12 in Collected Works of Bernard Lonergan (Toronto: University of Toronto Press) with the title *The Triune God: Systematics.* It is scheduled for publication in 2006.

6 Bernard Lonergan, *Divinarum personarum conceptionem analogicam evolvit B. Lonergan, S.I.* (Rome: Gregorian University Press, 1957, 1959).

7 He can be felt almost 'groaning' toward this position in the reflections on 'wisdom' in the first section of the notes 'De intellectu et methodo' (1959). These will be issued in translation as part of volume 22 of Collected Works of Bernard Lonergan, *Early Works on Theological Method I.*

8 Lonergan, *Method in Theology* 162.

9 Ibid. xi.

Chapter 2

1 Unless I am mistaken, it is only in *Method in Theology* that the language of 'principal function,' which implies other functions, is used. In earlier writings, the understanding of the mysteries of faith would seem to be the *only* function that Lonergan acknowledges.

2 There is a curious bit of history here. In his Latin treatises Lonergan continues to employ the Aristotelian notion of science, *certa rerum per causas cognitio,* a certain knowledge of things through their causes. This is true even as late as 1964, in *De Deo trino, Pars systematica* 7 (which of course was originally published in 1957). Yet he had moved beyond such a notion even by the time of *Insight,* which he completed in 1953. See the contrast between emergent probability and the Aristotelian world view: Bernard Lonergan, *Insight: A Study of Human Understanding,* vol. 3 in Collected Works of Bernard Lonergan, ed. Frederick E. Crowe and Robert M. Doran (Toronto: University of Toronto Press, 1992) 151–52. And sharp contrasts between the Aristotelian and modern notions of science are drawn at least by the time of 'Dimensions of Meaning' in 1965 (in *Collection,* vol. 4 of Collected Works of Bernard Lonergan, ed. Frederick E. Crowe and Robert M. Doran [Toronto: University of Toronto Press] at 238–40). Prior to that, a more thorough treatment of the issue in relation to theology is found in the Latin notes 'De methodo theologiae' and the Regis lectures on method in 1962, and it may be that the nuances in that treatment explain the continued use of this phrase in the Latin systematic works. The classical notion of science provides perhaps the key element in Lonergan's interpretation of Aristotle, but it seems that Lonergan is doing more than interpreting Aristotle when he employs this notion of science in the Latin works; he seems to be affirming

the Aristotelian notion; and the two methodological works just cited state why, at least at this period, he believed there was something to be affirmed in this notion. But more work remains to be done on the issue of interpreting the development of his thought on the notion of science.

3 Lonergan, *Method in Theology* 336.

4 'The systematic investigation and presentation itself entails also a very specific understanding of truth, namely, *truth as coherence*, as the mutual agreement of all that is true.' Wolfhart Pannenberg, *Systematic Theology*, vol. 1, trans. Geoffrey W. Bromiley (Grand Rapids: Eerdmans, 1991) 21. '[C]oherence is ... the basic thing in the concept of truth. The aspect of judgment – correspondence of judgment and fact – and the consensus of those who judge are then a derived element in the concept of truth.' Ibid. 53.

5 Lonergan, *Method in Theology* 345.

6 See Bernard Lonergan, *De Deo trino, Pars systematica* 21–23.

7 As we will see shortly, Lonergan has a quite specific and determinate set of criteria for what can qualify as 'dogma.' Moreover, he made it abundantly clear that the areas of Trinity, Incarnation, and grace are areas in which the basic categories have been determined. Sacramental theology and the theology of the church, where the latter is intrinsically connected with a theory of history, were for Lonergan areas in which major developments remain to be done, even as regards the establishment of the basic categories. See below, p. 222, note 23.

8 Lonergan, *Method in Theology* 336.

9 Lonergan, *Method in Theology* 345–46. Aquinas speaks of the *ordo disciplinae* in the Prologue to the *Summa theologiae*, contrasting it with *librorum expositio* and with the more incidental treatment of issues dictated by a given *occasio disputandi*. The latter two procedures are examples of the 'roundabout' functioning of intelligence in the way of discovery.

10 See Lonergan, *De Deo trino, Pars systematica* 34. The first chapter of this work, sections 5 and 6, contains Lonergan's most complete presentation of the contrast between the two ways.

11 That question will be addressed below, especially in chapter 7.

12 Lonergan, *Method in Theology* 345.

13 Ibid. 346.

14 Ibid. 343. I have wondered whether a sentence on 'special basic relations' was omitted here. Lonergan's typescripts, available in the Lonergan archives in Toronto, do not reveal such a sentence. Curious! The four-point hypothesis that we will cite below from Lonergan offers a suggestion as to what at least some special basic relations would be: created participations in the divine relations of active spiration (paternity-filiation) and passive spiration.

15 The categories are treated ibid. 281–93.
16 The issues are most starkly drawn in Milbank's major work, *Theology and Social Theory* (London: Blackwell, 1993).
17 These exigences are treated in Lonergan, *Method in Theology* 82–83.
18 For Lonergan's critical appropriation of the so-called linguistic turn, see ibid. 254–57. It is not true that he did not take this turn. He took it and relativized it. He never took it in the fashion that is emphasized exclusively in Wittgenstein and his many followers and imitators, but in fact he had already accounted for one dimension in the linguistic turn in his 1946–49 articles on *verbum* in Aquinas. Again, the account differs from that of the Wittgensteinians, as original meaningfulness in language differs from ordinary meaningfulness. But more of this later. A valuable dialectical and systematic study is Michael Vertin, 'Transcendental Philosophy and Linguistic Philosophy,' *Method: Journal of Lonergan Studies* 19:2 (2001) 253–80.
19 Bernard Lonergan, *The Ontological and Psychological Constitution of Christ*, trans. Michael G. Shields, vol. 7 in Collected Works of Bernard Lonergan (Toronto: University of Toronto Press, 2002) 89, 91.
20 See especially Bernard Lonergan, *Philosophy of God, and Theology* (Philadelphia: Westminster, 1973).
21 See Lonergan's statement, 'The *via inventionis* would cover the first four or perhaps five previous specialties.' 'Christology Today: Methodological Reflections,' in *A Third Collection* 96, note 10.
22 Such questions are particularly significant, I think, when one is attempting to understand what someone like Pannenberg is up to. As I indicated above, there is almost no *ordo doctrinae* exposition in his *Systematic Theology*. For all practical purposes the entire work is written in the *ordo inventionis*. Many exegetical and historical investigations are pursued, but all of them for the sake of results that Pannenberg might call 'systematic' but that are better called 'dogmatic.' One does not get beyond a quite rudimentary sense of 'system' if one never moves to the *ordo doctrinae*.
23 I began to address the relationship of Lonergan and Balthasar in Robert M. Doran, 'Lonergan and Balthasar: Methodological Considerations,' *Theological Studies* 58:1 (March 1997) 61–84. There I was concerned principally with Balthasar's theological aesthetics.
24 'Theological Dramatic Theory' is the subtitle of the five-volume work by Hans Urs von Balthasar, *Theo-drama* (San Francisco: Ignatius Press, 1988–94).
25 Hans Urs von Balthasar, *Theo-drama*, vol. 2: *Dramatis Personae: Man in God*, trans. Graham Harrison (San Francisco: Ignatius Press, 1990).
26 Bermard Lonergan, *Grace and Freedom: Operative Grace in the Thought of St Thomas Aquinas*, vol. 1 in Collected Works of Bernard Lonergan, ed. Frederick E. Crowe and Robert M. Doran (Toronto: University of Toronto Press, 2000).

27 See Lonergan, *Insight* 610.
28 The comment occurs in Lonergan's 1957 lectures on existentialism. See Bernard Lonergan, *Phenomenology and Logic*, vol. 18 of Collected Works of Bernard Lonergan, ed. Philip J. McShane (Toronto: University of Toronto Press, 2001) 348.
29 See Lonergan, *De Deo trino, Pars systematica* 43.
30 See Lonergan, *The Ontological and Psychological Constitution of Christ* 79: 'The proper aim ... of speculative theology is so to understand the revealed word of God and so to formulate the "in respect to itself" that the same truth is clearly discernible amid cultural variations and in different periods in the past, and is more easily preserved for the future.'

Chapter 3

1 Lonergan, *Method in Theology* 322: '[T]he dogmas of DS 3020 and 3043 refer to the church's declarations of revealed mysteries.' Ibid. 323: 'The meaning of a dogma is not a datum but a truth. It is not a human truth but the revelation of a mystery hidden in God.' One reader of this manuscript asked whether I was not interpreting these passages too strictly. I was ready to qualify my interpretation a bit until I discovered the following statement in Lonergan's 1971 Dublin lectures on *Method in Theology*, which were delivered after he had completed the manuscript of the book. '[T]he dogmas that the Vatican I is talking about are truths revealed by God which human reason could not discover if they were not revealed.' This is taken from the typescript of these lectures prepared by Nicholas Graham.
2 With Lonergan we may distinguish primary sources, church doctrines, dogmas, theological doctrines enunciated in distinct traditions, methodological doctrine, and finally those theological doctrines that one selects by applying a methodological doctrine to the multiple choices presented in dialectical encounter with all of the above and with the situation that prevails in one's own cultural matrix. See Lonergan, *Method in Theology* 295–98, but relate these pages to considerations presented here.
3 Translated from Bernard Lonergan, *De Deo trino, Pars systematica* (Rome: Gregorian University, 1964) 234–35. The passage appeared originally in the 1957 version of the same material, *Divinarum personarum ...* at p. 214.
4 'On the third day he rose from the dead.' 'For us and for our salvation,' etc., etc., etc.
5 See Bernard Lonergan, *The Way to Nicea: The Dialectical Development of Trinitarian Theology*, trans. Conn O'Donovan (Philadelphia: Westminster Press, 1976) 47–48.
6 See Lonergan, *De Deo trino, Pars systematica* 21.
7 See Lonergan, *Insight*, § 1.6 ('The Notion of Mystery') of chapter 17. In this

context in *Insight*, of course, 'mystery' means precisely these dynamic images. But their necessity is grounded in the ontological sense of 'mystery' that we are using here.

8 Lonergan, *Insight* 570–71. Lonergan's language is often what we have since come to regard as exclusive language (e.g., 'man' in this quotation). I have no doubt that he would have changed his usage, but I have no intention of changing it for him. He will be quoted as he wrote.

9 Again, I refer the reader to my article 'Lonergan and Balthasar: Methodological Considerations,' *Theological Studies* 58:1 (March 1997) 61–84. There will of course be some differences; thus I say, 'more or less.' I owe to a discussion with Neil Ormerod the suggestion that Balthasar's contributions are in the area, not of the cognitive function of meaning (where he is weak), but of meaning's constitutive function.

10 Lonergan acknowledges the plurality of theologies of the redemption, as well as the permanent character of mystery in any legitimate theological treatment of it. See his lecture 'The Redemption,' in *Philosophical and Theological Papers 1958–1964*, ed. Robert C. Croken, Frederick E. Crowe, and Robert M. Doran (Toronto: University of Toronto Press, 1996) 3–28, esp. 24–28. Here 'mystery,' which is 'the fundamental category' for understanding redemption, is related to 'the secret counsel of God.' While Lonergan distinguishes mystery in this sense from mystery 'in the theologian's sense of a truth that we cannot adequately understand in this life' (ibid. 24), still all the mysteries of faith are truths that we cannot adequately understand in this life *because* they are realities hidden in God. The very reason that we cannot adequately understand them is precisely that they are hidden in the counsel of God. For Lonergan the clue to the intelligibility of the redemption lies in 'the victory of suffering, of accepting the consequences of sin, the evils of this world, in the spirit that animated Christ ... the transformation of the world that arises when evil is transformed into good by the Christian spirit' (ibid. 28). And that intelligibility is 'not a single but a multiple intelligibility. It is not something that is going to be fitted into some single formula, some neat reason' (ibid. 13). (In my own view, the work of René Girard can help theology find more adequate expressions of this intelligibility, even though Girard's work itself stands in need of at least some qualification.) Again, in *De Deo trino, Pars systematica* 21, Lonergan mentions the redemption as an example of a mystery of faith that has not received the kind of dogmatic formulation that Christological and Trinitarian affirmations have been accorded.

11 Lonergan, *Method in Theology* 312: 'In general, the meaning of these doctrines is not systematic but, commonly, it is post-systematic.' Ibid. 314: '[T]he ongoing context that runs from Nicea to the third council of Constantinople derives from the doctrines of the first three centuries of Christianity but

differs from them inasmuch as it employs a post-systematic mode of thought and expression.' Ibid. 278–79: '[T]here is theoretically differentiated consciousness. As already explained, there was a slight tincture of this in the Greek councils at Nicea, Ephesus, Chalcedon, Constantinople III.'

12 Bernard Lonergan, *De Verbo incarnato* (Rome: Gregorian University Press, 1964), thesis 17.

13 If I may offer a topical example, many of the controversies surrounding Mel Gibson's movie The Passion of the Christ had to do with the way Gibson told the story. For many, myself included, this was not an appropriate narrative of the redemptive act of the passion and death of the Incarnate Word of God. It was not the best way to tell the story. My suggestion is that we may not be able to do more with certain elements of the Christian mystery than refine the way we tell the story. But let me emphasize that this is a suggestion, nothing more.

14 Lonergan, *Method in Theology* 63, 67.

15 See ibid. 67.

16 Ibid. 63.

17 See ibid. 67.

18 Ibid. 329.

19 Hans Urs von Balthasar, *Seeing the Form*, vol. 1 in *The Glory of the Lord: A Theological Aesthetics*, trans. Erasmo Leiva-Merikakis (San Francisco: Ignatius Press, 1982), on the last of the unnumbered pages of the 'Foreword.'

20 Ibid. The emphasis is added, in order to indicate that Balthasar is expressing precisely what I am saying. The emphasized words coincide as well with Lonergan's emphasis on the permanence of mystery, and they bring out an essential aspect of the category of 'elemental meaning.' The 'one dimension more' is the incarnate meaning embodied in the deed itself. (Further developments of the notion of elemental meaning will be introduced later in this book. See below, pp. 128–33.)

21 Lonergan, *Method in Theology* 320.

22 On the ontology of meaning, see chapter 19 in Doran, *Theology and the Dialectics of History.*

23 Karl Barth is very clear on this when he takes on Bultmann's demythologization of the resurrection, at least as Barth understood this. Barth is correct in everything that he says in this particular regard. See Karl Barth, *Church Dogmatics*, III/2, 437–54. For a more recent scriptural study, see N.T. Wright, *The Resurrection of the Son of God* (Minneapolis: Fortress Press, 2003).

24 The most complete articulation of what I mean by psychic conversion is found in *Theology and the Dialectics of History* (Toronto: University of Toronto Press, 1990) chapters 2, 6–10 passim. A further development of the notion will be offered below, at pp. 124–40.

25 Lonergan, *Method in Theology* 343.

26 See Lonergan, *Grace and Freedom*, chapters I–3 and I–4.
27 Lonergan, *Insight* 756.
28 Ibid.
29 The problem of the conceptual objectification of elemental meaning is raised in other terms in my paper 'Primary Process and the "Spiritual Unconscious,"' chapter 15 in *Theological Foundations I: Intentionality and Psyche* (Milwaukee: Marquette University Press, 1995). The issue is approached again below, at pp. 124–33.
30 'The metaphysics of Thomas is ... the philosophical reflection of the free glory of the living God of the Bible and in this way the interior completion of ancient (and thus human) philosophy. It is a celebration of the reality of the real, of that all-embracing mystery of being which surpasses the powers of human thought, a mystery pregnant with the very mystery of God, a mystery in which creatures have access to participation in the reality of God, a mystery which in its nothingness and non-subsistence is shot through with the light of the freedom of the creative principle of unfathomable love.' Hans Urs von Balthasar, *The Glory of the Lord: A Theological Aesthetics*, vol. 4: *The Realm of Metaphysics in Antiquity*, ed. John Riches (San Francisco: Ignatius Press, 1989) 406–407.
31 On operators, see Lonergan, *Insight* 490–92; on questions as operators, ibid. 493–94.
32 Lonergan, 'Natural Right and Historical Mindedness,' in *A Third Collection* at 175.
33 Lonergan, 'Mission and the Spirit,' in *A Third Collection* at 29. The expressions 'tidal movement' and 'passionateness of being' are metaphysical, and so derived, rather than drawn directly from intentional consciousness itself, and so basic. They both refer to the operator 'in the general case,' that is, 'the upwardly directed dynamism of proportionate being that we [call] finality.' Lonergan, *Insight* 490. The grounding of these terms in intentionality analysis is rendered possible by the fact that the basic structure of conscious intentionality is 'open at both ends.' See Bernard Lonergan, 'Philosophy and the Religious Phenomenon,' in *Philosophical and Theological Papers 1965–1980*, vol. 17 in Collected Works of Bernard Lonergan, ed. Robert C. Croken and Robert M. Doran (Toronto: University of Toronto Press, 2004) 400.

Chapter 4

1 Lonergan, *Method in Theology* 132.
2 Ibid. 349.
3 Ibid. 298.
4 This is a very brief statement of some of the dynamics that Lonergan traces

in the chapter on doctrines. I will not treat the issue more thoroughly here, since my point is simply that among the doctrines affirmed in the sixth functional specialty and submitted to further scrutiny in the seventh are those that in the chapter on doctrines Lonergan calls theological doctrines.

5 See Lonergan, *De Deo trino, Pars systematica* 16–17.

6 These criteria can be complemented by some suggestions that Lonergan presents in *Divinarum personarum* 16 ('*Sexto ...*') regarding the sources from which theological hypotheses can acquire a certain measure of truth. Briefly, (1) such hypotheses can be supported by natural knowledge of God and of creatures, (2) they can be bolstered by being in harmony with what we know from revelation, and (3) the deductions that can be made from a hypothesis can be so strongly in agreement with what we know from these other sources that they lend strong support to the hypothesis itself.

7 For Lonergan's late, nuanced articulation of his relation to Aquinas, see 'Aquinas Today: Tradition and Innovation,' in *A Third Collection*, ed. Frederick E. Crowe (Mahwah, NJ: Paulist Press, 1985) 35–54. Just as illuminating is 'Horizons and Transpositions,' in *Philosophical and Theological Papers: 1965–1980*, vol. 17 in Collected Works of Bernard Lonergan, ed. Robert C. Croken and Robert M. Doran (Toronto: University of Toronto Press, 2004) 409–32. There Lonergan begins by distinguishing between deducing logical conclusions from Aquinas, which he is *not* doing, and transposing Thomist insights into a different horizon, which is precisely what he *is* doing. (Lonergan's original delivery of 'Horizons and Transpositions' is now available on audio cassette from the Lonergan Research Institute, Toronto.)

8 See Lonergan, *Grace and Freedom*, chapters I-6 and II-5.

9 See especially Bernard Lonergan, *De ente supernaturali: Supplementum schematicum*, ed. Frederick E. Crowe, Conn O'Donovan, and Giovanni Sala (Toronto: Regis College edition, 1973), in particular thesis 5. Just as pertinent is Lonergan's *De scientia atque voluntate Dei*, also available in a Regis College edition from the same editors. The latter work also contains one of Lonergan's earliest and most extensive presentations of the issues around contingent predication regarding God and the consequent created conditions of such predication. On this issue, see below, pp. 76–77. English translations of both of these works by Michael G. Shields are available at the Lonergan Research Institute, Toronto; these translations will eventually be published as part of the volume of the Collected Works on Lonergan's early Latin theology (currently anticipated as vol. 19).

10 On advancing positions (and reversing counterpositions) the *locus classicus* is Lonergan, *Insight* 413–15.

11 Bernard Lonergan, 'Christology Today: Methodological Reflections,' in *A Third Collection* 93–94. The bracketed additions are necessary if one is to speak of 'three.' Lonergan goes on briefly to spell out the Christological

implications, 'the possibility of a single divine identity being at once subject of divine consciousness and also subject of a human consciousness.' Ibid. 94.

12 Frederick E. Crowe, 'Complacency and Concern in the Thought of St. Thomas,' *Theological Studies* 20 (1959) 1–39, 198–230, 343–95; now available in Crowe, *Three Thomist Studies,* ed. Michael Vertin (supplementary volume of *Lonergan Workshop* 16 [2000]) 71–203.

13 For a serious, balanced, and insightful attempt to draw attention to this analogy in the context of contemporary Trinitarian theology, see Anne Hunt, 'Psychological Analogy and Paschal Mystery in Trinitarian Theology,' *Theological Studies* 59 (1998) 197–218.

14 See Lonergan, *Method in Theology* 122–23, 278, 283, 340–41; and note the following (edited) comments transcribed from a question-and-answer session in Boston in 1970: 'Theology in the phase of interiority ... speaks of being in love as distinct from acts of loving. That being in love, in terms of interiority, is equivalent to what sanctifying grace is in terms of theory. That being in love stands to acts of loving as God the Father, who is named *Ho theos* in the New Testament ... stands to the Holy Spirit, *to pneuma,* proceeding love. So being in love stands to acts of love, then, as the Father does to the Holy Spirit.' Being in love is prior to knowledge; acts of loving follow on knowledge. But that same being in love, as correlated with the divine mission of the Holy Spirit, flows, not from our knowledge and inner word, but from God's knowledge and eternal Word.

The same analogy is present in the passage from 'Christology Today' cited at note 11 above.

In fact, Lonergan's basic four-point systematic hypothesis, linking as it does the four divine relations and four created *entia supernaturalia,* seems to call for some further nuances beyond what can be gathered from this comment of Lonergan's. But more of that later.

15 I have spoken of Rahner's failure to grasp the analogy. Just as basic, though less harmful perhaps from a doctrinal point of view, is von Balthasar's neglect of the same points. He presents his own analogy, but it is not the analogy of nature that was desired by the First Vatican Council. It is rather an analogy drawn from within the mysteries of faith (the Paschal Mystery). It is legitimate and helpful, but it is not enough. And if such analogies are regarded as the only valid aids to theological understanding, we are right back into a variant of the Augustinian side in the medieval conflict of Augustinians and Aristotelians. The basic issue today, as then, is the question, Are general categories, categories shared with other disciplines and derived from them, possible and desirable in systematic theology? Balthasar's answer, I have no doubt, would be yes, but he provides little help in specifying the invariant basis of such categories. The type of analogy that he provides for the Trinitarian processions does fulfill Vatican I's prescription

to theologians to show the interconnection of the mysteries with one another; but it does not satisfy the same council's desire for analogies with what we know naturally. The more consistently one overlooks that exigence, the more one will restrict oneself to special categories in theology; and the more one so restricts oneself, the less will one's theology play the role of mediating between a cultural matrix and the significance and role of a religion within that matrix.

Balthasar, of course, goes a long way toward meeting these objections elsewhere in his theology, by reason of the aesthetic and dramatic analogies that he employs to understand central Christian mysteries. The point that I am making now is directed solely against his hesitations regarding the Thomist psychological analogy for understanding Trinitarian processions. Moreover, there is a further danger in bypassing the Thomist contribution to a theology of God, and it appears in Balthasar's inner-Trinitarian dramatics, where, it would seem, the possibility is left open that the processions of Son and Spirit are based in free divine decisions. On Thomist grounds, this would make Son and Spirit contingent realities, and so creatures. Needless to say, Balthasar does not want these implications, but there is no way of avoiding them on his basic presuppositions, unless those presuppositions are taken, not literally, but figuratively. What is so repugnant, existentially, about affirming that *ipsum esse subsistens* is from all eternity necessarily constituted as dynamic Agape-Understanding generating an infinite Judgment of Value, and the two spirating the proceeding Love that is the Holy Spirit? Nothing, except that it is difficult to understand unless one understands the analogue in created human consciousness.

16 Bernard Lonergan, *Understanding and Being*, vol. 5 in Collected Works of Bernard Lonergan, ed. Elizabeth A. Morelli and Mark D. Morelli (Toronto: University of Toronto Press, 1995) 19. The context is a reference to an article by Peter Hoenen in which it is claimed that very few Scholastic philosophers – Hoenen does not in fact specify 'seven' – acknowledge the fact that *intelligere* in the texts of St Thomas usually means 'to understand.' The article is 'De origine primorum principiorum scientiae, *Gregorianum* 14 (1933) 153–84.

17 Lonergan, *Understanding and Being* 19.

18 John Webster, 'Hermeneutics in Modern Theology: Some Doctrinal Reflections,' in *Scottish Journal of Theology* 51:3 (1998) 307–41, at 316.

19 See Robert M. Doran, *Subject and Psyche*, 2nd rev. ed. (Milwaukee: Marquette University Press, 1995) 109–24.

20 See below, pp. 78–79, 144–46.

21 See below, pp. 170–95, summarizing key points from *Theology and the Dialectics of History*.

22 See below, pp. 79–82. For details, see *Theology and the Dialectics of History*, chapter 19.

Chapter 5

1 See above, p. 215, note 9.
2 Lonergan, *Method in Theology* 343. For further and more detailed statements on the bases of the categories employed in theology, see ibid. 282–83.
3 '[T]he use of such analogies seems an extremely simple matter. In point of fact there is nothing more complicated and difficult than their first emergence.' Lonergan, *Grace and Freedom* 175.
4 See Robert M. Doran, 'Consciousness and Grace,' *Method: Journal of Lonergan Studies* 11 (Spring 1993) 51–75; 'Revisiting "Consciousness and Grace,"' *Method: Journal of Lonergan Studies* 13 (Fall 1995) 151–59; and '"Complacency and Concern" and a Basic Thesis on Grace,' *Lonergan Workshop* 13 (1997) 57–78.
5 See below, the section entitled 'Complicating the Structure,' beginning on p. 179.
6 See Doran, *Theology and the Dialectics of History*, chapter 4, and parts 3 and 4 passim. The basic statement on the scale of values is Lonergan, *Method in Theology* 31–32. For a summary statement, see below, pp. 171–72.
7 Contrast the position of Karl Barth, *Church Dogmatics* III/2 (Edinburgh: T. & T. Clark, 1960) 3–19 passim. At least regarding these comments it may also be said that Barth does not make an adequate distinction of systematics and doctrines, of understanding and judgment.
8 Regarding this refinement, see my *Psychic Conversion and Theological Foundations: Toward a Reorientation of the Human Sciences*, 2nd rev. ed., forthcoming (Milwaukee: Marquette University Press, 2006) passim.
9 *Theology and the Dialectics of History* offers such a grounding for liberation emphases, through a development of Lonergan's notion of the scale of values.
10 H. Daniel Monsour, 'Harmonious Continuation of the Actual Order of This Universe in God's Self-communication' (unpublished paper delivered at the Lonergan Research Institute Seminar, Toronto, 13 November 2003) 21. The paper is being readied for publication.
11 Monsour, 'Harmonious Continuation ...' 21, with phrases quoted from Lonergan, 'Finality, Love, Marriage,' *Collection* (CWL 4), ed. Frederick E. Crowe and Robert M. Doran (Toronto: University of Toronto Press, 1988) 22. On the five sets of special categories, see Lonergan, *Method in Theology* 290–91. These will be important again later in our discussion of the question of a unified field structure for systematics.
12 See Lonergan, *Insight* 763–64.
13 Monsour, 'Harmonious Continuation ...' 22.
14 Ibid. 23.
15 Ibid. 26.

16 Robert M. Doran, 'Lonergan and Balthasar: Methodological Considerations,' *Theological Studies* 58 (March 1997) 61–84.
17 See below, esp. pp. 179–95.

Chapter 6

1 See below, pp. 197–203.
2 Lonergan, *Method in Theology* xi.
3 Bernard Lonergan, 'The Mediation of Christ in Prayer,' in *Philosophical and Theological Papers 1958–1964* 160–82. Major influences that directed Lonergan to the notion of mediation were his study of the work of Jean Piaget in the spring and early summer of 1959, in preparation for his Cincinnati lectures on the philosophy of education, and his reading of Henri Niel, *De la Médiation dans la philosophie de Hegel* (Paris: Aubier, 1945).
4 Ibid. 162. In addition to the applications of the notion of mediated immediacy indicated in chapter 4 above, it would be interesting to attempt to relate Lonergan's notion of mediation to Karl Rahner's notion of symbol. Symbol as understood by Rahner might provide one instance of immediacy and mediation as these dynamics are understood by Lonergan. See Rahner, 'The Theology of the Symbol,' in *Theological Investigations*, vol. 4, trans. Kevin Smyth (New York: Crossroad, 1982) 221–52.
5 Lonergan, 'The Mediation of Christ in Prayer' 162.
6 Ibid. 168.
7 Ibid. 170.
8 Details on the two times of the temporal subject are provided in *De Deo trino, Pars systematica* 196–204, in a section on the analogy of the eternal and temporal subjects.
9 Lonergan, 'The Mediation of Christ in Prayer' 174–76. We might add that mutual self-mediation is the arena of drama emphasized by Balthasar. Drama requires and arises from the interplay of multiple freedoms, each in some way mediating the emergence of the other's own self-determination. Theo-drama entails the interplay of divine and human freedom, where again each in some way mediates the other's self-determination, though the theological explanation of this is complex: as Lonergan is reported to have said in response to the question, Do we make any difference to God? 'We make an eternal difference to God.'
10 See Lonergan, *Phenomenology and Logic* 302. Essentially the same definition appears in the notes that Lonergan distributed for these lectures. See ibid. 209–10.
11 Lonergan does distinguish a mediating and a mediated phase in theology. The first phase (research, interpretation, history, and dialectic) mediates from the past into the present. The second phase (foundations, doctrines,

systematics, and communications) expresses the results of that mediation on the level of one's own time. My present point is, however, that in either phase there is involved more than a self-mediation of Christian constitutive meaning, and more than the simple mediation of that meaning to the cultural matrix. There is involved also the mutual self-mediation between that constitutive meaning in its present form and the meanings and values constitutive of particular cultural matrices, whether past (first phase) or present (second phase). Let me add, though, that this statement, with regard to the first phase, must be carefully nuanced. The mutual self-mediation that occurs in the first phase might involve contemporary acknowledgment of past neglect on the part of the church. Or it might entail the sort of conflicts in interpretation and history that are brought to the table in dialectic; contrast, for example, Barth and Bultmann on the resurrection. In either case, the aspect of mutual self-mediation emerges in dialectic; it cannot be allowed to control the methods or results of interpretation and history, whose questions, respectively, are simply, What did so-and-so mean? and, What was going forward? The evaluative aspect of mutual self-mediation becomes explicit only in dialectic.

The further question regarding the type of mediation that allows us to speak in the first place of a mediating and a mediated phase will be treated shortly.

12 David L. Fleming, S.J., *The Spiritual Exercises of St. Ignatius: A Literal Translation and A Contemporary Reading* (St Louis: The Institute of Jesuit Sources, 1978) 20, § 22.

13 See below, pp. 170–79 and 180–82.

Chapter 7

1 See Lonergan, *De Deo trino, Pars systematica* 21–23.

2 On the scissors metaphor, see Lonergan, *Insight*, index: Heuristic method, scissors action of.

3 I draw here on two papers by Monsour: 'The Categories "Gratia Increata et Creata" and the Functional Specialty Systematics,' presented for discussion at a Lonergan Research Institute Graduate Seminar, Toronto, 18 November 1999, and 'The Four-point Hypothesis and the Special Theological Categories,' delivered at the Lonergan Workshop, Boston College, June 2001, and to be published in the proceedings of that workshop.

4 The most complete discussion of the dogmatic-theological context occurs in the 1962 lectures on 'The Method of Theology' delivered at Regis College, Toronto. These are now available in audio form, as Lonergan delivered them, on compact disc from the Lonergan Research Institute. A written transcription will form part of volume 22 of Lonergan's Collected Works, *Early Works on Theological Method I.*

5 Lonergan, *Method in Theology* 241.
6 Ibid. 310.
7 The theological elaboration of this hypothesis and its transposition into the terms and relations of intentional and nonintentional consciousness will be the core of the first volume in the systematics that I hope to write next.
8 See Lonergan, *Insight* 747.
9 Translated from Lonergan, *De Deo trino, Pars systematica* (Rome: Gregorian University Press, 1964) 234–35.
10 Henri Rondet, *The Grace of Christ: A Brief History of the Theology of Grace*, trans. Tad W. Guzie (Westminster, MD: Newman Press, 1967).
11 'Scheeben was a man who certainly got hold of a large number of fertile ideas in theology that are still exerting an influence and fructifying in the field, but his theoretical expression of his findings, such as the quasi formal causality by which the Holy Ghost inhabits the soul, runs into endless theoretical difficulties.' Bernard Lonergan, in lecture 3 of the 1962 institute on 'The Method of Theology.'
12 See Rahner's famous and important early paper 'Some Implications of the Scholastic Concept of Uncreated Grace,' in *Theological Investigations*, vol. 1, trans. Cornelius Ernst (London: Darton, Longman & Todd, 1961) 319–46.
13 References to specific page numbers in each paper will be given in the text, as the '(3)' here.
14 I believe Monsour is more insistent on the heuristic rather than logical role of systematic conceptions than Lonergan himself was when he wrote the first chapter of *De Deo trino, Pars systematica*, from which Monsour is drawing the notion. In the section of that chapter where he discusses these notions Lonergan is very attracted by a logical ideal. In my interpretation of that chapter he is still coming to grips with the logical ideals that he scrutinized in preparation for his 1957 lectures on mathematic logic at Boston College, now published as Part 1 of volume 18 in his Collected Works, *Phenomenology and Logic*.
15 See Bernard Lonergan, *The Ontological and Psychological Constitution of Christ*, vol. 7 in Collected Works of Bernard Lonergan, trans. Michael G. Shields (Toronto: University of Toronto Press, 2002) 76–105.
16 Actually, I think the categories are worked out *ambulando*, that is, while one is doing systematics (or any other functional specialty): one returns to foundations, that is, to one's own self-appropriation, for the grounds of the categories as they are needed.
17 Bernard Lonergan, 'Questionnaire on Philosophy: Response,' in *Philosophical and Theological Papers 1965–1980* (see above, p. 207, note 4) 359–60.
18 Lonergan, *Method in Theology* 290.
19 Ibid. 291, emphasis added.
20 Ibid.
21 Ibid.

22 Ibid.

23 In a discussion period at the 1962 Institute at Regis College, Toronto, on 'The Method of Theology,' Lonergan expressed a conviction that the sacraments and the church are two areas in systematic theology in which an enormous amount of work needs to be done. In fact, he said, there is needed even doctrinal development in these areas. 'The fundamental developments are: the trinitarian doctrine in which the key element is the consubstantial; christological doctrine: one person and two natures; the idea of the supernatural, habit and act. There is then the field in which the categories are not yet fully developed. For example, categories as to the instrumental causality of the sacraments; they have to be developed more fully. There is also *everything regarding history and the mystical body, and the church*; all these need further development.' (Emphasis added.)

24 Robert M. Doran, 'Bernard Lonergan and the Functions of Systematic Theology,' *Theological Studies* 59:4 (1998) 569–607; 'System and History: The Challenge to Catholic Systematic Theology,' *Theological Studies* 60 (1999) 652–78; and 'Reflections on Method in Systematic Theology,' *Lonergan Workshop* 17 (2002) 23–51.

25 Lonergan, *Method in Theology* 343. Two comments must be made on this passage. First, as I mentioned above (see p. 209, note 14) it does not mention 'special basic relations.' I would like to raise the question whether the four-point hypothesis provides a clue as to where we might find special basic relations. The relation between sanctifying grace and charity as created participations, respectively, of active and passive spiration might be the source of special basic relations.

Second – and this is related to the first point – the 'corresponding element' that identifies the basic term or relation may be found either in intentional consciousness, as Lonergan says, or in nonintentional consciousness, as is the case in what St Ignatius Loyola calls 'consolation without a cause' as interpreted by Karl Rahner and Lonergan as consolation with a content but without an apprehended object. A conscious state that is not a response to an apprehended object is, at least in its initial moment, nonintentional. Ignatius even saw the difficulties that arise when it shifts into the realm of the intentional, difficulties that in no way detract from the value of the experience but that must be monitored carefully by the discerning subject.

26 See Bernard Lonergan, 'Natural Right and Historical Mindedness,' *A Third Collection*, ed. Frederick E. Crowe (Mahwah, NJ: Paulist Press, 1985) 169–83.

27 More will be presented in chapter 10 below regarding systematics as a theological theory of history.

Chapter 8

1 See below, pp. 144–49 for an expansion on the first two of these anticipations.
2 A wonderful statement of such integration is Lonergan's 'Natural Right and Historical Mindedness,' in *A Third Collection* 169–83.
3 Lonergan, *Divinarum personarum* 19.
4 Ibid.
5 In several articles in *Method: Journal of Lonergan Studies,* I study the relations between the two versions of the first chapter of Lonergan's systematic work on the Trinity. See above, p. 207, note 1.
6 Lonergan, *Method in Theology* 172–73.
7 Yves M.-J. Congar, *A History of Theology,* trans. and ed. Hunter Guthrie (New York: Doubleday, 1968) 84.
8 For an interpretation of one instance of such integration, see Lonergan's 'Introduction: Subject and Soul,' in *Verbum.*
9 If I may repeat something that Lonergan once said as he was heading to give a lecture: 'They asked me to speak about the demise of Thomism. I had a mind to say that we are marking its seventh centenary!'
10 See chapter II-1 of the Collected Works edition of *Grace and Freedom.* This is the first chapter of Lonergan's doctoral dissertation. In this chapter Lonergan is proposing one example or model (his claim, in fact, is much stronger than this) of the kind of explanatory history that I mentioned above.
11 Bernard Lonergan, 'Method in Catholic Theology,' in *Philosophical and Theological Papers: 1958–1964* 44. See also Lonergan, *Grace and Freedom,* chapter 1. In a moment I will speak of the potential complementarity of Lonergan and Hans Urs von Balthasar. A number of questions remain, however. One of them has to do with the notion of freedom. It may be asked whether Balthasar appreciates the seriousness of the methodological issue in medieval theology that this question exhibits. He presents a different and far more positive reading of Anselm's position on freedom in his chapter on Anselm in *The Glory of the Lord: A Theological Aesthetics* 2: *Studies in Theological Styles: Clerical Styles* (San Francisco: Ignatius Press, 1988). See also the comment on Anselm (in the context of a discussion of Boethius) in vol. 4 of the same work, *The Realm of Metaphysics in Antiquity* (San Francisco: Ignatius Press, 1989) 328. Within the total problematic of grace and freedom, Anselm's definition of freedom is incoherent. He is speaking psychologically of freedom as a quality of graced habits. What was required but had yet to emerge, Lonergan emphasizes, was a philosophical doctrine of freedom as a natural potency. Anselm's emphasis left anomalous certain aspects of the relation of human freedom with divine grace. Only with Philip's discovery of the theorem of the

supernatural was speculation on nature itself set free to make a purely philosophical analysis of freedom. Anselm's theological emphasis (rooted in Augustine) on a freedom that is an ease of good action is, surely, a valid emphasis; but it could not solve some of the problems on which it was brought to bear. It is integrated by Aquinas when the 'specific theorem' on grace that derives from Augustine is finally coordinated with the 'generic theorem' released by the theorem of the supernatural. The result is Aquinas's position on moral impotence and the liberation effected by grace, a position of which Lonergan makes capital again in chapter 18 of *Insight.*

12 Lonergan, *Method in Theology* 288–91.
13 Lonergan, 'Method in Catholic Theology' 45–46.
14 Bernard Lonergan, *Topics in Education,* ed. Robert M. Doran and Frederick E. Crowe, vol. 10 in Collected Works of Bernard Lonergan (Toronto: University of Toronto Press, 1993) 242.
15 It is interesting to note that all three of these achievements, at least in the form that I am emphasizing, came into prominence only after the Second Vatican Council. None of them was a formative influence on the Council itself. Two of the figures whom I am singling out (Balthasar and Lonergan) had already done a great deal of their work by the time the Council began and were later named by Pope Paul VI as original members of the International Theological Commission. But neither of them nor any theologian of liberation played a prominent role at the Council. Lonergan was officially a *peritus,* but he remained very much in the background. As hard as it may be to fathom, Balthasar was not even invited to the Council, despite the enormous contributions that he had already made to theology and to the church.
16 For a clear statement of the differences between Lonergan and Kant, see Giovanni B. Sala, *Lonergan and Kant: Five Essays on Human Knowledge,* trans. Joseph Spoerl, ed. Robert M. Doran (Toronto: University of Toronto Press, 1994). Chapter 1 is sufficient to establish the present point.
17 Robert M. Doran, 'Lonergan and Balthasar: Methodological Considerations,' in *Theological Studies* 58:1 (1997) 61–84.
18 There remain emphases, however, in Balthasar's notion of freedom *in* God, *in* the Trinitarian processions themselves, that will need clarification and, possibly, correction.

Chapter 9

1 Lonergan mentioned the contribution of psychic conversion as one indication of the openness of the method to further refinement. See especially 'Questionnaire on Philosophy,' in *Philosophical and Theological Papers 1965–1980* 381.

2 For the latter point, see Bernard Lonergan, 'Philosophy and the Religious Phenomenon,' *Philosophical and Theological Papers 1965–1980* 400.
3 Lonergan, *Method in Theology* 6.
4 To be exact, more is required than simply appealing to this distinction. What is required is precisely the self-appropriation to which Lonergan invites one. In particular, what will prove decisive, I believe, is Lonergan's distinction between consciousness as experience and consciousness as perception. The 'foundations' that are criticized by anti-foundationalist literature are, I wager, all based on an at least implicit assumption that consciousness is some sort of perception of self. Related to this, I think, is the fact that anti-foundationalism is as wedded to conceptualism as are the varieties of 'foundationalism' that it attacks. The difference is that it has despaired of conceptualism and, at least in many instances, sees no alternative but a fairly thoroughgoing relativism.
5 See Lonergan, *Method in Theology* 110.
6 See Thomas G. Dalzell, 'Lack of Social Drama in Balthasar's Theological Dramatics,' *Theological Studies* 60:3 (1999) 457–75.
7 'Nor in the last resort can one reach a deeper foundation than that pragmatic engagement.' Lonergan, *Insight* 356.
8 Ibid. 412.
9 Ibid. 424–25.
10 See Lonergan, *Philosophy of God, and Theology* (see above, p. 210, note 20) 12.
11 These notes have been translated by Michael Shields and will appear as part of volume 22 in Collected Works of Bernard Lonergan, *Early Works on Theological Method I.*
12 Lonergan, *Method in Theology* 305, emphasis added.
13 Ibid. 282.
14 Ibid. 285–86.
15 Ibid. 303.
16 Ibid. 282.
17 Ibid. 289.
18 See ibid. 290.
19 Ibid. 343.
20 See the section above, pp. 76–77, on the further implications of the proposed unified field structure. And see below on the social doctrine of grace.
21 Lonergan, *Method in Theology* 285.
22 Ibid.
23 Ibid. 343.
24 Ibid. 287.
25 Lonergan, *Insight* 457.
26 On the latter theme, see my efforts in *Psychic Conversion and Theological Foundations: Toward a Reorientation of the Human Sciences*; see above, p. 218, note 8.

27 See below, pp. 195, 204.
28 Lonergan, *Method in Theology* 287.
29 '[W]hat in a philosophic context I have named being in love in an unrestricted manner, in a theological context could be paralleled with Karl Rahner's supernatural existential.' Lonergan, 'Philosophy and the Religious Phenomenon' 402.
30 See Bernard Lonergan, 'Christology Today,' in *A Third Collection* 93–94.
31 Lonergan, *Method in Theology* 338.
32 Ibid. 340.
33 Ibid. 132.
34 Ibid. 336.
35 Ibid. 340.
36 Ibid. 341.
37 See below, pp. 123, 187–203.
38 See below, pp. 125–26, where I will argue that perhaps it is best that the level of consciousness that we have been calling 'experience' is better named 'reception.'
39 The expressions 'procession of an operation' and 'procession of a product' are attempts to render the Latin phrases 'processio operationis' and 'processio operati,' respectively. 'Processio operationis' is the emergence of act from potency, 'processio operati' the emergence of act from act. See Bernard Lonergan, *Verbum: Word and Idea in Aquinas,* vol. 2 in Collected Works of Bernard Lonergan, ed. Frederick E. Crowe and Robert M. Doran, chapter 3 passim.
40 This is the central point of my book *Psychic Conversion and Theological Foundations* (see above, p. 218, note 8).
41 Bernard Lonergan, '*Insight* Revisited,' in *A Second Collection,* ed. Bernard J. Tyrrell and William F.J. Ryan (London: Darton, Longman & Todd, and Philadelphia: Westminster, 1974; latest reprint, Toronto: University of Toronto Press, 1996) 277.
42 Ignatius Loyola, *Spiritual Exercises,* trans. Henry Keane, S.J. (London: Burns, Oates, and Washbourne, 1952) 61–62.
43 See Eric Voegelin, 'The Gospel and Culture,' in *Jesus and Man's Hope,* ed. D.C. Miller and D.Y. Hadidian (Pittsburgh: Pittsburgh Theological Seminary, 1961) passim.
44 Bernard Lonergan, 'Religious Knowledge,' in *A Third Collection* 144.
45 See above, pp. 35–36.
46 'It is of the nature of love that it does not proceed except from a conception of the intellect.' Thomas Aquinas, *Summa theologiae,* 1, q. 27, a. 3, ad 3m.
47 Lonergan, *Method in Theology* 122–23.
48 Bernard Lonergan, 'Mission and the Spirit,' in *A Third Collection* 23.
49 Robert M. Doran, *Theology and the Dialectics of History,* chapters 8 and 9.

50 Lonergan, *Insight* 555.
51 For a more complete argument on the relevance to psychic conversion of the distinction of consciousness and knowledge, see chapter 3 of *Theology and the Dialectics of History*. On the permanent distinction of the two dimensions of consciousness, Lonergan says elsewhere: 'We are conscious in a twofold way: in sense consciousness we are more passive, as we undergo sensations and images, desires and fears, delights and sorrows, joys and sadness; in intellectual consciousness we are more active, as we inquire in order to understand, understand in order to speak, weigh evidence in order to judge, take counsel in order to decide, will in order to act.' Translated from Lonergan, *De Deo trino 2: Pars systematica* (Rome: Gregorian University Press, 1964) 71–72. *Insight*'s principle of correspondence would harmonize these two dimensions of consciousness in a permanent dialectical tension that I will call a dialectic of contraries (rather than a dialectic of contradictories). And let us note the passive element in 'intellectual consciousness' as well, something highlighted perhaps better in *Verbum* than in *Insight. Intelligere est pati.* And see below, pp. 124–43, where recent developments in my thinking on psychic conversion open upon new dimensions precisely with regard to what is received in empirical consciousness.
52 On conversion to phantasm as a natural orientation, see Lonergan, *Verbum* 171–72.
53 Lonergan, *Insight* 556.
54 Bernard Lonergan, 'The Subject,' in *A Second Collection* 83.
55 The addition of 'received meanings and values' to this inventory of empirical consciousness marks the recent development in my thinking to which I have referred several times. I will argue for it below, pp. 124–43.
56 See Lonergan, *Insight* 646–47.
57 Lonergan, *Philosophy of God, and Theology* 38.
58 See chapter 4 in *Subject and Psyche.*
59 Lonergan, 'Mission and the Spirit,' *A Third Collection* 29–30, emphasis added.
60 Lonergan, 'Natural Right and Historical Mindedness,' *A Third Collection* 175, emphasis added.
61 Bernard Lonergan, 'Philosophy and the Religious Phenomenon' 400.
62 Ibid. 401–402.
63 Lonergan, *Insight* 225.
64 See Robert M. Doran, 'Aesthetics and the Opposites,' chapter 4 in *Theological Foundations*, vol. 1: *Intentionality and Psyche.* This paper appeared originally in *Thought* (1977) 117–30.
65 Lonergan, *Insight* 225.
66 1 John 4.16.
67 For a series of extremely practical exercises oriented to such identification and negotiation, see Eugene T. Gendlin, *Focusing* (New York: Everest House,

1978). Lonergan was very affirmative of Gendlin's work, and in fact he gave me a copy of this book. I used Gendlin's earlier work *Experiencing and the Creation of Meaning* (Toronto: Free Press of Glencoe, 1962) in my doctoral dissertation, *Subject and Psyche.*

68 Lonergan, *Method in Theology* 33.

69 Ibid. 273. The work of René Girard develops the notion of *ressentiment.*

70 For one expression of such an objection, see Michael Vertin, 'Lonergan on Consciousness: Is There a Fifth Level?' *Method: Journal of Lonergan Studies* 12:1 (1994) 16: '[T]he existence of exactly four levels of conscious intentional operations, together with the fact of two basic phases in any discipline that studies the past and takes a stand on the present, means that there are exactly eight functional specialties in theology and, more broadly, in scholarly human studies.'

71 See Robert M. Doran, 'Primary Process and the "Spiritual Unconscious,"' chapter 15 in *Theological Foundations,* vol. 1: *Intentionality and Psyche.*

72 As we will see in the next chapter, this something more finds its systematic place in Lonergan's notion of the dialectic of history, where history is understood in terms of progress, decline, and redemption.

73 See Lonergan, *Insight* 745.

74 Ibid. 721.

75 Ibid.

76 Ibid. 724.

77 Ibid. 723.

78 See Lonergan, *Method in Theology* 116. For more on faith as knowledge born of religious love, see ibid. 116–18. On religious beliefs, see ibid. 118–19.

79 Lonergan once spoke in an aside of 'the flowering of eros into agape.' That is what I mean by affective conversion. It is the cumulative product of the entire conversion process.

80 Lonergan, *Insight* 744–45, emphasis added.

81 Ibid. 763.

82 Ibid. 585.

83 See the 'Editorial Symposium' in *Horizons* 16:2 (1989) 316–52, and especially the contribution of Fred Lawrence, 'On the Relationship between Transcendental and Hermeneutical Approaches to Theology' 342–45. See also Donna Teevan, *Lonergan, Hermeneutics, and Theological Method* (Milwaukee: Marquette University Press, 2005).

84 On psychic conversion and hermeneutics, see my paper 'Psychic Conversion and Lonergan's Hermeneutics,' in *Lonergan's Hermeneutics: Its Development and Application,* ed. Sean E. McEvenue and Ben F. Meyer (Washington: Catholic University of America Press, 1989) 161–208, reprinted in *Theological Foundations,* vol. 2, *Theology and Culture,* chapter 14. See also chapter 20 of *Theology and the Dialectics of History.* And see the developments discussed below, pp. 124–43.

85 See Avery Dulles, *Models of Revelation* (New York: Doubleday, 1985) 131–54.
86 Lonergan, *Insight* 610.
87 I cannot repeat here the argument of *Theology and the Dialectics of History*, but on the present point see especially chapter 8 of that book.
88 Lonergan, *Insight* 255.
89 This section is based upon a paper that I prepared for the 2003 Lonergan Workshop at Boston College, 'Reception and Elemental Meaning: Expanding the Notion of Psychic Conversion.' The paper was the subject also of a Faculty / Advanced Degree Seminar at Regis College in January 2004, and has been published in *Toronto Journal of Theology* (2005).
90 See above, p. 213, note 19. Note that 'Gestalt' here is an aesthetic term. It does not mean 'form' in the sense of a metaphysical element, even though it is not unrelated to such a discussion – after all, von Balthasar did include two volumes on metaphysics precisely in his theological aesthetics, and 'Gestalt' does convey in part the notion of intelligibility.
91 See, for instance, ibid. the second unnumbered page of the Foreword.
92 Lonergan, *Insight* 243.
93 Ibid. 212, emphasis added.
94 On *Verstehen* and *Befindlichkeit*, see Martin Heidegger, *Being and Time*, trans. John Macquarrie and Edward Robinson (New York: Harper and Row, 1962) 182. 'State-of-mind is *one* of the existential structures in which the Being of the "there" maintains itself. Equiprimordial with it in constituting this Being is *understanding*. A state-of-mind always has its understanding, even if it merely keeps it suppressed. Understanding always has its mood.'
95 Lonergan, *Insight* 302.
96 Ibid. 303.
97 Ibid. 299.
98 Ibid.
99 Lonergan, *Method in Theology* 74.
100 Ibid. 80. I hope it does not complicate things too much to suggest that the major authenticity or inauthenticity issues in the minor formal and actual intelligibility of presentations. If these are traceable to inauthenticity, then the major formal and actual intelligibility of the subject's creative operations is what can restore some integrity to the tradition.
101 Ibid. 255–56.
102 Ibid. 348, emphasis added.
103 Ibid.
104 Ibid. 348–49.
105 Ibid. 349. With regard to the eighth functional specialty, communications, we may add what Lonergan wrote in chapter 5: '[C]ommunications produces data in the present and for the future.' Ibid. 135.
106 Bernard Lonergan, 'Time and Meaning,' in *Philosophical and Theological Papers 1958–1964*, Collected Works of Bernard Lonergan, vol. 6, ed. Robert

C. Croken, Frederick E. Crowe, and Robert M. Doran (Toronto: University of Toronto Press, 1996) 104–105.

107 Ibid. 105.

108 For a development of the notion of the ontology of meaning, see chapter 19 in my book *Theology and the Dialectics of History*. See also below, pp. 146–49.

109 Bernard Lonergan, 'The Analogy of Meaning,' in *Philosophical and Theological Papers, 1958–1964* 205–206.

110 Ibid. 206 note 50.

111 Ibid. 206.

112 Lonergan, *Method in Theology* 356.

113 Ibid.

114 See Doran, *Theology and the Dialectics of History*, part 4 passim.

115 Lonergan, *Insight* 243.

116 Dulles, *Models of Revelation* 131–54.

117 Lonergan, *Method in Theology* 357.

118 Ibid.

119 Ibid.

120 Ibid. 358.

121 Bernard Lonergan, *De Deo trino: Pars systematica* 257–58; the translation is by Michael Shields, in preparation for the Collected Works edition.

122 Ibid.

123 Max Scheler, *Ressentiment*, trans. William W. Holdheim (New York: Free Press of Glencoe, 1961) 77–78.

124 Lonergan, 'Natural Right and Historical Mindedness,' in *A Third Collection* 174–75.

125 More work needs to be done on the intentional and nonintentional elements in genuine religious experience.

126 Bernard Lonergan, 'Religious Experience,' in *A Third Collection* 127.

127 Ibid. 116–17.

128 Lonergan, *Insight* 204–205.

129 Lonergan, 'Religious Experience' 127.

130 Ibid.

131 Bernard Lonergan, 'Religious Knowledge,' in *A Third Collection* 130.

Chapter 10

1 See my article 'System and History' (see p. 222, note 24 above). For an overview of the issue of 'system and history' in Lonergan's early writings, see Patrick Brown, 'System and History in Lonergan's Early Historical and Economic Manuscripts,' paper written for the Convention of the American Catholic Philosophical Association, 2000, and now available online in *The Journal of Macrodynamic Analysis* (www.mun.ca/jmda) 1:1. The concern in

Brown's paper is largely with Lonergan's 'vision of the possibility of an increased informing and directing of the historical flow by theory and of theory by history,' which, Brown says correctly, 'forms a kind of theme with many variations over Lonergan's career as a thinker.' The four meanings of 'system and history' that I have disengaged here may be interpreted as four of the variations that this theme displays in Lonergan's work.

2 Lonergan, *Method in Theology* xi.

3 A very serious question can be raised, of course, whether there is even possible a shift in basic terms and relations when these terms and relations are derived from interiorly and religiously differentiated consciousness. A correct articulation of the structure of such consciousness is not subject to radical revision. On the other hand, we must ask whether the following changes in the expression of that structure represent homogeneous expansions or higher viewpoints: the advance from a three-levelled structure of intentional consciousness to a four-levelled structure, the affirmation of a fifth level constituted by God's gift of love (and so in its initial moment nonintentional), the recognition of a movement from above as well as the movement from below, the acknowledgment in 'Philosophy and the Religious Phenomenon' of the openness of intentional consciousness on both ends to other operators, and the acceptance of psychic conversion, with its implications for our understanding of the level of empirical consciousness.

4 Lonergan, *Method in Theology* xi.

5 Lonergan, *Divinarum personarum* 19.

6 Ibid. The emphasis is added in the translation.

7 Paul Ricoeur, *Time and Narrative*, 3 vols., trans. Kathleen McLaughlin and David Pellauer. See especially vol. 1, part II (Chicago: University of Chicago Press, 1984), 'History and Narrative.' Interestingly, this volume is dedicated to Henri-Irenée Marrou. Lonergan and Ricoeur consulted many of the same authors regarding historical method, including Marrou.

8 '[D]ialectic stands to generalized method as the differential equation to classical physics, or the operator equation to the more recent physics. For dialectic is a pure form with general implications; it is applicable to any concrete unfolding of linked but opposed principles that are modified cumulatively by the unfolding; it can envisage at once the conscious and the nonconscious either in a single subject or in an aggregate and succession of subjects; it is adjustable to any course of events, from an ideal line of pure progress resulting from the harmonious working of the opposed principles, to any degree of conflict, aberration, breakdown, and disintegration; it constitutes a principle of integration for specialized studies that concentrate on this or that aspect of human living, and it can integrate not only theoretical work but also factual reports; finally, by its distinction between insight

and bias, progress and decline, it contains in a general form the combination of the empirical and the critical attitudes essential to human science.' Lonergan, *Insight* 268–69.

9 I have spoken of diachronic structuralism in a different context in 'Self-knowledge and the Interpretation of Imaginal Expression,' in *Theological Foundations*, vol. 2: *Theology and Culture* 426–31.

10 As I mentioned above, the section of *Divinarum personarum* from which our quotations were taken does not appear in the 1964 edition of the same material, *De Deo trino, Pars systematica*, where Lonergan is more concerned with addressing the logical ideals that he lectured on in 1957 (the year in which *Divinarum personarum* was first published) and that he wrestled with in the 1959 course 'De intellectu et methodo.' Only vague and somewhat uncertain references to such a hermeneutics and explanatory history are given by Lonergan in *Method in Theology* (see pp. 172–73). I regard this as unfortunate.

11 On the ontology of meaning, see Doran, *Theology and the Dialectics of History*, chapter 19. This is probably the least understood of my own proposals. None of the reviews of the first printing of *Theology and the Dialectics of History* that I have seen even mentions chapter 19. Neil Ormerod does mention it in a review occasioned by the second printing. See his review in *Theological Studies* 64:1 (March 2003) 167–69. Coelho, *Hermeneutics and Method* (see above, p. 207, note 2) 236, note 123, gets the point.

12 I regard Lonergan's apparent downplaying of the hermeneutics of *Insight* as unfortunate. He has moved from a hermeneutics of the intentionality of the text to a hermeneutics of the intention of the author. The latter goal is sometimes, though by no means always, an impossible objective, and to stress it as much as Lonergan does diverts attention from the positive and indeed unique features of the hermeneutic proposals of chapter 17 of *Insight*.

13 The page is numbered A472, and can be found as the first item in file 7 of Batch V in the Lonergan papers, Archives, Lonergan Research Institute, Toronto.

14 Lonergan here used the singular noun for each of the last three specialties.

15 This is precisely the step that is missed if one wishes to dispense with a 'turn to the subject.' One *cannot* move from indirect to direct discourse without passing through the 'mediating subject.' It is *impossible*. It does not happen. And it is far better to pass through the subject knowingly than to do so blindly.

16 These pages are numbered A474, and they constitute the fourth item in the seventh folder of Batch V in the Lonergan papers, Archives, Lonergan Research Institute, Toronto.

17 A study of Lonergan's development would show the influence of both Jean Piaget and Edmund Husserl on this transition.

18 Transcribed by Nicholas Graham from the tape of the first lecture in an institute at Regis College, Toronto, on 'The Method of Theology' in the summer of 1962 (now available on compact disc through the work of Greg Lauzon at the Lonergan Research Institute, Toronto, and to be published in vol. 22 of Collected Works of Bernard Lonergan, *Early Works on Theological Method I*). It may be that the elimination from *Method in Theology* of the material on mediating and mediated objects is due to a concern that attention would be shifted from operations, which are the concern of the book, to objects.

19 Clearly Lonergan's initial conception compacts into history what later became dialectic; the conversion that later would be acknowledged to occur outside theology was initially the fourth functional specialty.

20 Added by hand (the rest of the page is typed) after the list of operational specializations is the comment 'explanation = intelligibility immanent in affect-laden images.' It would seem that the comment belongs with the description of 'communications,' though the manner in which it is written and placed on the page makes it impossible to be sure of this. It could also go with the seventh specialty, though it is doubtful that Lonergan had come to such a conception, which can be developed in terms of the role of psychic conversion in systematics.

21 The comments quoted in this paragraph appear on the same twelfth page of A474.

22 Notice again that what eventually became the functional specialty 'dialectic' has not yet emerged in its specificity. When it does, the distinction of positions and counterpositions becomes its concern.

23 Emphasis added.

24 Two of these papers have been published. See Bernard Lonergan, 'Pantôn Anakephalaiôsis,' in *Method: Journal of Lonergan Studies* 9:2 (1991) 139–72; and 'Analytic Concept of History,' *Method: Journal of Lonergan Studies* 11:1 (1993) 5–35.

25 Bernard Lonergan, '*Insight* Revisited,' in *A Second Collection* 271–72.

26 A good start is made by Michael Shute, *The Origins of Lonergan's Notion of the Dialectic of History: A Study of Lonergan's Early Writings on History* (Lanham, MD: University Press of America, 1993).

27 See, for example, Ronald McKinney, 'Lonergan's Notion of Dialectic,' *The Thomist* 46 (1982) 221–41; and Glenn Hughes, 'A Critique of "Lonergan's Notion of Dialectic" by Ronald McKinney, S.J.,' *Method: Journal of Lonergan Studies* 1 (1983) 60–67, with a response by McKinney and a counter-response by Hughes.

28 Bernard Lonergan, 'Natural Right and Historical Mindedness,' in *A Third Collection* 170.

29 Ibid. 172.

30 Ibid.

31 Ibid.

32 Ibid. 174.

33 Ibid. 175.

34 A position on infrastructure and superstructure is worked out in chapter 12 of *Theology and the Dialectics of History*, where I engage in a sort of 'random dialectic' with Marx. It will be summarized later in this chapter, when we treat the scale of values.

35 Lonergan, 'Natural Right and Historical Mindedness' 176. The formulation here (the 'single object that can gain collective attention') recalls the overlooked title of chapter 7 of *Insight*, 'Common Sense as Object.' Lonergan in that chapter and in its title is already dealing with the embodiments of constitutive meaning in the collective realities that constitute a society, without yet having developed the language of 'constitutive meaning.'

36 Ibid.

37 Lonergan, *Method in Theology* 85–99. For a metaphysical analysis of the same issue, see chapter 19 of *Theology and the Dialectics of History*, 'The Ontology of Meaning.'

38 Lonergan, 'Natural Right and Historical Mindedness' 177.

39 From references elsewhere in Lonergan's work, we may presume that he is thinking here of Eric Voegelin's analysis of the cosmological mentality in the opening pages of *Israel and Revelation*, vol. 1 of Voegelin's *Order in History* (Baton Rouge, LA: Louisiana State University Press, 1956).

40 Lonergan, 'Natural Right and Historical Mindedness' 177. 'Poets and orators, prophets and wise men, bring about a development of language and a specialization of attention that prepare the way for sophists and philosophers, mathematicians and scientists. There occurs a differentiation of consciousness, as writing makes language an object for the eye as well as the ear; grammarians organize the inflections of words and analyze the construction of sentences; orators learn and teach the art of persuasion; logicians go behind sentences to propositions and behind persuasion to proofs; and philosophers exploit this second-level use of language to the point where they develop technical terms for speaking compendiously about anything that can be spoken about; while the more modest mathematicians confine their technical utterances to relations of identity or equivalence between individuals and sets; and similarly the scientists have their several specialized languages for each of their various fields' (ibid.). In the posthumously published paper 'Philosophy and the Religious Phenomenon,' what here are first and second plateaus become three stages, so that there are in all four stages of meaning: linguistic, literate, logical, and methodical. 'In the linguistic stage people speak and listen. In the literate they read and write. In the logical they operate on propositions; they promote clarity, coherence,

and rigor of statement; they move towards systems that are thought to be permanently valid. In the methodical stage the construction of systems remains, but the permanently valid system has become an abandoned ideal; any system is presumed to be the precursor of another and better system; and the role of method is the discernment of invariants and variables in the ongoing sequences of systems.' 'Philosophy and the Religious Phenomenon' (see above, p. 214, note 33) 405.

41 Lonergan, 'Natural Right and Historical Mindedness' 177. 'On this plateau logic loses its key position to become but a modest part within method; and logical concern – with truth, with necessity, with demonstration, with universality – enjoys no more than marginal significance. Science and history become ongoing processes, asserting not necessity but verifiable possibility, claiming not certitude but probability. Where science, as conceived on the second plateau, ambitioned permanent validity but remained content with abstract universality, science and history on the third plateau offer no more than the best available opinion of the time, yet by sundry stratagems and devices endeavor to approximate ever more accurately to the manifold details and nuances of the concrete.' Ibid. 178.

42 Ibid. 177.

43 Ibid.

44 See also the section entitled 'The Second Enlightenment' in his paper 'Prolegomena to the Study of the Emerging Religious Consciousness of Our Time,' in *A Third Collection* at 63–65.

45 Ibid. 179.

46 Ibid.

47 Ibid.

48 Ibid.

49 Ibid. 180.

50 Ibid.

51 Ibid.

52 Ibid. 180–81.

53 Ibid. 182.

54 Lonergan, *Insight* 214–31.

55 I have emphasized dream analysis as such a practice. Much more accessible is the technique set forth by Eugene T. Gendlin in *Focusing* (New York: Everest House, 1978).

56 Lonergan, 'Mission and the Spirit' 29.

57 Ibid. 29–30, emphasis added.

58 Lonergan, 'Philosophy and the Religious Phenomenon' 400, emphasis added.

59 Ibid.

60 Lonergan, *Method in Theology* 290.

61 Ibid.

62 Lonergan, 'Mission and the Spirit' 29–30. The issue in Jungian psychology is more complex than Lonergan here intimates. Much of my early work in articulating psychic conversion consisted in dialectical engagement with Jung on the basis of Lonergan's intentionality analysis. For my most complete statement on Jung, see chapter 10 of *Theology and the Dialectics of History.*

63 For illustrations, I would refer the reader to the papers 'Aesthetics and the Opposites' and 'Dramatic Artistry in the Third Stage of Meaning,' both contained in my *Theological Foundations*, vol. 1: *Intentionality and Psyche.* Let me also call attention to Lonergan's understanding of what I was about in earlier writings: 'With me [Doran] would ask: "Why?" "Is that so?" "Is it worthwhile?" But to these he would add a fourth. It is Heidegger's *Befindlichkeit* taken as the existential question: "How do I feel?" It is not just the question but also each one's intelligent answer, reasonable judgment, responsible acceptance.' Bernard Lonergan, 'Reality, Myth, Symbol,' in *Myth, Symbol and Reality*, ed. Alan Olson (South Bend, IN: University of Notre Dame Press, 1980) 37; now in Lonergan, *Philosophical and Theological Papers 1965–1980* at 390.

64 See Lonergan, *Insight* 555.

65 This is clear, I believe, already in Lonergan's talk of genuineness in chapter 15 of *Insight*, where neither element of the tension is neglected or overruled in favour of the other. Furthermore, as was just mentioned, there is talk in chapter 17 of *Insight* of the correspondence between operators of intellectual and sensitive development.

66 Lonergan, *Insight* 258, emphasis added.

67 Ibid. 268–69, emphasis added.

68 See also Doran, *Theology and the Dialectics of History*, chapters 6–10.

69 See also ibid. chapters 11–14.

70 See ibid. chapters 15–17.

71 Voegelin, *Israel and Revelation* 56.

72 See Eric Voegelin, *The New Science of Politics* (Chicago: University of Chicago Press, 1952) 70.

73 Karl Jaspers, *The Origin and Goal of History*, trans. Michael Bullock (New Haven: Yale University Press, 1953).

74 Lonergan, *Method in Theology* 31–32. On the question of the derivation of the scale of values, see below, p. 181.

75 Lonergan, *Insight* 258.

76 Ibid. 263–67.

77 Doran, *Theology and the Dialectics of History*, chapter 17.

78 On dramatic artistry, see Lonergan, *Insight* 212–14; see also Doran, 'Dramatic Artistry in the Third Stage of Meaning,' chapter 7 in *Theological Foundations*, vol. 1: *Intentionality and Psyche.*

79 Joseph Schumpeter, *Imperialism/Social Classes: Two Essays* (New York: New American Library, 1951) 6.
80 Hannah Arendt, *The Origins of Totalitarianism* (New York: Harcourt, Brace, Jovanovich, 1973).
81 Lonergan, *Insight* 251–57.
82 Lonergan, *Method in Theology*, chapter 2.
83 The tape recordings of these lectures are now being transferred to compact disc. Quotations here are from a transcript made by Nicholas Graham.
84 See Lonergan, *Topics in Education* 55–56.
85 Lonergan, 'Natural Right and Historical Mindedness' 175.
86 Ibid. 174.
87 Ibid. 175.
88 Ibid. 176.
89 Ibid.
90 Bernard Lonergan, 'Mission and the Spirit,' in *A Third Collection* 29–30.
91 See above, p. 90.
92 Lonergan, *Insight* 501.
93 Bernard Lonergan, 'Theory of History,' unpublished manuscript dated around 1937, p. 4.
94 Lonergan, 'Natural Right and Historical Mindedness' 174.
95 Ibid. 169.
96 Ibid. 169.
97 Lonergan, *Insight* 258. Emphasis added to draw attention to 'natural dialectic' or the 'dialectic of contraries' as opposed to the 'dialectic of contradictories.'
98 Doran, *Theology and the Dialectics of History* 96.
99 Ibid. 96–97.
100 Ibid. 104.
101 Lonergan, *Insight* 497–99.
102 Lonergan, *Method in Theology* xi.
103 'We are not seeking the whole foundation of [doctrines, systematics, and communications] – for they obviously will depend on research, interpretation, history, and dialectic – but just the added foundation needed to move from the indirect discourse that sets forth the convictions and opinions of others to the direct discourse that states what is so.' Lonergan, *Method in Theology* 267, at the beginning of the chapter on the functional specialty 'Foundations.'
104 One can watch Lonergan begin to work out his own notion of horizon, in the last two chapters of *Phenomenology and Logic*.
105 On dialectical, complementary, and genetic relations among horizons, see Lonergan, *Method in Theology* 236–37. The reader will do well to ponder the significance of Lonergan's reflections in chapter 14 of *Insight*, where it is

clear that one ought not begin reading another author with an explicitly adversarial purpose. Even so-called counterpositions can teach us something, and the search is always to learn, to broaden one's horizon, to advance positions even while reversing counterpositions. Again, in the words of *Method in Theology*, 'dialectic' is 'a generalized apologetic *conducted in an ecumenical spirit*, aiming ultimately at a comprehensive viewpoint, and proceeding towards that goal by acknowledging differences, seeking their grounds real and apparent, and *eliminating superfluous oppositions*.' Lonergan, *Method in Theology* 130, emphasis added.

106 See Bernard Lonergan, 'Theology in Its New Context,' in *A Second Collection* (see above, note 177) 55. Here Lonergan dates at approximately 1680 the time when at least Catholic theology started to fall behind the times.

107 A constructive analysis from Lonergan's stance of what have come to be contrasted as modern and postmodern emphases can be found in Lonergan's discussion of a first and a second Enlightenment. See Bernard Lonergan, 'Prolegomena to the Study of the Emerging Religious Consciousness of Our Time,' in *A Third Collection*, 63–65; on the social alienation that is part of the context for a second Enlightenment, see ibid. 60–63. On Lonergan and the postmodern, see Fred Lawrence, 'The Fragility of Consciousness: Lonergan and the Postmodern Concern for the Other,' *Theological Studies* 54:1 (March 1993) 55–94; Lawrence, 'Lonergan, the Integral Postmodern?' *Method: Journal of Lonergan Studies* 18 (2000) 95–122; Doran, *Theology and the Dialectics of History* 153–58 and 459–67; James L. Marsh, 'Post-modernism: A Lonerganian Retrieval and Critique,' *International Philosophical Quarterly* 35:2 (June 1995) 159–73; and a recent book, *In Deference to the Other: Lonergan and Contemporary Continental Thought*, ed. Jim Kanaris and Mark J. Doorley (Albany: State University of New York Press, 2004).

108 For seminal ideas along these lines, see Bernard Lonergan, 'Aquinas Today: Tradition and Innovation,' in *A Third Collection* 35–54.

109 See Lonergan, *Method in Theology* 94–96. In the fifth of his lectures on mathematical logic (1957), Lonergan says that the modern differentiation first of philosophy from science and then of philosophy from theology sets the context that makes his own starting point in cognitional theory so important. See Lonergan, *Phenomenology and Logic* 119–21.

110 On metaphysical equivalence, see Lonergan, *Insight* 526–33.

Index

www.ingramcontent.com/pod-product-compliance
Lightning Source LLC
La Vergne TN
LVHW090806070826
844660LV00022B/1100

* 9 7 8 1 4 8 7 5 9 1 4 6 5 *